ID62.4 .I4844 2004

International
entrepreneurship in
c2004.

MW01119626

2009 03 09

HUMBER COLLEGE
LAKESHORE CAMPUS
LEARNING RESOURCE CENTRE
3199 LAKESHORE BLVD. WEST
TORONTO, ONTARIO M8V 1K8

International Entrepreneurship in Small and Medium Size Enterprises

THE McGILL INTERNATIONAL ENTREPRENEURSHIP SERIES

Series Editor: Hamid Etemad, *McGill University*, *Canada*

The two fields of International Business and Entrepreneurship have traditionally covered seemingly unrelated and practically different disciplines. One covered larger-scale, multi-point business operations by mainly large Multinational Enterprises (MNEs) in international markets; and the other addressed entrepreneurial initiatives primarily in the context of smaller-scale and domestic operations.

International Entrepreneurship is the emerging field dedicated to both the grounded practice and scholarly inquiry in the unfolding competitive environment and the corresponding entrepreneurial strategy for achieving success internationally and remaining competitive at home. It neither assumes an a priori geographical limitation in its scope or concentration, nor a theoretical barrier in conceptualization and formulation of its entrepreneurial initiatives and associated strategies. It embraces the richness of theory and practice in its constituent fields of International Business and Entrepreneurship as well as others. It strives to examine, develop and highlight the underpinning of entrepreneurial initiatives at home and beyond that result in riches and also learns to avoid the ruins.

Elgar's McGill International Entrepreneurship Series is a bold entrepreneurial quest for excellence. It is a joint initiative between Edward Elgar's traditional dedication to publications in entrepreneurship and the McGill University's pioneering efforts in International Entrepreneurship. The primary aim of this series is to present cutting-edge advances in this rapidly developing and dynamic field.

Titles in the series include:

Globalization and Entrepreneurship
Policy and Strategy Perspectives
Edited by Hamid Etemad and Richard Wright

Emerging Paradigms in International Entrepreneurship
Edited by Marian V. Jones and Pavlos Dimitratos

International Entrepreneurship in Small and Medium Size Enterprises

Orientation, Environment and Strategy

16510l

Edited by

Hamid Etemad

McGill University, Canada

THE McGILL INTERNATIONAL ENTREPRENEURSHIP SERIES

Edward Elgar
Cheltenham, UK • Northampton, MA, USA

© Hamid Etemad 2004

All rights reserved. No part of this publication may be reproduced, stored in a retrieval system or transmitted in any form or by any means, electronic, mechanical or photocopying, recording, or otherwise without the prior permission of the publisher.

Published by
Edward Elgar Publishing Limited
Glensanda House
Montpellier Parade
Cheltenham
Glos GL50 1UA
UK

Edward Elgar Publishing, Inc.
136 West Street
Suite 202
Northampton
Massachusetts 01060
USA

A catalogue record for this book
is available from the British Library

Library of Congress Cataloguing in Publication Data
International entrepreneurship in small and medium size enterprises : orientation, environment and strategy / edited by Hamid Etemad.
    p. cm. — (McGill international entrepreneurship series)
    Includes bibliographical references.
      1. International business enterprises—Management. 2. Small business—Management. 3. Competition. 4. Strategic planning. 5. Entrepreneurship. I. Etemad, Hamid. II. Series.

    HD62.4.I5544 2004
    658´.022—dc22

                           2004046963

ISBN 1 84376 194 7

Typeset by Cambrian Typesetters, Frimley, Surrey
Printed and bound in Great Britain by MPG Books Ltd, Bodmin, Cornwall

Contents

PART III   HIGH TECHNOLOGY AND STRATEGY

Figures

Tables

Contributors

Dr Gabriele Beibst is Professor of Marketing in the Department of Business Administration at the University of Applied Sciences (UAS) Jena. She has been the President of UAS Jena since 2001. She is also a principal member of the GET UP–Thüringer Existenzgründer Initiative. Her research interests and publications are in marketing, university-based start-ups and international entrepreneurship.

Dr Jim Bell is Professor of International Business Entrepreneurship at Magee College, the University of Ulster, Northern Ireland. His teaching and research interests cover a wide area, including international marketing and internationalization of knowledge-based SMEs as well as international business education. He has published widely in these and related areas. He was chair of the Sixth McGill International Entrepreneurship Conference at the University of Ulster, 19–22 September 2003.

Dr Bee-Leng Chua is with the Chinese University of Hong Kong (CUHK), and teaches in the Faculty of Business Administration. Her work in entrepreneurship education includes establishing the Asia Moot Corp® Business Plan Competition in 1998. Her current research interests and publications are in career decisions, entrepreneurship and pro-social behaviors.

Mr Hankyu Chu is currently a PhD candidate at the Faculty of Management, McGill University. The focus of his area of research is on the process of learning and development of competence in knowledge-intensive firms. His work aims to formulate a theory of situated competences. He is an accomplished graduate of the Graduate School of International Studies, Chung-Ang University, South Korea.

Dr Steve Conway is a Senior Lecturer in Innovation at the University of Leicester Management Centre in the UK. His research interests and publications are focused on the nature and role of social networks and organization networks in the shaping and developing of technological innovation in the practice of entrepreneurship and in knowledge creation.

Dr Hamid Etemad is Professor of Marketing and International Business at the Faculty of Management, McGill University. He is the co-founder and

Convenor of the McGill International Entrepreneurship Conference Series and is the Series Editor of Edward Elgar Publishing's McGill International Entrepreneurship Series of publications. He has served as the past president of the Administrative Sciences Association of Canada and is the current Director of the Business and Management Research Center at McGill University. The focus of his recent research interests is on electronic marketing, globalization of SMEs, management of knowledge, intellectual property and technology, the network of strategic alliances and multinational enterprise–host country relations. He has published widely and has edited numerous books and scholarly journals, including the *Canadian Journal of Administrative Sciences*, *Global Focus*, the *International Marketing Review*, the *Journal of International Entrepreneurship*, *Small Business Economics*, and the *Journal of International Management*.

Dr Oswald Jones is Professor of Innovation and Entrepreneurship at Manchester Metropolitan University Business School. His research interests and publications are in the areas of innovation and technology management, as well as social capital, entrepreneurial networks and entrepreneurial processes. He recently coedited (with Dr Fiona Tilley) *Competitive Advantage in SMEs: Organising for Innovation and Change* (Wiley, 2003).

Ms Supara Kapasuwan is a lecturer in international business at the Faculty of Business Administration, Dhurakijpundit University, Bangkok, Thailand. She is currently a doctoral candidate in business administration at the College of Business and Economics, Washington State University. Her research interests include international entrepreneurship, interorganizational networks and organizational learning.

Dr Norris Krueger Jr is a Clinical Professor of Entrepreneurship and serves as the Program Manager for the Kauffman-supported TEAMS initiative. He continues to teach a wide array of entrepreneurship courses at Boise State University in Idaho. His current research interest is in understanding how we learn to see opportunities and how this understanding helps promote a more entrepreneurial mindset in organizations, communities and newer domains such as social entrepreneurship. He is a widely-published author and highly-cited expert on entrepreneurial cognition.

Dr Arndt Lautenschläger is a research associate in the GET UP–Thüringer Existenzgründer Initiative at the University of Applied Sciences in Jena. In this position, he is committed to creating an enabling infrastructure for knowledge-based start-ups from the academic sector. His research interests and publications are in university-based start-ups, entrepreneurship education and international entrepreneurship.

Dr Yender Lee is a Professor of the National Taipei College of Business in Taiwan. He teaches Management Information System (MIS) and marketing courses. His research interests and publications are in knowledge networks, knowledge management, data mining and electronic commerce. His PhD work at McGill University was focused on knowledge networks, technology management and management of information systems.

Harry Matlay is Reader in SME Development at the University of Central England Business School and is leading the activities of the newly-established Organisational Learning and Innovation Unit in Birmingham, UK. His research interests and publications are in entrepreneurship, organizational learning and knowledge management, with a special focus on SMEs. His other interests include training and innovation. He is the editor of the *Journal of Small Business and Enterprise Development*, UK.

Dr Rod B. McNaughton holds the Eyton Chair in Entrepreneurship and is Director of the Institute for Innovation Research and Associate Director of the Centre for Business, Entrepreneurship and Technology, at the University of Waterloo. He specializes in international marketing strategy with a focus on the internationalization of small knowledge-intensive firms. His research interests and publications focus is on choosing international channels of distribution, exporting and export policy, market orientation and value creation, strategic alliances, foreign direct investment and the venture capital industry.

Dr Jay Mitra is Professor of Entrepreneurship, Director of the Centre for Entrepreneurship Research and Development, and Director of the Business and Management Research Institute, at Luton Business School, University of Luton. He is also the Scientific Coordinator of the OECD's LEED programme project on Entrepreneurship Education. A focus of his wide publications is on different aspects of new venture creation and the development and management of acclaimed postgraduate programs on entrepreneurship.

Dr Kent E. Neupert is Professor of International Business and Research Director of the Global Business Consortium at the University of Idaho. He is also the director of the Northwest Venture Championship, an international business plan competition that he launched in 2002. In addition to teaching in the MBA and undergraduate programs, he initiates and coordinates research on international business, business strategy and entrepreneurship. His research interests and publications are in international business, entrepreneurship and business strategy areas.

Dr Jerman Rose holds the James Huber Chair of Entrepreneurship and is the Director of the Center for Entrepreneurial Studies at Washington State University. He has extensive experience in teaching and training activities in both higher education and industrial settings in the United States and abroad, as well as practical experience in the creation and operation of small and medium-sized enterprises. His research interests and publications are focused on entrepreneurship and small business management topics.

Dr Philip Rosson was appointed to the Killam Chair of Technology, Innovation and Marketing at the School of Business Administration at Dalhousie University in 2002. He teaches courses in Internet marketing and marketing strategy. He has served as co-editor of the *Canadian Journal of Administrative Sciences* and Dean of the Faculty of Management at Dalhousie University. He has published widely, with a special emphasis on the growth strategies of small and medium-sized companies, particularly in foreign markets.

Dr Khaled Soufani is Professor of Finance in the John Molson School of Business at Concordia University in Montreal. He specializes in financial and business economics, with many publications in the area of entrepreneurial finance. He teaches corporate finance, economics and international business. The focus of his research and publications is on business, economic and financial affairs as well as topics related to the growth and development of SMEs in both the domestic and the international environment.

Dr Terence Tse is in the final year of a PhD in management at the University of Cambridge, UK. His thesis focuses on strategic innovation for e-commerce retailers. He was formerly a merger and acquisition analyst in Montreal and New York. He also co-founded IdeaBistro, a Toronto-based Internet company, which serves the Canadian dental industry. His research interests and publications are in e-commerce strategy and financial economics.

Preface

This book is the third volume in Elgar's McGill International Entrepreneurship Series. The series is dedicated to advancing knowledge in the emerging field of International Entrepreneurship. McGill International Entrepreneurship (MIE) initiatives started in the late 1990s. In its inaugural international conference in September 1998, it brought together leading scholars from the fields of international business and entrepreneurship to stimulate interaction between entrepreneurship and international business fields.

The natural, gradual and interactive process that enriches a field with the heritage, accumulated knowledge stock and knowledge creation and diffusion principles and processes of another field, that is, the process by which a field evolves by becoming increasingly interdisciplinary and multidisciplinary, has not been foreign to either of the two fields. However the rapid globalization of the environment, liberalization of trade and investments and rapid advances in technology in the latter parts of the 20th century have accelerated the actual process of infusion of the two fields, as well as others, and accentuated the rather critical need to formalize the emerging interdisciplinary field. The MIE initiative proved to be highly responsive to that need by providing flexible instruments for its scholarly expression. This volume is one of the manifestations of that expression.

I have met the scholars who have contributed to this volume, and other volumes in Elgar's MIE series, at the First and Second Biennial McGill Conferences on International Entrepreneurship in September 1998 and 2000 at McGill, in Montreal, followed by the 2001 conference at the University of Strathclyde, in Glasgow. We have all become a part of the family of MIE scholars as well as the broader International Entrepreneurship network. The scholarly papers included in this volume were selected from papers written for, and presented at, the second McGill biennial international entrepreneurship conference, which was run more like an intensive-research workshop than a formal conference. Papers submitted to this conference series, and the publications emanating from it, are normally subjected to a rigorous peer review process in several stages. The chapters in this volume are not an exception. They were first reviewed before acceptance for presentation at the conference; they were then peer reviewed blindly and revised accordingly before selection as potential chapters for inclusion in this book. I have further edited them and asked for additions, clarifications and revisions, when appropriate, before submitting the collection to

Edward Elgar Publishing for their editorial examination. This examination has normally been long, detailed and methodical. Each chapter has been copy-edited for form, consistency and accuracy. Without the patience, cooperation and diligence of all concerned, especially authors under continuous time and academic pressures, this collection would not have assumed book form.

The scholarly inception of this volume, and many other similar scholarly publications, lies in the MIE Conference Series, the success of which must be attributed mainly to a host of highly interested and dedicated scholars, and supportive colleagues, staff and assistants. In addition to conference proceedings, these conferences have produced a number of edited volumes as well as coherent collections of papers in thematic issues of scholarly journals for high impact. A selective list of publications, emanating from the first four MIE conferences, is presented in Table 1.[1]

In our rapidly emerging IE community, my former and current doctoral students have risen to the scholarly challenges that International Entrepreneurship presented to all of us. Yender Lee, now a Professor of Management Information Systems and Management of Technology at the National Taipei College of Business in Taiwan, and I conducted the first diligent and laborious, epistemological and bibliographic search for the early roots of International Entrepreneurship in the mid-1990s. Our research discovered that international entrepreneurship has been functioning for a long time. Documentation of internationally-oriented entrepreneurs, who practiced entrepreneurship across nations, dates back at least to a French wine merchant, Cantillon, in the 17th century, who took the highly localized French wines to international markets, and even much farther back, to traders of international trading routes.[2] The international traders of the ancient trading caravans trekked the trading routes of antiquity that linked many cities for more than three millennia. The true practice of International Entrepreneurship parallels the early history of international trade and appears to be the recent discovery of a lost practice going back to antiquity.[3] These traveling traders must be viewed as the early ancestors of the modern international entrepreneurs who are increasing their activities in real and cyber space.[4]

The old city of Xian (shee-yan), the seat of the old Chinese dynasties, and Empire later on, in the Middle Kingdom (that is, the current People's Republic of China) was one of the easternmost stages of the 'Silk Road' that ran thousands of miles across the Central Asian planes and the lands ruled by the old Persian Empire, Assyrian kingdom, Egyptian dynasties and what we now call Central Europe. Local products served as the wellsprings of goods for barter trade elsewhere as well as the exchange currency for obtaining the goods of other nations. The group of international traders, traveling with trading caravans, the ancient version of international trade delegations, exchanged many goods on their long routes, from silk, gunpowder, compasses and other novelties from China,[5]

Table 1   The collection of leading-edge publications in the MIE Conference Series, presented in chronological order

I.   Selected papers from the Inaugural McGill International Entrepreneurship Conference (at McGill, Montreal, September 1998) appeared in the following:

two dedicated sections of the *Journal of Global Focus*, **11**(4) and **8**(2), Hamid Etemad, guest editor; two special issues of the *Journal of International Marketing*, **7**(4) and **8**(2), Hamid Etemad and R.W. Wright, guest editors; *International Entrepreneurship: Globalization of Emerging Businesses* (JAI Press, 1999).

II.   Selected papers from the Second McGill International Entrepreneurship Conference, held in parallel with the 1999 ENDEC (at Nanyang University of Technology, Singapore, 1999), appeared in the following:

Journal of Small Business Economics, **16**(2), L.P. Dana, guest editor; *Journal of Euromarketing*, **9**(2), L.P. Dana, guest editor; *Global Marketing Co-operations and Networks* (The International Business Press, 2000); *International Entrepreneurship: An Anthology* (ENDEC, 1999, L.P. Dana, editor).

III.   Selected papers from the Third McGill International Entrepreneurship Conference (at McGill, Montreal, September 2000) have appeared in the following:

a special issue of the *Journal of International Management*, **7**(3), Hamid Etemad and R.W. Wright, guest editors; a special issue of the *Journal of Small Business Economics*, **20**(1), Hamid Etemad and R.W. Wright, guest editors; two edited book volumes in the McGill International Entrepreneurship Series (Edward Elgar Publishing Ltd), Hamid Etemad, series editor. These books are *Globalization and Entrepreneurship: Policy and Strategy Perspectives*, June 2003 (Hamid Etemad and R.W. Wright, editors), and the current volume: *International Entrepreneurship in Small and Medium Size Enterprises: Orientation, Environment and Strategy* (Hamid Etemad, editor).

IV.   Selected papers from the Fourth McGill International Entrepreneurship Conference (The 2001 Annual Conference at the University of Strathclyde, Glasgow, September 2001) have appeared in the following:

Journal of International Entrepreneurship, **1**(2) and (3); a volume in the McGill International Entrepreneurship Series published by Edward Elgar Publishing Ltd entitled: *Emerging Paradigms in International Entrepreneurship* (Marian V. Jones and Pavlos Dimitratos, editors, 2004).

exotic spices from the Indian subcontinent, Persian rugs and other woven fabrics from countries of the Persian Empire to olive oils, minerals and other Mediterranean goods in ancient Assyria, Egypt and what became the Roman Empire later on.

Unfortunately, the modern theories of international business and international trade have drawn attention away from the inherent entrepreneurship function and the vital role of entrepreneurs, who went through a time-consuming, laborious and risky process to make trade and investments possible. Similarly, entrepreneurship has focused on the entrepreneurs and entrepreneurial process without much concern for the broader theories that explained the flow of trade and investment. With Hankyu Chu, a current doctoral student, we have begun to combine concepts from numerous fields, including entrepreneurship and international business, for studying the inner dynamics of young and fast-growing firms in internationally oriented regional industrial clusters. Individual entrepreneurs, similar to the international traders of the past, travel the obstacle-ridden roads of industrial and corporate entrepreneurship in the globally competitive regional clusters, and play a critical role in such complex groupings. If small firms grow in industrial regional clusters much faster than their counterparts elsewhere, it is mainly because of their entrepreneurial efforts and international orientation within highly progressive enterprises and conducive environments. It is this combination of entrepreneurial efforts, enterprise capabilities and enabling environment that excel young entrepreneurs and their enterprise into the regional industrial clusters and into global markets by extension.

From its inception, the MIE series has encouraged a holistic and integrated approach, if not a paradigm, to reflect the true reality of international entrepreneurship and the internationalization process in small and medium-sized enterprises. Fortunately the emerging paradigm appears to slowly capture both the bilateral relations and the multilateral interactions among the various components influencing international entrepreneurship: internationally oriented entrepreneurs who interact with their markets and environments within and outside the firm structure; growth-oriented and entrepreneurially oriented enterprises that interact with other firms and markets within and outside their environment; and continuously evolving environments that are shaped and reshaped by the competitive dynamics of entrepreneurs and enterprises acting in their own self-interest as well as the socioeconomic forces that affect local and international markets within and outside a country's immediate boundaries. The main components of this emerging paradigm and their respective interactions are schematically presented in Figure 1. The basic design of this volume also adheres to the emerging holistic and integrated paradigm.

Finally, as MIE series editor, and on behalf of all authors shaping this volume, I hope that we have collectively succeeded in advancing the state of our thoughts and knowledge on International Entrepreneurship.

Hamid Etemad

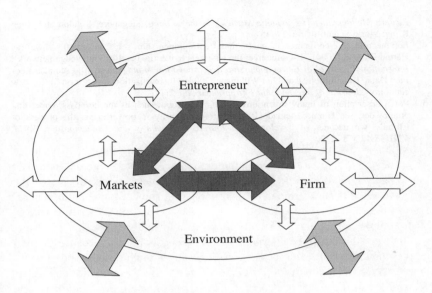

Figure 1   Interrelations among influential components

NOTES

1. Selected papers from the Third Biennial McGill International Entrepreneurship Conference (The 2002 Annual Conference at McGill, Montreal, September 2002) are in the process of being published in prominent scholarly media, all under the guest editorship of Hamid Etemad. The tentative list of the forthcoming journals in 2003/4 includes *Canadian Journal of Administrate Sciences*, *Journal of Entrepreneurship Theory and Practice*, *Journal of Small Business Economics*, *Journal of International Entrepreneurship*, *International Journal of Entrepreneurship and Innovation Management*, *Management International Review*, and possibly others. The Sixth McGill International Entrepreneurship Conference at the University of Ulster in September 2003 (The 2003 Annual Conference) will follow the above tradition. In addition to the conference proceedings, similar efforts are under way for placing a coherent and cutting-edge set of prominent publications in books and special issues of journals with high impact.
2. The highlights of the research into the scholarly roots of International Entrepreneurship as a field of scholarly enquiry, which we have termed 'the knowledge network of international entrepreneurship', is presented in Hamid Etemad and Yender Lee (2003), 'The emerging knowledge network of international entrepreneurship: theory and evidence', *Journal of Small Business Economics*, **20**(1), 5–23, and Hamid Etemad and Yender Lee (2000), 'The development path of an emerging knowledge network in international entrepreneurship', *Proceedings of Administrative Sciences Association of Canada, Entrepreneurship Division*, **21**(21), 72–82.
3. For brief historical highlights of international entrepreneurship in Europe going as far back as the 1600s see Hamid Etemad (2004), 'Marshaling relations: the enduring essence of international entrepreneurship', in Leo-Paul Dana (ed.), *Handbook on Research in Entrepreneurship*, Cheltenham, UK, and Northampton, MA, USA: Edward Elgar Publishing, and, for a brief review of bazaars and caravans of ancient Assyria, Persia and China, also see Leo-Paul Dana and Hamid Etemad (2000), 'The bazaar economy', in Leo-Paul Dana, *Economies of the*

Eastern Mediterranean: Economic Miracles in the Making, Singapore, London and Hong Kong: World Scientific, pp. 27–45.

4. For the role of e-commerce in international entrepreneurship, see Chapter 10, as well as Hamid Etemad (2004), 'E-commerce: the emergence of a field and its knowledge network', *International Journal of Entrepreneurship and Innovation Management*. And see also Leo-Paul Dana, Hamid Etemad and Ian Wilkinson (2004), 'Internetization: a new term for the new economy', *Journal of International Entrepreneurship*, **2**(1).

5. For a description of many inventions of Chinese origin, such as the compass, paper and gunpowder, see Hamid Etemad (1996), 'From obscurity to powerhouse: the process of China's two decades of development', *Journal of Business and Contemporary World*, **VIII**(3&4), 171–222.

Acknowledgments

This book is the culmination of cooperation among many interested groups. Each group assisted the publication process in its own special ways with overwhelming openness and good will. I am deeply grateful and indebted to all of them. Among them are many scholars, friends and colleagues, supporting staff of my home faculty and university, and the professional staff of Edward Elgar Publishing. Undoubtedly contributions of many others will loom larger as time marches on. In the absence of that foresight, I shall remain indebted to them in advance.

The contributions of numerous individuals and institutions stand out. The critical roles and full participation of scholars in the McGill International Entrepreneurship (MIE) conferences cannot be exaggerated. This diverse and accomplished group of researchers and scholars has been both the powerful engine and the inspiring force behind the conference series. The success of the MIE conference and publication series is a scholarly tribute to them (see the Preface for a selective list of publications).

Without the financial support and moral encouragement of John Dobson and the John Dobson Foundation's dedication to excellence in entrepreneurship (and international entrepreneurship by extension), we could not have achieved what we have attained routinely at MIE. Not only is John Dobson a highly successful international entrepreneur in his own right, he has been the enabling force behind entrepreneurship studies in Canada for the past two decades. Furthermore the support of the John Dobson Foundation for entrepreneurship education across the country has made entrepreneurial studies rewarding and successful. Our scholarly community has benefited tremendously from John's genuine support and encouragement and, on behalf of all who have benefited, I would like to extend a special thank you to him and to the Foundation.

The list of individuals at the Faculty of Management at McGill University, and especially former students who have become friends and colleagues, extending a helpful hand, is a long one. Suffice it to say that the MIE Conference Series has enjoyed the unwavering support of Dean Gerold Ross and the directors of research centers, including Jan Jorgensen and Margaret Graham. The efforts of my colleague and MIE co-founding father, Peter Johnson, have been invaluable to MIE from its inception. Peter's years of experience as a student of entrepreneurship in different capacities, including owner–manager of his own firms, an executive of the Power Corporation, new product manager of Dupont Corporation, senior consultant at Cooper and Lybrand and a member of many corporate boards, to name a few, make him especially indispensable as a friend and colleague. My former colleague and director of the Business and Management Research Centre, Cheryl McWatters, was a source of constant moral support and encouragement. My current colleagues, Emine Sarigollu and Dennis Senik, have always extended a helping hand whenever needed.

Lorraine Vezina, my secretary for more than a decade, has been indispensable. She has gradually become one of the principal supporting pillars, functioning simultaneously as the MIE Conference coordinator, and the back-up person of last resort, who finds timely solutions to administrative and support-related problems with clam and patience.

We have all benefited from, and enjoyed, the services of the capable staff of the McGill International Executive Institute that has housed and supported the MIE conference series graciously and professionally over the past six years. These efforts merit full recognition. Special thanks go to my bright and dedicated students, Amanda Skoda, Isabella Dagenais and Marie-Hélène Perron, who managed to excel as undergraduate students while assisting with numerous aspects of the MIE conference series. These academic entrepreneurs did not shy away from the challenges of new fields and new concepts along with their much older professors.

Ironically, the signs of an excellent editor and a quality publishing house are lost when authors and editors face no major problem as the manuscript travels through the various preparatory stages. This gives the erroneous impression that there were no problems to solve in the first place. Our personal experience, however, indicates otherwise. Publishing, regardless of form and milieu, is riddled with problems. Professional editors and their staff in supportive publishing houses dissolve problems before they can develop. Experience, patience and methodical attention to detail – in a word, professionalism – characterize Elgar and are among Elgar's special qualities, rarely found elsewhere. Alan Sturmer, the Acquisition Editor of Elgar's North American Operations (Northampton, Massachusetts), stands among a host of truly capable and genuinely dedicated professionals. Again the team is large and I will not be able to recognize them all. I must make do by only highlighting a short list of those with whom I have had direct and repeated contacts over the past years. The Associate Editor, Tara Gorvine, at the Northampton office and the Senior Desk Editor, Karen McCarthy, in the United Kingdom office shouldered the real brunt of preparing the manuscript. I know full well that their proven competencies and diligent efforts behind the scenes avoided many unforeseen difficulties. At the interfaces of Edward Elgar, the scholarly community and society at large are two capable marketing executives: Katy Wight, in charge of the North and the South American markets, and Hilary Quinn, marketing in the rest of the world. As compared to other experiences, I can hardly characterize my interactions with the Elgar organization as work, as it was done so professionally and pleasantly. I always knew that we were on the right path, which always turned out to be short and fruitful.

My final thanks and gratitude must be extended to my wife, Shokouh Kazeroonian-Etemad and my son, Farshid C. Etemad. My wife has been an illuminating pillar of support, at the same time pursuing her own research and scholarly endeavors. She has helped me, and the process, as a capable academic reader and reviewer, with many insightful and constructive suggestions. All my computational and data-handling needs as well as electronic problems have been routinely directed to Farshid. He is a capable young professional on whom his parents, other professionals and institutions depend highly. In the final analysis, the solitary and prolonged nature of scholarly work deprives the family of their fair share of quality time. It even shifts the burden of certain time-consuming responsibilities to other family members. My case is no exception. My involvement with this volume, the McGill International Entrepreneurship Conference Series and the Elgar–McGill International Entrepreneurship Book Series is but a small manifestation of the time and effort dedicated to such scholarly endeavors. My wife and son have been very generous with their time and unfailing support throughout the decades. I shall remain eternally indebted to both of them for this and also for the time, not rightfully mine, that I have spent on my work, and can never pay them back.

Hamid Etemad
McGill University, Montreal, Canada
September 2003

1. The emerging context of international entrepreneurship: an overview, interrelations and extensions

Hamid Etemad

INTRODUCTION TO THE VOLUME

Markets used to be segmented: large companies competed in international markets while smaller businesses remained local or regional. However, the global competitive environment is changing dramatically. The drivers of globalization are removing the barriers that segregated the competitive space of the small and the large firms in the past. Firms of all sizes have begun to share the same competitive space. It is becoming increasingly difficult for independent small firms to thrive in their traditional markets unless they are globally competitive (Etemad, 1999, 2003a).

As smaller firms are forced to compete with global players even at home, the tendency is to seek successful patterns of internationalization, experiment with them and even emulate them, in the hope of becoming globally competitive. In spite of their obvious benefits, such practices may also be fraught with dangers. Although emulating successful strategies is likely to reduce short-term risks and costs, they may also expose SMEs to the hazards of herding behavior (Knickerbocker, 1973), where competitors emulate each other to avoid the risk of falling dramatically behind. When the successful strategies of multinational enterprises (MNEs) are emulated, or even variants of their models and strategies are adopted, the added danger is that SMEs may suffer doubly: not only may their relatively smaller size and inexperience disadvantage them, they may also find themselves strategically defenseless in direct competition with the much larger and more competitive MNEs, especially those whose integrated strategies were emulated in order to enter and compete in the international competitive markets (Etemad, 1999). By adopting these or similar strategies, SMEs may even compromise their conventional advantage in their own base markets (that is, their conventional, local, domestic markets), where they have traditionally held local advantage over the others. This is bound to happen, especially to

SMEs, whenever they borrow or emulate a variant of a group's strategy. However, as the emerging modes of international business competition involve both the small and the large enterprises in international markets, which are home markets to their local competitors, each must devise certain strategies to empower their competition.

Ideally, a distinctive set of capabilities and competencies could serve as the basis for an equally distinct set of competitive advantages and competitive strategies to enable SMEs to set their own respective 'basis of competition' (Christensen and Bower, 1996). Etemad (2003a, 2003b) has consistently argued that paramount among such capabilities is the ability of SMEs to establish and then manage their relations with the others, especially at home, where they have their strong knowledge base, social capital and social network. Some of these relations are personal, socioculturally-based and uniquely synergistic (Dana *et al.*, 2001; Etemad, 2003a, 2003b), if not symbiotic with SMEs' local operations (Etemad, 2003c, 2003d), which may include a rich and long-established set of collaborative networks. These locally based resources and relations constitute advantages that empower SMEs' strategy at home and could even be leveraged for competing in international markets. While these strategies are potent against the others, especially against foreign-based firms, at home, they may be impotent in international markets, especially when they are emulations of others' strategies, as stated earlier. Unfortunately the traditional theories of internationalization, including theories of MNEs, do not offer much guidance on such competitive matters and are becoming increasingly less potent than in the past as a plethora of rich and diverse strategies are facing one another in the converging global environment (Etemad, 2003b). On the other hand, however, small entrepreneurially oriented enterprises find it easier to overcome barriers to entry when they can leverage their distinct advantages (for example, assets, capabilities and relations) abroad, especially when such barriers are also falling.

THE OBJECTIVE AND STRUCTURE OF THE VOLUME

The primary objective of this volume is to discuss the emerging patterns of SMEs' growth and international expansion in response to the ever-changing competitive environment, dynamics of competitive behavior, entrepreneurial behavior and strategy. These patterns appear to be increasingly different from those of the past and are continually defining, and redefining, the enterprise in new and innovative ways in relation to its changing environment, competitors, other stake-holders (for example, buyers, suppliers and associates) and their respective competitive or behavioral strategies. In such a changing environment, managing enterprises' commercial, industrial and even political relations with these external agents exceptionally well, regardless of size and location, assumes greater importance, as these relations can serve as relatively distinct bases for empowering SMEs' distinct strategy and competitiveness. The context of these relations, however, changes from one firm to the other and from one time period to the other, especially as firms grow in size, market coverage and the way in which they learn how to compete globally. Naturally their interactions with others would evolve from relatively simple, personal and largely localized relationships in the earlier stages to more complex, functional and wider scope (for example, products, markets, strategy and geography) during the later stages of the enterprise's life cycle, requiring higher degrees of strategic attention to, if not institutionalization of, previously entrepreneurial strategies than ever before. Managing such a multitude of rich and diverse relations and interactions, especially in their more formalized and institutionalized forms, appears to assume even greater importance to the health and success of the enterprise as markets become more integrated, richer and more punishing at the same time. Etemad (2003a, 2003b, 2003c) examines such relations from a wide perspective, ranging from those of MNEs to SMEs both historical and contemporary, to suggest that managing relations remains the essence of the entrepreneurial challenge for growth and prosperity in today's globally competitive arena.

This volume consists of three parts, which examine the basis and the requirements of growth and expansion in smaller enterprises from three different perspectives: (a) managing the interactive impact of an enterprise's strategy in relation to its environment; (b) managing the impact of entrepreneurial characteristics and traits on the evolutionary path of the smaller firm's internationalization strategy, including their effects on the choice, formulation, development and implementation of competitive strategy; and (c) managing the impact of enabling factors, such as high technology and electronic commerce, which entrepreneurs deploy to compete effectively in innovative ways globally.

Each of the above perspectives forms the main theme of a part in this volume. Following this introduction, this chapter provides an overview of each chapter, discusses its contributions or implications and presents the interconnections among the chapters within each part as well as with the other 11 chapters. In the process it also discusses the effects of the three interactive themes of the book while examining the impact of change on international entrepreneurship in terms of enterprise–environment interactions, patterns of entrepreneurial orientation and the evolution of strategy in internationalizing SMEs.

PART I: ENTERPRISE–ENVIRONMENT INTERACTIONS AND INTERNATIONALIZATION

This part of the book considers the characteristics of systems and subsystems embedded in the SMEs' environment, which may facilitate, if not enable, the internationalization of such firms. The three chapters of this part provide examples of the way internationalizing enterprises interact with, and build on, the local institutional relations, including those of governments and their corresponding policies, universities and their creative capacity, and other competing enterprises. These interactions with others within the environment can help, or hinder, SMEs' further internationalization.

. While the first chapter of this part, by Hamid Etemad and Hankyu Chu, has a constructionist and theoretical approach, grounded in the extensive literature of regional cluster, exploring the impact of a nurturing environment on eventual internationalization of initially small firms emanating from regional clusters and then entering competitive international markets, the orientation of Chapter 3, co-authored by Rod McNaughton and Jim Bell, is strongly empirical and factual. Their message, however, remains complementary to that of Chapter 2 and resonates well with the theme of Part I of the book: that international success is predicated on a supporting environment, especially when it is in full harmony with the entrepreneurial objective of succeeding globally. McNaughton and Bell's chapter focuses on the financial structure and the financial needs of SMEs for internationalization in relation to the financial dimension of their environment, while Gabriel Beibst and Arndt Lautenschläger concentrate in Chapter 4 on effective knowledge creation and transfer from universities to their spun-off firms. The earlier discussion of trust, social embeddedness, absence of opportunism and symmetric access to information, presented in Chapter 2, resonates well with Beibst and Lautenschläger's discussion in chapter 4 as they are usually very critical to knowledge- and transaction-intensive firms, especially in the early spin-off stages, when they are highly vulnerable.

In Chapter 2, Etemad and Chu study the dynamics of successful regional clusters and their impact on the internationalization of firms emanating from such regions. They suggest that a regional cluster is a distinct place, where Marshallian external economies attract firms to the region and the Schumpeterian creative destruction threatens their survival. It is this set of attractions and insecurities that combines to make up a successful cluster. The principal research question of this chapter is: what accounts for successful regional clusters – is it the collection of superior firms, the superior environment or a set of dynamic conditions and interactions that empower firms differentially?

What distinguishes firms in successful clusters from others is both efficiency and innovative dynamism. Their collective innovativeness and efficiency appear to be mainly due to geographical proximity and social embeddedness which combine to allow for symmetric access to the critical information and resources necessary for the efficient exchange of goods, services and ideas among members of a regional cluster, which confers both efficiency and innovativeness. Innate Marshallian instincts urge firms to seek the requisite efficiency within the region in order to reach competitive levels that can stand up to competition beyond the region. This initial need for economic efficiency calls for effective access to pertinent information among members. The geographic and social closeness provides for low incidence, even the absence, of opportunism, which characterizes a typical buyer–supplier relation elsewhere. The need for Marshallian economies and the consequent efficiencies, reinforced by closeness, interdependence and the absence of information asymmetry, cultivates closer economic relations, reinforces their socioeconomic interdependence and strengthens their sense of belonging to the social community of the region. This dynamic inter-firm relationship combines with the region's supportive environment to distinguish firms and successful clusters from the others.

The need for competitiveness within the region parallels the Schumpeterian dynamism that underpins creative destruction. The destructive forces of creative firms within the region, complemented by a supportive environment, facilitate joint action of regional firms directed against the others, especially those which neither have developed the economic efficiency of the Marshallian type nor are yet creative enough, solely or collectively. Such firms in general, and the latter firms in particular, are unable to stop open market warfare and the destruction brought upon them by the innovative force of the Schumpeterian type emanating from firms in successful regions. The key to the success of the firm within the region, and the region by extension, seems to be in their willingness to band together to create both the external economies and the necessary potent innovations by reducing their own complementary divergences to inflict competitive pains on others.

Etemad and Chu argue that the essence of firms' success in regional clusters must, therefore, lie in their willingness to take sustained joint action, while bearing the normal stresses and strains of collaboration and close competition, to achieve the requisite innovativeness that enables them to stop destructive forces from within while unleashing them on firms without. The concept of embeddedness in the socioeconomic life of the regional community, animated, conferred and even reinforced by the social institutions of the region, is what sets growing firms and an expanding region apart from the others. The social institutions charged with the task of social animation across firms must necessarily act as public institutions even when they are not technically publicly owned. This characteristic enables them to play a non-discriminatory, catalytic and at times stimulating role, especially where firms and also the region are in the formation stages of a life cycle, when the urge for opportunism – through acquisition and takeovers – by larger firms, from within and outside the region, is strong.

The combination of social embeddedness and social animation, Etemad and Chu argue, can have an implicit effect similar to social capital, where only socially embedded firms can gain access to it, and exploit it, without much additional cost when operating in concert with others within the region, while not being available to others outside the region. This has given rise to the observation that firms in successful clusters are members of the sociocultural networks (that is, embedded in the sociocultural environment of the region) and their success is the result of socioculturally specific cooperative behavior among firms in the regions supported by the nurturing environment prevailing in the region.

Chapter 2 presents some 26 propositions, grounded in theory, that portray relations between families of concepts rooted mainly in sociocultural systems with equally strong economic overtones, including cooperative behavior, trust and joint actions. Etemad and Chu argue convincingly that the sociocultural factors in the region must be dominant as the economic aspects alone are almost universally accessible elsewhere, including special economic zones (SEZs), free trade zones (FTZs) and pockets of industrial concentration spread all around the world.[1] However not all of these economic regions have been successful or have developed distinct regional competencies not readily replicable elsewhere. This insight resonates well with the comparative work of Saxenian (1994) pointing to a very different pattern of social behaviors within the San Francisco Bay Area's Silicon Valley, as compared to Boston's Route 128. It also explains the reasons behind the successes of enterprises within, or associated with, SEZs and FTZs as growth and development agents, where local governments have consistently acted as social animators, strongly and actively over time.

In the study of the People's Republic of China (PRC)'s growth and development in the 1980s and 1990s, Etemad (1996) found local authorities' social animation function to be both catalytic and stimulating in the success of enterprises in these zones, which in turn provided strong support for other enterprises in the interior of China. The local authority played an active role in the success of the initial four SEZs (Shanghai, Shenzen, Tianjin and Xiamen), followed by those of the 14 coastal FTZs (called the 'Fourteen Open Coastal Cities'), which acted as catalytic agents in reducing the perceived, if not the real, transaction costs and opportunism (Williamson, 1979, 1981; Joshi and Stump, 1999) of internationally oriented operations in their own regions first and then extended them to their own respective hinterlands in PRC's vast interior as well. The patterns of such dynamism and their role in the internationalization of the enterprise are well documented and confirmatory of the process discussed by Etemad and Chu in Chapter 2. Combined these arguments suggest that the manifestations of the sociocultural milieu in a region exhibit features similar to social capital, which at least facilitates a distinct pattern of interactions among the members that stimulates confidence-seeking and trust-building behaviors.

As a relational concept, trust can lead to the joint action necessary for enhanced efficiency and increased innovative capacity, which, in the course of time, bring about increased competitiveness and prosperity in the region. Naturally trust can only be earned (or gained) through experiential social interactions. Social regional institutions must play a critical role in facilitating and supporting sustained intraregional inter-firm relations, which appear to be functioning catalytically across firm and industry boundaries, yet tend to remain very local. With the help of social institutions in the region, higher collaboration and trust are more likely to develop between individuals and respective enterprises (Barkema *et al.*, 1996, 1997) in close proximity (Gulati, 1995a; Gomes-Casseres, 1997) than between those separated by both geographical and sociocultural distance, in spite of enhanced communications due to globalization. Individuals embedded in the socio-cultural life of a region can perceive lower costs associated with intraregional inter-firm interactions, especially for transaction-intensive relations, such as research and development in cutting-edge innovations.

Accumulated trust seems to militate against opportunistic behaviors in the region and especially among the collaborating partners pursuing innovative endeavors jointly (Forrest and Martin, 1992). Such nurturing characteristics are critical to the growth of firms and the region, especially if smaller firms with much higher levels of vulnerability are to be attracted. Naturally, small firms can concentrate on innovation and relative economic efficiency in such nurturing environments without the customary fears of insolvency and demise due to asymmetric information flow from, and the opportunistic behaviors of, others (especially collaborating partners in the region). Instead they can even develop synergistic relations with other partners in the regional cluster and thereby contribute to the growth of their own constellation (Gomes-Casseres, 1996, 1997) as well as that of the region. The evolutionary path of constellations (Gomes-Casseres, 1996; Yoshino and Rangan, 1995) would inevitably force them through internationalization transformation, taking them beyond the region and into the international markets, and internationalizing their previously regional supply and value chains, if not their strategic orientation.

The last section of this chapter examines how successful clusters achieve higher and faster economic growth than other regions through an effective creation and transfer of knowledge within a region. Knowledge, as an input to innovation, tends to be tacit and requires intensive interaction among individuals for its effective transfer and efficient use. A successful region, where trust is embedded in the social relations among the members within the region, facilitates the interaction and exchange of knowledge. Therefore the region tends to exhibit higher capacity for innovation, leading to higher economic prosperity.

The overriding implication, if not the lesson, of this chapter is that firms are attracted to supportive environments, which can provide for the agglomeration of Marshallian external economies that culminate in deployment of innovative forces destructive to others. A strongly adaptive, interactively supportive and even dialectically dynamic relationship between a firm and other firms within a region and their environment stands out as the compelling message of this chapter, which complements those of the next two chapters.

In Chapter 3, McNaughton and Bell suggest that both the act and the pace of internationalization are influenced by two ignored dimensions: the firm's capital structure and the financial environment within which it operates. They draw upon the wide and rich experience of venture capitalists in Australia. Australian venture capitalists not only finance the early stages of SMEs' growth and development, they have also acquired a much broader perspective on the subject of financing entrepreneurial ventures than the entrepreneurs, whose views are generally limited to one or a few experiences. They suggest that the small size of the Australian market forces growth-oriented SMEs to consider internationalization sooner than larger markets. However a combination of factors affect the growth and internationalization of such firms. They are all related to financial structure, including the ways in which Australian SMEs have traditionally financed their growth in relation to both the structure of the private capital community and the public equity markets, which at best serve as impediments, if not as barriers, to the growth and internationalization of small firms in most cases.

The small size of the private capital (that is, the venture capital community) and the highly conservative requirements of public equity markets seem to have discouraging effects on entrepreneurs and a negative impact on raising successive rounds of capital to finance early and optimal internationalization. As a result, and because of the shortage of capital, entrepreneurs either impede their firms' internationalization or alternatively look for the necessary capital from sources that are not conducive to rapid growth and optimal internationalization.

McNaughton and Bell's empirical research paints a vivid picture of the financial environment's impact on the growth rate of small firms aspiring to internationalize. Although this chapter concentrates on growing firms' financial structure and financial relations with the private and public financial communities in Australia, some of the broader factors discussed by Etemad and Chu in Chapter 2 seem to be operating in the background. The less than optimal relationship between the firms and the financial community could be attributed to, for example, information asymmetry, fear of opportunism and weak (or even absence of) trust between the firm and the venture capital community. While the literature of industrial clusters documents the profound impact of these factors (that is, contributing positively when present), their absence or negative impacts must be equally negative. McNaughton and Bell find that successive rounds of capital-raising activity and easy access to sources of capital – both private and public – are required for rapid internationalization. Naturally either the absence of capital or the conservative behavior of the venture and equity capital communities, in terms of high rates, stringent requirements or impatience, may not only eclipse SMEs' growth, it may also divert them from achieving optimal internationalization. The chapter reports on capital-seeking internationalizations with less than optimal results.

The managerial implications of this research are noteworthy and deserve serious attention. Those entrepreneurs whose expectations and decisions lead them to pursue less than aggressive objectives and select relatively conservative financing strategies, in response either to the stringent domestic equity requirements or to the less than highly-supportive overall environment (that is, non-supportive, if not hostile, in some cases), are bound to achieve lower growth rates than their counterparts with more positive outlooks facing supportive environments elsewhere. McNaughton and Bell refer to a report by McKinsey & Company (1993) that documented some of these problems as early as 1993. Ironically it suggested the concept of 'born globals' as an option for ameliorating problems associated with small domestic market size and the financial community's conservative behavior. The chapter suggests that there is still a strong need for the financial community to recognize and respond to promising entrepreneurial initiatives, especially when they entail rapid internationalization. In the absence of a responsive Australian financial community, McNaughton and Bell contend, firms with high growth prospects will be forced to seek supportive financing outside Australia.

The entrepreneurial challenges of this chapter are equally engaging. Australian entrepreneurs need to develop a deeper understanding of the financial communities' requirements, based on the wealth of accumulated experience, which can assist them with their early financing problems. Reportedly the challenges facing entrepreneurs, the financial community and the Australian government remain unresolved and, as a direct result, the internationalization of small and medium enterprises is forced to assume a slower rate than those of other countries with both conducive financial environments and financial structure.

While the financial structure and financial dimension of the environment are relatively tangible, the impact of other intangible entrepreneurial inputs, such as knowledge, competence and orientation, among other experientially based behaviors, is not well understood or well measured, and naturally receives little consideration. On the one hand, embryonic firms in high technology suffer more from the added symptoms of smallness, inexperience and the inherent uncertainties of high technology than their counterparts elsewhere. On the other hand, the older firms in their sector show strong reaction to their new and high-technology offerings when the latter have the potential to restructure older businesses, and even to put them out of business altogether. This is a typical Schumpeterian creative destruction (Schumpeter, 1934), which makes survival very difficult for small firms in the embryonic stages of their life cycle as their larger and established counterparts, especially when facing premature technological obsolescence, may conspire to slow their progress, if not eliminate them altogether. Within this category of firms, new technology-based firms (NTBFs), when spun off by universities and run by previously university-based academics (that is, former scientists, turned scientific or technological entrepreneurs), are particularly vulnerable and face tremendous challenges. In most cases they are underprepared and feel profoundly ill-at-ease in the embryonic stages of their enterprise.

In Chapter 4, Beibst and Lautenschläger focus on a number of complicated issues. Theoretically, new technology-based firms spun off by university researchers should stand a high chance of success as most successful high-technology firms have had a university-based pedigree and started in regions with supportive universities active in cutting-edge research and development, knowledge creation and transfer. The experience of Silicon Valley in the San Francisco Bay area, Boston's cluster of firms, the Silicon Triangle in North Carolina (all in the USA) and the Cambridge–Oxford area cluster (in the UK), to name a few, provide ample confirmatory evidence of the contribution of universities to the success of technology-based firms in their respective regional clusters.

Beibst and Lautenschläger provide a short overview of university-based start-ups, combined with a literature review to suggest that two factors, economies of scale and international orientation, are critical to the survival and success of these high technology-based firms. In spite of their high-technology status, which may suggest that they are in technology supply-push modes, these firms must be responsive to their buyers in order to generate the large scale necessary for achieving scale economies. Naturally, and owing to the small size of their domestic markets in the early stages of the technology, these firms must also adopt an international orientation and be prepared to attract international customers and therefore compete in global markets, which by definition are more competitive and need higher entrepreneurial and managerial competencies than those required of their domestic counterparts. However this chapter's empirical findings show that the academic and scientific entrepreneurs, based broadly in the USA, Ireland, Israel and Munich, are initially ill-prepared to deal with these and similar complex issues. The chapter also explores empirically whether these new entrepreneurs are aware of the internationalization imperative necessary to the success, if not survival, of their business. The authors report that mere access to cutting-edge technology is not sufficient; strong entrepreneurial competencies in a supportive environment are also necessary. These empirical findings resonate very well with the the theme of Part I and the message of previous chapters. Beibst and Lautenschläger report that there is ample evidence to suggest that an international orientation is even more critical to international success than a cutting-edge technology, which necessitates that the universities and their spun-off businesses inculcate the values of, if not actually taking the necessary steps to implement, globally thinking and globally acting entrepreneurship to ensure success.

PART II: ENTREPRENEURIAL CHARACTERISTICS AND INTERNATIONALIZATION

Part II of the book turns from the interactive impacts of the environment and entrepreneurship to focus on the potential impacts of entrepreneurial characteristics on internationalization. Although the three chapters contained in Part II examine distinct aspects of entrepreneurial characteristics, the influence of the environment is omnipresent in the background. In each of the chapters, however, entrepreneurial characteristics empower entrepreneurial actions even in the face of non-cooperative and non-interactive, if not hostile, environments. Traditionally entrepreneurs are viewed as assertive, creative and influential members of their respective socioeconomic and cultural environments. These characteristics are usually attributed to the entrepreneur's personal traits. Chapter 5 presents a vivid example of the lifelong efforts of an exceptionally successful British entrepreneur, James Dyson, who capitalized on his extensive social network to accomplish highly ambitious objectives far beyond the immediate reach and resources of a typically young enterprise. This example provides insights into the enabling impact, as well as limiting aspects, of entrepreneurs' social networks and their respective effects on the entrepreneur's internationalizing efforts. Chapter 6 elaborates on culturally rooted entrepreneurial traits leading to decisions and behaviors that have an effect on SMEs' growth and internationalization. Chapter 7 presents the findings of a cross-cultural research study of potential future entrepreneurs via self-assessment.

In Chapter 5, Oswald Jones and Steve Conway present an in-depth study of a successful and fascinating entrepreneur who understood the value of social networks very well, built them systematically and exploited them masterfully for his firm's growth and internationalization.

Jones and Conway approach the case carefully and methodically. They first review the literature on the psychological characteristics of individual entrepreneurs and point out that even highly independent entrepreneurs find it necessary at times to depend on the resources of their social network. In fact successful entrepreneurs learn how to capitalize on both the strong and the weak ties in their social network to achieve their goals on the one hand and benefit their network members on the other hand. Ironically a highly successful entrepreneur, such as James Dyson, found himself repeatedly in need of external resources and could not marshal them without the help of his social network. In this situation most successful entrepreneurs rely on their own innate characteristics and find the path of least resistance. For example, Dyson succeeded repeatedly in identifying and leveraging the necessary resources of his network for expanding to where his network had already extended. Conversely, he was restrained from achieving his full potential where the network became weak, thin or non-existent. Dyson's network was rich, dense and deeply rooted in the UK. As a result Dyson could draw upon it to finance his entrepreneurial initiative and attain his impressive achievements.

Jones and Conway challenge the classic portrayal of entrepreneurs as independent and heroic individuals who rely on themselves alone for a host of capabilities, including developing insights, risk taking, resourcefulness and even motivating others to follow them. They argue, however, that a substantive literature, confirmed by a host of lifelong cases such as that of Dyson, paints a different picture, if not pointing to the contrary: that entrepreneurs are highly ingenious in depending on their own social network, which is at times protected from, and even opaque to, others. In other words they are not as independent as the psychological approaches portray them. However their acute sense of establishing a balance between trust-based dependence and self-based independence driven by their innate need for high achievement is what sets them apart from the others. We therefore expect this balance to vary from one entrepreneur to another (according to the entrepreneur's individual traits) and not necessarily to vary from one culture to another. Chapter 6 provides a rich and complementary perspective on this balance in terms of potential trade-offs between entrepreneurially based traits and culturally rooted practices.

Chapter 6 considers Thailand's manifestations of culturally rooted and distinct entrepreneurial practices. Here Supara Kapasuwan and Jerman Rose present their longitudinal and in-depth examination of entrepreneurial traits in a special class of firms owned, operated and managed by their original founders from the start-up stage. They contend that the practice of delegating authority and responsibility (or lack thereof) in fast-growing small enterprises (that is, with a relatively high growth rate as compared to others in the environment) is based on the evolution of socioculturally rooted entrepreneurial tendencies. They trace the pattern and impact of delegation of authority and responsibility overtime in fast-growing small firms from start-up to high growth and early maturity. They suggest that the pattern of delegation holds the potential to set the enterprise on its way to becoming a successful medium-sized enterprise with a strong presence in international markets, or to follow a road to stagnation domestically. They also report that the Thai pattern defies the predictions of the Western linear growth models leading to delegation of authority and responsibility.[2]

The conventional wisdom, based on the 'linear growth' assumption, is that such firms would eventually reach the limits of their founder's managerial capabilities at the helm of the enterprise, beyond which further growth either slows down or stops altogether. The implicit assumption behind the proposed 'stages of small business growth models', rooted in the sociocultural tenets of the West, is constant, if not decreasing, returns to scale for the founder's managerial capabilities. With this assumption omnipresent, all founder–managers will eventually reach the outer limits of their capabilities, at a point beyond which a professional management team must be put in place if further progress along the firm's evolutionary path is to continue unimpeded. Such transitional models imply that the entrepreneur, who had created, learned experientially (that is, endured the 'growing pains' of start-up stages) and matured over the early life cycle of the enterprise, would reach a point beyond which he was incapable of further growth and thus must delegate his responsibilities to others. The set of assumptions leading to the above implications and consequent practices appear to ignore the universal sense of patriarchal ownership and control and the entrepreneur–founder's beliefs and practices beyond the Western cultures. Kapasuwan and Rose argue that most such models are developed in the West and function well within a typical Western environment, where the succession of professional management is a part of formal planning for continued growth and not necessarily linked to the founder's managerial capabilities. The implicit assumption behind such delegation models is that they are independent of the entrepreneurs' innate traits (see Chapter 5 for more detailed discussion) and the sociocultural context within which they operate. Kapasuwan and Rose challenge the cultural aspect of this assumption for Eastern cultures. They also challenge the validity of such models for growing family enterprises in an Eastern environment such as Thailand.

On the basis of a review of the literature, they further argue that the entrepreneurial traits of Thai founder–managers put their enterprises on an evolutionary path that differs from that of their Western counterparts: (a) the enterprise may not reach the hypothesized limitation of entrepreneurial capabilities as fast as the theory proposes; (b) founder–managers' capabilities may have been enhanced along the way by the recruitment of family members; and (c) these family members enrich and strengthen the firm's managerial capabilities even though they may not have occupied the ranks of management officially.

Kapasuwan and Rose present the longitudinal case study of two founder–manager entrepreneurs in Thailand's fish processing industry that supports their contentions. In both cases the growth continued unabated with the original founder managing the firm. In the first case, where a professional manager, with broad and successful past experience, was brought on board, the sociocultural context of the firm rendered the manager ineffective and the original founder had to step in to resume his responsibilities in order to remedy the situation. In the second case the start-up continued to grow without many detectable fluctuations or slow-downs.

The authors suggest that the Thai founder–managers studied resort to their own culturally rooted traits and use their close family and social networks, developed within the context of both the family and the firm over time, to enhance their own capabilities, and as a result growth continues unimpeded. The clear implication of their study, although not generalizable because of the study's limitations, is that the sociocultural embeddedness of the Thai entrepreneurs allows them to leverage their family relations and networks to extend their capabilities beyond the linear limits implied by Western theory. The implications of this study stand out and can be stated clearly:

1. the cultural context of such firms separates them from their counterparts in the West, which may render Western theories less applicable, if not inapplicable, to societies such as Thailand;
2. the characteristics of entrepreneurs from, and embedded in, such environments, may not be those postulated by or derived from such theories, as entrepreneurial traits may be manifestations of deep-rooted sociocultural characteristics and long accepted social norms;
3. the firm–environment interactions in general, and those of family firms in particular, may be much more supportive and cooperative than those of the West (which are adversarial for the most part) and thus grow beyond the Western expectations;
4. the family firm embedded in an Eastern culture may grow and gain competitiveness at a higher rate than its counterparts in the West thanks to the close family dynamics.

Combined, these implications suggest that caution must be exercised in applying, or extending, Western based models to societies within which firm and family operate differently, such as Thailand.

On the other side of the coin, however, culturally embedded entrepreneurial practices may face added complexities in international environments. Although culturally embedded start-ups may grow for a long time and not reach the limits of the individual founder–manager's abilities (as predicted by the Western theories) in their own home environment, as discussed earlier, achieving similar growth paths in international markets is not certain. The uncertainty is in part due to the fact that neither the family nor the social networks are extendable to foreign markets. Similarly, culturally embedded practices may not be as potent in international markets as they are at home; furthermore, when the social network can be extended beyond the home environment, they may not be capable of offering as much potency to compensate for similar local social networks supporting the local professional management teams managing the internationalizing firm (see Chapter 5 for the detailed case of James Dyson).

One must also consider the possibility that the need for a transition to a professional managerial team may have been obscured by sustained growth of the firm while operating in its original cultural milieu[3] and drawing on family members as if they were regular employees, which may erroneously lead the culturally embedded founder–manager (and entrepreneurs, by extension) to conclude that there is no need to consider professional management even in international markets. In the absence of a similar supportive sociocultural milieu, the internationalization of these firms must necessarily suffer as neither is their cultural embeddedness helpful to their internationalization process nor are the founder–manager's culturally and entrepreneurially optimal practices at home (including the recruitment of family members for managerial posts) as potent abroad (even when they can be easily extended beyond the home base). In the international markets, such socioculturally rooted competencies cannot be regarded as potent capabilities for propelling the company forward. Ethnocentricity (Chakravarthy and Perlmauter, 1985) may in fact impede progress abroad. Furthermore, as the potentially low rate of learning by doing associated with the above factors (owing to potential cultural incompatibilities) may have an adverse impact on experimental accumulation of potent managerial capabilities in international markets, the growth rates are likely to slow down, which may in turn expedite the need for transition from a family enterprise type of management team and associated operations (Redding, 1990) to a professional manager or a managerial team. While the possibility of recruiting family members for potential management positions, growing on the job and learning at an even faster rate than professional managers, provides for managerial consistency and puts the non-family type of professional managers at a relative disadvantage at home, local professional managers may serve the firm much better abroad. This is a characteristic that family enterprises may not fully recognize, and could not easily remedy, if they do not question the applicability of practices at home and extend their home-based practices abroad when embarking on internationalization.

Although these, and similar, complications form a rich agenda for future research on family or owner-operated firms operating internationally, a host of troubling issues remain. Consider, for example, the conflict between culturally rooted managerial styles at home and abroad or across Eastern and Western cultures. How could entrepreneurs of family enterprises delegate authority and responsibility to non-family members abroad when they had not done so at home? Irrespective of the extent of delegation, would they be able to identify the true nature of emerging problems in international markets through their own cultural, perceptual and even managerial perspectives? Would the familiar and successful home-based solutions be applied once problems were identified abroad? How would entrepreneurs of such family enterprises recognize their own limitations and finally delegate to others, not to their family members, but to international professionals? How and when would the general problem of limited personal capacity, and even technical competence, be approached and solved? How would these problems affect their choice of strategy and rate of internationalization and international entrepreneurship?

Chapter 7 provides answers to some of the above questions, in addition to a series of generic questions concerning entrepreneurial competencies and capabilities across cultures. In this chapter, the research team of Kent Neupert, Norris Krueger and Bee-Leng Chua explores some of the root causes of the problems identified above. They examine the concept of entrepreneurial self efficacy (ESE) and explain that previous research had found that the entrepreneurial self-efficacy construct would be a good indicator of a person's belief in his own abilities to perform the wide range of tasks required to create a new venture. They also point to the previous research indicating that one's perception of entrepreneurial opportunities for new ventures could become increasingly credible when one was involved in stimulating processes such as formal business planning.

Neupert, Krueger and Chua extend the context of earlier research on the self-efficacy construct, and its application, to entrepreneurial activities in new international settings and contexts. Their findings support those of earlier research and reconfirm the relationship between ESE and 'entrepreneurial intentions'. In order to test ESE measures for their applicability to participants in international business plan competitions, they formed a sample of non-US international respondents. Their findings are generally supportive: not only does ESE appear to be a good proxy measure for performance in business plan competitions, but also the measure of 'intention to enter and compete' in such events appears to be reflective of strong belief in one's entrepreneurial abilities. The authors also examined a potential relationship between ESE and entrepreneurship education programs and explored their corresponding implications: the presence of the originator of the idea in the business competition team helps and, in the same vein, the exposure of entrepreneurship students to local community entrepreneurs may foster their interest in entrepreneurship and stimulate their desire to gain added capabilities in order to support their entrepreneurial intentions successfully beyond graduation.

Therefore the family of ESE and related measures must be viewed as welcome signs, as they will provide us with some tangible systems of measurements for previously intangible, if not unknown, aspects of entrepreneurship, especially in the international settings. Scholars may be able to identify the high correlates, if not the actual predictors, of entrepreneurial success in international markets in order to assist internationalizing entrepreneurs. Consider, for example, a potential application to Britain's James Dyson's case, discussed in Chapter 5. In the absence of such measures and in spite of an impressive array of successes in his domestic markets in Britain, Dyson's much less successful foray in international markets is an indication that much still remains unknown about entrepreneurship in general and, by extension, international entrepreneurship in particular (see Chapter 5 for details). A partial list of questions, for example, might include the following. Under what circumstances do entrepreneurial successes at home lead to similar results in the international markets? Is the former a prerequisite of the latter? What possible role can education play in translating success in domestically oriented entrepreneurial initiatives and intentions to their international counterparts? And finally, how should we account for intangible characteristics of international entrepreneurs?

The cross-cultural implications of some of these concerns resonate well with Kapasuwan and Rose's research that found detectable divisions in delegation of authority and responsibility, from the accepted Western models, documented in the case of Thai entrepreneurs. This is another indication of the need for further cross-cultural research, especially on internationalization topics related to, and at the interfaces of, environment, entrepreneurial characteristics and strategy formulation.

Chapter 6 provides a set of constructs and measurements that lay the initial foundation for a systematic understanding of the factors that influence entrepreneurial success, especially in the embryonic stages of an enterprise. By logical extension, the knowledge of which pattern of personal traits (or professional profiles) and corresponding entrepreneurial practices, among others, could lead to entrepreneurial success and which other traits do not lead to a successful entrepreneurial career, especially in the earlier stages, facilitates an individual entrepreneur's quest for success in international markets. Therefore ESE and similar measures may even help the aspiring entrepreneurs to assess their own potentials for future successes and thereby seek to enhance and enrich their own capabilities in order to avoid the agony of failure, or slow growth, uncharacteristic of the successful entrepreneurs. Likewise, such measures may also save potential partners, the investment community and even society from indiscriminately high expectation of success from all entrepreneurial endeavors. Stimulating educational programs and institutions may also use ESE-type measures to trace the impact of various curricular components of their entrepreneurial curriculum for their potential or actual differential effects on future successes. For both their educational and demonstrative effects, an active involvement of the entrepreneurial community with students in entrepreneurship programs would expose them to the entrepreneur's 'real life and experience' and might stimulate, improve and even strengthen their entrepreneurial intentions; this in turn might be traced with ESE-type measures over time. Such applications resonate well with this chapter's suggestion as they would allow for even mildly interested students to examine themselves realistically, leading them either to enhance their competencies in relation to their entrepreneurial intentions and interests regarding the tasks at hand or to select alternative courses of action.

Equally important, at the policy level, is the potential educational role of successful entrepreneurs in encouraging entrepreneurship. According to this research, not only may exposure to local entrepreneurs popularize their success stories and successful practices in dealing with a host of challenging problems in their respective projects (including environmental adversity), which may in turn inspire nascent entrepreneurs, it also helps to create a portfolio of the best entrepreneurial practices against which proposed projects and prospects could be measured. The creation of benchmarks is of critical importance, especially to international entrepreneurship, for which such benchmarks are *not* well established. Consider, for example, the potential use of such benchmarks (or the knowledge portfolio of best practices) in two cases discussed earlier in this book. If James Dyson, highly successful in British markets on the strength of his domestic social network (see Chapter 5 for details), had been exposed to the international counterparts of his own case earlier on, he would have recognized the necessity of developing, for example, the requisite international network for his ultimate success in international markets. With that recognition, Dyson could have taken the necessary steps early on and propagated an even stronger international social network than his domestic one to ensure success. For an entrepreneur of James Dyson's caliber, extending his social network beyond the British Isles would probably not have constituted a challenge, but it could have come as a natural routine.

Another notable application of measurements is to the cross-cultural bases of international entrepreneurship. Similar to Dyson's case, if successful domestic entrepreneurs, such as those in Thailand (see Chapter 6 for details), were exposed to the benchmarks of success in international markets, they would certainly take the necessary steps to master them before attempting to enter such markets. By a logical extension, an early exposure to the challenges and disappointments of many potentially influential factors, including the inherent challenges and impact of new technology, could serve as an early warning system to entrepreneurs. Such exposure assumes greater importance when domestic entrepreneurs decide to embark on international markets, especially when they deploy inherently riskier strategies to reach those markets, including those based on high technology, where operational risks and rewards are higher, while markets are richer and larger, and competition is likely to be more intense than in their respective domestic markets. Inevitably the required resources and entrepreneurial capabilities for operating in such markets must be measurably higher than those of the entrepreneur's home base.

The combined research in Part II of the book portrays an attractive system. On the one hand, a system of measurements (for example, ESE-type measures and constructs as presented in Chapter 7) is emerging to trace entrepreneurial evolution (and even building up entrepreneurial capabilities to meet the requirements) and, on the other hand, there will be a battery of documented success stories and best practices on which entrepreneurial strategy can be based and measured. Armed with the above evidence and measurements, international entrepreneurs can deal with the added complexities of the international markets. One such added complexity is that the local competitors are embedded in the local sociocultural and technological environment (see Chapter 2 for detailed discussion of social embeddedness and Chapters 5 and 6 for British and Thai examples, respectively) and are naturally more knowledgable with better access to local resources (including social capital and social networks) and more dexterous in their own environment than others entering their markets from elsewhere (for example, international entrepreneurs). In contrast, international entrepreneurs face the opposite and suffer from the ills of foreignness (Hymer, 1976). Technology can be viewed as another complicating factor as it may assume a Janus face in international markets: it may further enable the international entrepreneur to achieve a 'level playing field' against competitors or it may fail of its own account, as a result, for example, of various mismatches: (a) with the entrepreneur's intentions and interest, and thus not enable the entrepreneur to attain his objectives, even though the focal technology may become a technical or technological marvel on its own merits; (b) with consumer expectations, and thus not achieve the necessary market acceptability, irrespective of the technological merits of the consequent goods and services; or (c) with the environment, and thereby magnify the international entrepreneur's early 'foreignness' disadvantages, instead of ameliorating them, which may seal the fate of the enterprise in those foreign markets.

Part III of the book will discuss some of these technological complexities, sometimes with unclear, but real, Janus faces.

PART III: HIGH TECHNOLOGY AND STRATEGY

In the internationalization process of entrepreneurial firms, the lines of demarcation between an action motivated by a deliberately formulated strategy in response to environmental change, and one initiated by the innate entrepreneurial characteristics, may lose their precision and even their clarity as events unfold. Cases presented in this volume are instructive. For example, James Dyson's indisputable success in Britain, and not so successful performance in international markets, could be equally attributed either to his inappropriate entrepreneurial aptitude for internationalization or to an inadequately formulated internationalization strategy and its corresponding implementation (see Chapter 5 for details). While the end results in a typical entrepreneurial case are clear, causes or combination of causes are not, which raises challenging questions for future scholarly inquiry. Such research may in fact show that a combination of the entrepreneurial and strategic factors were responsible and their combined impacts may have been further mitigated by environmental forces. However some clear resolution must emerge if young entrepreneurs are to use successful practices as guides and as benchmarks.

Thai entrepreneurship, and entrepreneurship in Eastern cultures by extension, portray another aspect of the above fuzziness. Aside from the narrow question of whether or not the Western models of delegation are applicable to the delegation of authority and responsibility in international markets (see details for Thailand in Chapter 6), the broader related question in international entrepreneurship is whether socioculturally rooted models and theories can be easily extended to other sociocultural systems or subsystems. Alternatively, where should internationalizing enterprises start when adjustments are necessary and must be adopted? The implications could be very profound. The case of international entrepreneurship, emanating from Thailand, where entrepreneurial traits and strategy formulation may have interacted, can serve as an instructive example. It is not difficult to imagine that the internationalizing Thai entrepreneurs must have anguished over the dilemma of deciding on a balance between two polar-extreme possibilities:

1. *Home-oriented strategy.* From a managerial perspective, a family of Thai-oriented strategies would be readily available and the socioculturally embedded traits, and their associated management practices in Thailand, could be easily extended internationally. Although such extensions would provide for consistency between the home and host market strategies, it would also expose them to the risk of using an ethnocentric internationalization strategy (that is, one based on home practices) where polycentric strategy (that is, strategy adopted for local conditions) would have been more potent, thereby yielding relatively inferior results at home and

abroad. By a logical extension, the management would then be compelled to face the added challenges of adopting home-centered strategies for each local market, one at a time, or entertaining the other polar extreme, or a combination of the two.

2. *Host-oriented strategy.* Such strategies would formulate a locally centered strategy for entry into each market based on the prevailing patterns of management practices abroad (or in the local market). However this would expose a typical Thai firm to the risk of inconsistencies, if not incompatibilities, between its practices at home and in international markets.

The former option would require training a host of family members (or close social allies) to extend the tradition of the Thai or family enterprise management practices (Redding, 1990) to international markets. The latter would delegate management authority and responsibilities to local managers in each of the international markets with the added risk that their management might not necessarily be compatible with the patterns practiced at home, which could render the home-based control measure totally ineffectual. As stated earlier, the practical solution may indeed lie somewhere in between the two polar extremes, where a balance of entrepreneurial traits and strategy formulation would interact with, or be further mediated by, the environmental factors. However the current state of literature does not reflect such formulaic strategy formulation; nor does it point to a tested and sound process for achieving the well-balanced optimal strategy. As a result, international entrepreneurs may have to rely on their entrepreneurial instincts to formulate a potent strategy and find innovative and competitive pathways to success in international markets. Ironically e-commerce and Internet-oriented international entrepreneurs were forced to face the above dilemma and devise their own ad hoc, but informed, solutions to tackle the problem. The extreme transparency of e-commerce would quickly expose inconsistencies and exploit inefficiencies, to the detriment of its practitioners.

While the conventional wisdom has pointed to SMEs' diseconomies of size and scale (due to their smallness) in the past, it has not pointed to a relatively low level of inefficiency due to the information intensity of their operations, especially for 'on-line' enterprises. Such conventional scale arguments implied that they would not be more competitive, or gain competitiveness at a higher rate, than their larger counterparts, especially in international markets which require even more explicit and tacit (Nonaka, 1995; Nonaka and Takeuchi, 1996) as well as more experiential information (Johanson and Vahlne, 1977, 1990; Johanson and Wiedersheim-Paul, 1975; Cavusgil, 1980, 1982; Eriksson *et al.*, 1997) than the others.[4] However this is no longer the case as these information-intensive enterprises are using information as the strategic arena of choice to gain efficiencies at rates not experienced before. Furthermore the public good aspect of information and the transformation of the Internet to a public knowledge network (discussed in Chapter 9), especially the readily available information on-line, have favored these firms. They are benefiting at differentially higher rates (than their larger and conventional counterparts) as they do not bear the full cost of supporting the information infrastructure to harvest the pertinent information for their own use and advantage. There is sufficient evidence to support the above argument and it suggests that on-line enterprises are using the advantages of information intensity and the knowledge networks (discussed in Chapters 9 and 10, respectively) readily accessible on the Internet to counter their diseconomies of size, scale and inexperience. These arguments run against the grain of the conventional wisdom and traditional strategy formulation in typical environments and invite scholars to confront new and challenging frontiers.[5]

While Chapter 8 documents the success of small on-line entrepreneurs, Chapter 9 focuses on developing a theoretical model to explain the efficiency-enhancing role of information and knowledge in businesses in general and through the Internet and the World Wide Web in particular. Chapter 10 follows the tradition of the resource-based view of the firm (Barney, 1991; Grant, 1996; Nelson and Winter, 1982) to suggest that smaller enterprises can exploit knowledge as a resource as potently as the others. In fact, Chapter 10 concentrates on the use of knowledge through knowledge networks (Etemad and Lee, 2000, 2003), which underlies the operations of the Internet and associated information- and knowledge-intensive strategies such as e-commerce. In contrast to Chapter 8's specific case examples, Chapter 9's theoretical arguments support general models of e-commerce, which is the explicit model in Chapter 10, in which information and knowledge intensity through the Internet underlies most e-commerce processes and Internet technologies used by the popularly called 'dot.com' or 'on-line' entrepreneurs.

As economic efficiency in any information-intensive market depends critically on the amount, the nature and the efficient use of information, especially in the emerging international markets, differential competitive gains will have to depend on better access to, and the use of, high-quality information. Therefore information-aware entrepreneurs should logically formulate strategies to increase their access to information and knowledge continually, improve upon the quality of information (and knowledge) on which they would base their strategic decisions, and exploit[6] the accessible information and knowledge as rapidly and efficiently as possible, as time is of the essence in e-commerce transactions. Therefore, if on-line entrepreneurs can succeed in implementing the above provisions, they will be able to gain higher competitiveness relative to others and consequently acquire market share at home and abroad, especially in those market segments based on higher information requirements, at one extreme, and in others based on the readily available information (or knowledge that can be mined) at the other extreme, that the larger and conventional firms may have been incapable of exploiting or simply missed.

As stated earlier, Chapter 8 is based mainly on specific e-commerce matters. The ten cases studied by Phillip Rosson in that chapter portray the above entrepreneurial instincts and reflect a true entrepreneurial orientation in action. The entrepreneurs that Rosson studied saw the emerging international marketing opportunities, through e-commerce, and responded to them accordingly. Their cases can be reflective of the enabling impact of the environment (for example, the advent of the Internet and e-commerce technologies providing opportunities), entrepreneurial traits (for example, the particular entrepreneurial traits of this group of entrepreneurs compelled them to take advantage of the emerging e-commerce opportunities), and/or strategy formulation (for example, formulating internationalization strategy by leveraging the emerging e-commerce technologies). As stated earlier, the most likely scenario in such cases is where all three sets of factors may have had some partial, yet interactive, impact on the ultimate decisions.

As technology is assuming a much higher importance in entrepreneurial actions, this part of the book focuses on the interaction of technology and internationalization of SMEs. Therefore the impact of technology on formulation of strategy and internationalization constitutes the main theme of Part III of this volume. The first four chapters of Part III explore technologically oriented strategies through which small firms can achieve competitiveness and gain international presence. Internet-based techniques and technologies underlie the first three chapters of this part, while the fourth presents a wide, rich and longitudinal and integrated perspective on the true entrepreneurial practices of a large number of micro and small enterprises over time, where the impacts of technology, environmental change and entrepreneurial intentions combine indiscernibly to produce the ultimate results.

In Chapter 8, Philip Rosson examines the role of the Internet and early e-commerce in the internationalization of small Canadian firms. The chapter starts with a review of exporting literature related to small and medium-sized enterprises. It then introduces the characteristics of competition in cyberspace with a view to the potential advantages, and also disadvantages, associated with SMEs' marketing on the Internet. While SMEs can leverage their restricted resources by taking advantage of the Internet characteristics to achieve international presence at a higher rate and with fewer additional costs than otherwise, disadvantages must be avoided as much as possible to guard against the lower consequent growth rates. Rosson draws on the literature to review pertinent aspects of e-commerce from the above (SMEs') perspective. He proceeds to examine a list of Internet marketing-related issues with a potentially higher impact on SMEs than on the larger enterprises. This list includes disintermediation, extreme price transparency, non-clarity of size (that is, smallness is not obvious), trust and liability, and privacy of information on the Internet, among others. The results of this examination are then incorporated into a general conceptual framework for start-ups' growth in the international markets through a simple and then an expanded exporting arrangement. This framework forms the context within which Rosson studied ten rapidly internationalizing start-ups. He presents the highlights of his in-depth interviews with these SMEs in short case studies. They cover a wide range of variations in terms of scope of activities, number of employees, annual sales and sales growth rates, service orientation and mode of serving customers in highly diverse sectors. With two exceptions, the cases can be viewed as successful 'Internet start-ups', which are still thriving in spite of the post 'September Eleven' economic slow-down and the melt-down of the high-technology sector in general and the massive bankruptcy of the dot.coms in particular.

The ten cases in Chapter 8 document and present brief personal stories of the entrepreneurs who started their enterprises with the help of the Internet. They also show how these entrepreneurs would spot opportunities, find innovative and ingenious ways to capitalize on those opportunities that others had ignored, and also avoid the adversities that entrap even the large enterprises at the same time. In fact they are vivid examples of international entrepreneurship, with local entrepreneurs seizing the moment to create lasting value locally and internationally.

The chapter ends with some noteworthy conclusions. First, Rosson synthesizes his research in terms of the lesson that other SMEs must study and learn before attempting similar cases.[7] Second, he identifies a pattern of best practices utilized throughout his sample. Although restricted to the cases studied, these derived suggestions resonate very well with the theme of Part II of the book as well as the specific findings of Chapters 5, 6 and 7, where entrepreneurial traits and visions combine with the best practices that entrepreneurs devised in isolation or adopted from others and improved upon.

Third, he briefly points to the emerging models of exporting on the Internet which are gradually combining the best practices adopted from both traditional and Internet marketing. These hybrid models are theoretically more efficient than their conventional counterparts as they capitalize intensively on the flow of information for managing their affairs much more favorably than conventional exporting cases.

While Rosson's chapter and its case studies provide empirical evidence for on-line entrepreneurial efforts leading to information- and technology-centered efficiencies in on-line SMEs, the next chapter provides theoretical arguments that support and explain them. Chapter 9 presents a theory of incremental efficiency gains of the Internet-based enterprises. Khaled Soufani and

Terrence Tse adopt a theoretical approach to show that the Internet-based enterprises, popularly referred to as 'dot.coms', constitute a new genre of firms. These firms are information-intensive and use their information intensity in the e-commerce's information-rich environment to improve upon the economic efficiency of their own operation as well as the efficiency of their supply and value chains with which they are associated (or of which they are a part). Consequently they improve upon the efficiency of the entire system to which they belong or within which they operate.

As the direct result of these firms' actions, the authors argue, consumers will be better served as their wishes will be better detected by the information-intensive processes in place for communicating with these firms and thus their expected value will be better realized than ever before. Additionally the information intensity required by these firms' operations spills over to the other members of their associated supply chain through information channels and eventually to other economic agents in the rest of the economy. In their theoretical treatment, the authors argue that overall improvements may result from the efficiency gains in each agent, isolated and independent of the others, which they call 'single stage efficiency gains' as well as the spillover effects in multiple stages and multiple enterprises, which they call the 'ripple effect'. Single stage improvements alone, even if the rest of their associated supply chain did not follow information-intensive processes and remained unaffected by them (which is highly unlikely) could be substantial. As dot.com-type enterprises often pursue information-intensive strategies to gain economic efficiency, relative to their conventional counterparts, in response to the information-aware customers, they can better satisfy the needs of the others as well. Satisfying such customers demands efficiencies of a higher magnitude that are bound to be forced upon the entire system. Soufani and Tse use the 'ripple effect' concept to refer to cases where all related economic agents in a value chain facilitate the flow of information up and down the chain to minimize the unnecessary waste associated with insufficient information, and consequently optimize value. It is implicit in the chapter that any gains in efficiency made by the members of a given value chain would increase their collective competitiveness as compared to the others and would set a new and higher basis for competition (Christensen and Bower, 1996). Given the abundance of information and the relatively low cost of searching on the Internet, competition is bound to become intense. As a direct result, firms must strive to mine information and increase their information intensity, in order to become more competitive than their rivals to win customers. Alternatively they must be prepared to lose market share to others, which would force the entire economy to gain further efficiencies.

The managerial and public policy implications of this chapter are clear and inescapable: those enterprises that fail to use the newly emerging information-

and knowledge-intensive networks on the World Wide Web to gain efficiency in order to match the efficiency gains of others are doomed to diminish with time. Similarly, operating conditions that do not minimize waste for gaining efficiency through mining of information intensively will be overtaxing the enterprise's quest to achieve global competitiveness. By a logical extension, countries that fail to contribute to furthering the efficiency of their overall information system in enhancing the productivity of their resources and increased competitiveness of their enterprises through national programs for efficiency gains will be bound to lose their market to globally efficient competitors domestically and internationally.

The managerial lessons and policy implications of this chapter resonate very well with the previous chapter as it provides a theoretical treatment for increased competitiveness of the smaller on-line firms in spite of the disadvantages of size and experience. The implicit information-intensive framework, supporting the operation of such firms, may have actually contributed to the strategic flexibility, and even agility, of these enterprises relative to larger and slower moving conventional counterparts. While Chapter 9 provides a theoretical argument for increasing information intensity of processes in business enterprises, the next chapter embarks on the systematic application of such information intensively through a knowledge network. It examines electronic commerce (e-commerce) and Internet technologies as integral parts of the internationalization strategy of the smaller firms, which aspire to compete in the larger, richer and also more competitive international markets, which have traditionally required more resources and experience, in spite of SMEs' constrained resources and relative inexperience.

In Chapter 10, Hamid Etemad and Yender Lee examine e-commerce from four complementary perspectives:

1. the impact of e-commerce on individual consumers, entrepreneurs and society as a whole;
2. the potential contribution of knowledge networks to value creation utilizing information- and knowledge-intensive strategies;
3. e-commerce as an information- and knowledge-intensive strategy drawing on pertinent information through knowledge networks in general and the Internet in particular to create and deliver incremental value;
4. the theoretical concept of knowledge networks as an aid to scholarly inquiry in this emerging field.

As stated earlier, the impact of this web-based and information-intensive business strategy on internationalization is differentially higher for small and medium-sized enterprises, especially in the earlier stages of the internationalization process, where information needs regarding international markets are even higher than for their domestic markets and the smaller enterprises are less capable of acquiring the necessary information.

On the first perspective, Etemad and Lee suggest that the information revolution in progress for about a decade began to affect different agents in society when e-commerce was ushered in, in 1991. Individual consumers, for example, began to take advantage of the readily available information in the mid-1990s to minimize their costs, both financially and temporally, while maximizing their expected (and derived) benefits, including increased convenience and expanded choice of potential purchases. Naturally, when an enterprise did not satisfy their expectations, they would 'click away' as easily as they had 'clicked in'. Individual entrepreneurs embarked on e-commerce as a part of the information revolution to take advantage of the expanded opportunities and responded to the newly emerging consumer behavior and expectations. They created on-line enterprises that were more responsive to unmet consumer needs and were also capable of extending their reach virtually to all corners of the world. While some of these entrepreneurs started virtual enterprises of their own and internationalized them rapidly, others within the established firms (called 'intrapreneurs' in the chapter) used the emerging information systems and information technology to champion the cause of internationalizing their firm's supply chains to gain further competitiveness and access to global customers regardless of time and distance, as discussed earlier.

The advent of e-commerce, Etemad and Lee suggest, changed the nature of global competition: it removed most advantages of large size, leveled the playing field, especially for agile and information-adept smaller enterprises, and enabled them to provide their goods and services to the international market through e-commerce in ways unimagined a decade earlier. Naturally the more competitive smaller enterprises seized the opportunity earlier and entered international markets faster than the others. Others become suppliers to the information-intensive international supply chain and thereby gained an international presence indirectly. Conversely, larger enterprises used e-commerce to internationalize their supply chain (popularly referred to as the 'back-end' or business-to-business – or B2B for short – of e-business) and gain added competitiveness. Etemad and Lee argue that e-commerce results in increased overall internationalization in information-oriented enterprises, especially SMEs, as it helps to meet one of the main and most difficult requirements of internationalization: competitiveness.[8] Their argument complements Soufani and Tse's concepts of 'single- and multiple-stage efficiency gains', 'spillover efficiency gains' and added information intensity in supply and value chains, as discussed earlier.

On the second perspective, Chapter 10 proposes the theoretical concept of knowledge networks as the infrastructure and also as an organizing framework for providing for information and knowledge needs in general and for the needs of the scholarly e-commerce community in particular,[9] supporting the actual practice of e-commerce, which is very young but growing rapidly, and delivering benefits to its members, users and practitioners similar to social networks and social capital (Gulati, 1995b), discussed in earlier chapters (for example, see Chapters 4 to 7).

The accumulated information and knowledge on the various parts of the knowledge network can serve the needs of its members on the other parts. The members of the network can update the state of their information and knowledge as well as that of the the entire network once a particular piece of knowledge becomes available on the network. Therefore access to such knowledge networks can allow for extracting benefits associated with the new information at relatively low costs, especially when information is viewed as a public good in a particular social network. When that particular social network decides to extend access (or not to restrict access) to non-members, it becomes a part of the broader societal network. Many members of the society can then benefit from it by drawing upon the network for their information and knowledge needs, on the one hand; and depositing their own information on the network for others' needs and potential use, on the other hand. Therefore an information-adept entrepreneur can exploit the emerging patterns and behavioral characteristics to their own advantage at very reasonable cost. In fact the public parts of the Internet have begun to exhibit characteristics similar to those of knowledge networks, and e-commerce entrepreneurs have been deploying information- and knowledge-intensive strategies to exploit the opportunities based on information intensity through e-commerce techniques and technologies to build on-line enterprises as well (these are variants of, and complements to, the main theme of the third perspective on e-commerce).

After a brief discussion of the knowledge networks theory essentials in the latter part of the chapter, Etemad and Lee present an application of the fourth perspective and uncover the knowledge network that underlies the scholarly publications in e-commerce. They suggest that this knowledge network is the foundation for supporting e-commerce at the scholarly level and has enabled e-commerce's rapid growth in the past 10 to 15 years. Using bibliometric epistemology and the Social Science Citation Index, they found that an article by J.Y. Bakos (1991) in *MIS-Quarterly*, 15, 295ff, introduced electronic commerce to the scholarly community. Three articles in practitioner-oriented journals followed in the next two years: J. Meyer (1992), 'The challenge of electronic e-commerce'; J. Kao (1993), 'The Worldwide Web of Chinese business'; and M.J. Cronin (1993), 'Internet business resources'.[10] Two books by Kalakota and Whinston, and Tapscott popularized the topic in 1996; they parallel the birth of the field of electronic commerce as a novel commercial endeavor based on intensive use of information and knowledge.[11] The chapter goes on to reveal five of the six essential characteristics of the scholarly knowledge network of e-commerce as articulated by Latour (1987): 'where', 'when', 'how', 'what' and 'by whom'. Etemad and Lee's research identifies the most popular and highly cited e-commerce documents (books and journal articles), authors and the associated titles and publication media, including books and journals, a partial list of which is presented in the chapter.

The lessons of this and the previous chapters in Part III of the book can be stated simply: the efficiency gains based on higher information intensity and the use of knowledge may not necessarily require higher resources (which smaller firms do not have) to eclipse their competitiveness and growth rate. Therefore smaller information-aware entrepreneurs and their enterprises can gain relative competitiveness through the use of information- and knowledge-intensive strategies, including e-commerce, at higher rates than their larger counterparts because of the potential efficiency gains inherent in information- and knowledge-intensive operations. Furthermore one can even argue that the public good aspects of information may allow for transforming isolated pools of information into something resembling intellectual capital for the use of the knowledge network with a difference: it is equally accessible to, and can benefit, those who are skilled in the information and knowledge areas and who can exploit them through the knowledge network, while disadvantaging others who cannot.

In Chapter 11, Harry Matlay and Jay Mitra report on the results of a massive research effort based on a longitudinal survey of micro and small enterprises in Britain. A very large sample of micro and small enterprises was first selected randomly and interviewed by telephone. The aim of this telephone survey was to collect qualitative data and to establish a comprehensive picture of these firms' globalization efforts in the British economy. A subsample of some 600 owner–managers from the above British survey of enterprises was then chosen and interviewed, once a year over the duration of the research study, from 1996 to 1998, to trace their globalization progress over time. Over the same period, some 60 'matched' detailed case studies were also conducted to explore their motivations and challenges, and the main strategies and approaches that these owner-managed enterprises utilized to achieve their globalization objectives, at times facing barriers and adverse condition. This chapter presents the refined highlights of the triangulated and corroborated results of these three distinct methods. It is based on a wealth of quantitative and qualitative data relating to the globalization attempts, successes and failures of the participating owner–managers and their respective enterprises.

Matlay and Mitra's research findings confirm numerous dominant themes of this book. For example, owner–managers in micro and small firms make most, if not all, of their decisions regarding globalization according to their own perception of global competition and processes, which resonates with other chapters and cases reported in Part II of the book. They distinguish between the internal and external sources giving rise to factors influencing these small business owner–managers' globalization objectives and tendencies. Their research suggests that the internal factors are related mainly to the owner–manager's own expectations, knowledge, skills and competencies (for more details on entrepreneurial attributes in other cases, see Chapters 3 to 6). As in the case of Australian SMEs (see Chapter 3), they found that the availability of external financial and skilled human resources directly influenced these entrepreneurs' globalization efforts at all stages of the process. However the impact of external factors affecting globalization in these firms was mediated by the owner–manager's own ability to participate in global networks in order to leverage them for the enterprise's globalization needs, which varied widely, ranging from sources of funds and specific marketing information about market opportunities abroad to actual access to local markets and physical channels of distribution. Although much more broadly-based, these findings are similar to those in Chapters 5 and 6 (discussing Dyson and Thai entrepreneurs).

Matlay and Mitra report that entrepreneurs with highly positive attitudes, expecting success with promising rewards, that is, with high needs for achievement (McClelland, 1961), view globalization in an equally positive light: not only can globalization provide them with a springboard for deploying high-growth expansion strategies, but it also motivates expanded operations to achieve globalization objectives. As with other cases in the book, entrepreneurs' own skills, expertise, capabilities and social networks played very significant roles in achieving their globalization objectives. Those entrepreneurs who exhibited high need for achievement acquired the necessary prerequisites in terms of specific information, knowledge and resources. This in turn enabled them (a) to foresee market trends and emerging market developments, (b) to identify emerging opportunities, (c) to reallocate human and financial resources, (d) to reorient their efforts, and (e) to employ innovative business strategies to respond to the opportunities and achieve high growth. Naturally the owner–managers of high-growth firms were good at strategy. For example, they approached human resource development proactively and arranged access to the necessary external financial resources in advance and as integral parts of their business plans and strategies. As a result, these entrepreneurs also achieved their globalization targets.

On the other hand, entrepreneurs who failed to foresee trends and to react to change in the global market in timely fashion invariably experienced relative stagnation and decline. Their reactive development of human resources and financing strategies, for example, appeared to have hindered organizational growth significantly in their firms. Furthermore these entrepreneurs' inability to raise funds from a variety of commercial and personal sources to build organizational capabilities and stimulate growth hampered the achievement of ambitious short to medium-term growth objectives.

Matlay and Mitra's extensive and longitudinal study leads to an inevitable observation: differences in individual abilities and aspirations of the founder–managers in small enterprises play critical roles in developing strategies for these firms' globalization and should not be ignored. These differences should, therefore, be identified and calibrated well in advance (see Chapter 7 for detailed discussion of entrepreneurial self-efficacy, ESE). Globalization strategies must take the enabling (or disabling) entrepreneurial characteristics into account and even base strategy formulation on them if globalization objectives are to be achieved. Stated differently, these enterprises are reflections of their founder–managers and seemingly similar and generic strategies are likely to yield different results owing to the strong influence of their founder–managers' entrepreneurial characteristics. The research results suggest that there is a need (a) to develop a good understanding of these entrepreneurs' motivational factors that influence their decision to expand globally (or not), (b) to work closely with them to provide for their globalization needs, and (c) to motivate public and private policies to enable them and their enterprises, for example, by influencing the composition or the nature of internal and/or external factors, to exploit future growth opportunities. Of equal importance is the impact of educational sessions, complemented by well-focused literature on the 'global market place', in raising the awareness and increasing the sensitivities of these founder–managers, and their enterprise as a whole by extension. However Matlay and Mitra caution that this literature is unlikely to have much appeal for these entrepreneurs if it does not reflect the peculiarity of the owner–managers' personal make-up and aspirations as well as organizational objectives and processes, which portray both the owner–manager and the sociocultural environment within which such micro and small enterprises are deeply embedded.

While Chapter 11 relates to earlier chapters in the book in many ways and at different levels, it also sets the stage for a better understanding of change over time: that the micro and small enterprises project a pattern of evolutionary change, from local, micro and small to medium and then large enterprises being active internationally in the later stage of their growth, which resonates well with all of the other themes of this volume. This chapter also covers the characteristics of micro and small enterprises managed mainly by their founders and owner–managers.

As indicated in discussions in previous chapters, the quantitative change in size over time would logically accompany corresponding qualitative change in management in terms of composition and nature (for example, from founder–manager alone to a professional team), orientation (for example, from independent owner–manager to interdependence and reliance on own social networks as well as supply and value chains), and strategies (for example, from competing in isolated domestic market niches to broader global competition) as firms traveled along the evolutionary path of growth and internationalization. Therefore, if internationalization can be viewed as the ideal mature stage in a typical enterprise's life cycle, micro enterprises must necessarily be viewed as in the early childhood of that life cycle, raised and nurtured by their founder–manager, and must be supported to realize their potential growth and development. As in organic life cycles, the process of growth and development of micro enterprises will depend on their initial pedigree as well as the forces of evolutionary change in their environment as they grow to become mature SMEs and multinational enterprises later on. This suggests that these enterprises use a more integrated and holistic approach over the span of their life cycle than the isolated and independent stages reflected in internationalization studies.

The last chapter of the book (Chapter 12) builds on the previous 11 chapters, adopting an evolutionary perspective. Its starting points are mainly the concepts and arguments presented in the various chapters of the book. However it builds upon them and extends them in order to develop a better understanding of the evolutionary path in firms' life cycles from young, micro-sized to large, multinational enterprises. Following the evolutionary tradition of environment and strategy in the enterprise (Barney, 1991; Doz, 1996; Kanter, 1984; Nelson and Winter, 1982; Teece *et al.*, 1997), Chapter 12 examines the evolutionary change in the environment and the corresponding change in strategy from four different perspectives, namely the patterns of change and the emerging trends in the socioeconomic aspects, the technological aspects, the organizational aspects, and converging forces and theories. The critical analysis of the four environmental perspectives, described in terms of the prevailing change and the emerging patterns, allows for thorough re-examination and further extension of pertinent concepts in order to extract logical lessons, implications and conceptual tools for internationalizing firms. Stated differently, the change in the environment is viewed in four interwoven layers, each corresponding to one of the four different perspectives, each building on the previous one, and thereby contributing to the understanding of the complexity that characterizes the internationalizing firm's environment. This increasing complexity in turn requires equally rich strategies to respond to them.

Each layer is decomposed in order to exploit the relevant influential concepts, constructs or theories present in the previous chapters and elsewhere. The sequential de-layering of the complexity allows for identifications of frontiers of the near-future and cutting-edge trends with potential impact on internationalizing firms. Each part builds on the pertinent concepts for providing powerful conceptual tools for analyzing the complex environment facing smaller firms aspiring to internationalize. While global competition is constantly adding to the complexity, each part's conceptual or theory-grounded tools and discussions are designed to unbundle them to provide a strategic flexibility equal to that of an internationalizing firm. The lessons and implications surrounding the discussion of the patterns of change and their associated trends are presented at the conclusion of each argument and they are also interspersed throughout the chapter.

NOTES

1. There are a large number of free trade and special economic zones around the world which provide concessionary incentives to value-adding investment and trade in these zones while exempting the zone activities from restrictions on operating within the environment of which the zone is a part.
2. For a comparison of cultural characteristics of Eastern and Western cultures, see Lodge and Vogel (1987).
3. These incompatibilities may result in different expectations: while the founder–manager sees no need for change, those from other environments expect a change from founder–manager to professional managers at any time, which delays major transactions within the firm until the installation of the new team.
4. For a critical review of this school of thought, see Leonidou and Katsikeas (1996).
5. The so-called 'born global' firms do not follow the received conventional wisdom. For more details, see McDougall *et al.* (1994), Oviatt and McDougal (1994), Knight and Cavusgil (1996).
6. Instead of 'exploitation', the concept of 'mining information' is used in e-commerce.
7. This part of Rosson's chapter relates well to the discussion regarding benchmarking and best practices presented earlier.
8. The internationalization of supply chains, in small and large firms alike, can result in increased competitiveness and better utilization of available resources as firms switch from relatively more expensive internal sources to relatively less expensive international suppliers, thereby reducing costs and releasing resources for more productive use at the same time.
9. Etemad and Lee have applied the theory of knowledge networks to trace the origin and the heritage of international entrepreneurship, management of technology and electronic commerce. Chapter 10 presents an application of the theory and its tangible manifestations on the scholarly side.
10. See the notes of Table 10.1 for more details on each of the above books and articles.
11. See Table 10.2 for the full citations.

REFERENCES

Barkema, H.G., I.E. Bell and J.A.M. Pennings (1996), 'Foreign entry, cultural barriers, and learning', *Strategic Management Journal*, **17**, 151–66.
Barkema, H.G., O. Shenkar, F. Vermeulen and J.H.J. Bell (1997), 'Working abroad with others: how firms learn to operate international joint ventures', *Academy of Management Journal*, **40** (2), 426–42.
Barney, J. (1991), 'Firm resources and competitive advantage', *Journal of Management*, special issue on the resource-based view of the firm, **17**, 99–120.

Cavusgil, S. Tamer (1980), 'On the internationalisation of firms,' *European Research*, **8**.
Cavusgil, S.T. (1982), 'Some observations on the relevance of critical variables for internationalization stages', in M. Czinkota and G. Tesar (eds), *Export Management: An International Context*, New York: Praeger, pp. 276–85.
Chakravarthy, B. S. and H.V. Perlmauter (1985), 'Strategic planning for a global business', *Columbia Journal of World Business*, **20** (Summer), 4–7.
Christensen, C. M. and J.L. Bower (1996), 'Customer power, strategic investment and the failure of the leading firms', *Strategic Management Journal*, **17**, 197–218.
Dana, Leo-Paul, Hamid Etemad and Richard Wright (2001), 'Symbiotic interdependence', in Dianne Welsh and Ilan Alon (eds), *International Franchising in Emerging Markets*, Riverwood, IL: CCH Publishing, pp. 119–29.
Doz, Y.L. (1996), 'The evolution of cooperation in strategic alliances: initial conditions or learning processes?', *Strategic Management Journal*, **17**, 55–83.
Eriksson, K., J. Johanson, A. Majkgård and D. Sharma (1997), 'Experiential knowledge and cost in the internationalisation process', *Journal of International Business Studies*, **28** (2), 337–60.
Etemad, Hamid (1996), 'From obscurity to powerhouse: the process of China's two decades of development', *Journal of Business and Contemporary World*, **8**, (3, 4), 171–222.
Etemad, H. (1999), 'Globalization and small and medium-sized enterprises: search for potent strategies', *Global Focus*, (formerly *Business and Contemporary World*), **11** (3), summer, 85–105.
Etemad, Hamid (2003a), 'Managing relations: the essence of international entrepreneurship', in Hamid Etemad and Richard Wright (eds), *Globalization and Entrepreneurship: Policy and Strategy Perspectives*, Cheltenham, UK and Northampton, MA, USA: Edward Elgar Publishing.
Etemad, Hamid (2003b), 'Marshalling relations: the enduring essence of international entrepreneurship', in L.P. Dana (ed), *Handbook of Research on International Entrepreneurship*, Cheltenham, UK, and Northampton, MA, USA: Edward Elgar Publishing.
Etemad, Hamid (2003c), 'Strategies for internationalization of entrepreneurial firms facing different competitive environments', in Hamid Etemad (ed.), *The Proceedings of the Third Biennial McGill Conference on International Entrepreneurship: Researching New Frontiers*, 13–16 September 2002, vol. 1.
Etemad, H. (2003d), 'The typology of competitive intensity, evolutionary path of the local subsidiary and the local SMEs' internationalization strategies', *2003 Proceedings of the Administrative Association of Canada, International Business Division*, 12–14 June.
Etemad, Hamid and Yender Lee (2000), 'The developmental path of an emerging knowledge network in international entrepreneurship', *Proceedings of Administrative Sciences Association of Canada, Entrepreneurship Division*, **21** (21), 8–12 July, 72–82.
Etemad, Hamid and Yender Lee (2003), 'The emerging knowledge network of international entrepreneurship: theory and evidence', *Journal of Small Business Economics*, **20** (1), February, 5–23.
Forrest, Janet E. and M.J.C. Martin (1992), 'Strategic alliances between large and small research intensive organizations: experience in biotechnology industry', *R & D Management*, **22**, 41–53.
Gomes-Casseres, Benjamin (1996), *The Alliance Revolution: The New Shape of Business Rivalry*, Cambridge, MA: Harvard University Press.

Gomes-Casseres, Benjamin (1997), 'Alliance strategies of small firms', *Small Business Economics*, **9** (1), 33–44.

Grant, R.M. (1996), 'Toward a knowledge-based theory of the firm', *Strategic Management Journal*, **17**, 109–22.

Gulati, R. (1995a), 'Does familiarity breed trust? The implications of repeated ties for contractual choice in alliances', *Academy of Management Review*, **38** (1), 85–112.

Gulati, R. (1995b), 'Social structure and alliance formation patterns: a longitudinal analysis', *Administrative Science Quarterly*, **40**, 619–52.

Hymer, Stephan (1976), *International Operations of National Firms: A Study of Direct Foreign Investment*, Cambridge, MA: MIT Press.

Johanson, Jan and Jan-Erik Vahlne (1977), 'The internationalization process of the firm: a model of knowledge development and increasing foreign commitments', *Journal of International Business Studies*, **8** (1), 23–32.

Johanson, Jan and Jan-Erik Vahlne (1990), 'The mechanism of internationalization', *International Marketing Review*, **7** (4), 11–24.

Johanson, Jan and Jan-Erik Vahlne (1992), 'Management of foreign market entry', *Scandinavian International Business Review*, **1** (3), 9–27.

Johanson, Jan and Finn Wiedersheim-Paul (1975), 'The internationalization of the firm: four Swedish cases', *Journal of International Management Studies*, **12** (3), October, 36–64.

Joshi, Ashwin W. and Rodney L. Stump (1999), 'Determinants of commitments and opportunism: integrating and extending insights from transaction cost analysis and relational exchange theory', *Canadian Journal of Administrative Sciences*, **16**, December, 334–52.

Kanter, E.M. (1984), 'Collaborative advantage: the art of alliances', *Harvard Business Review*, July–August, 96–108.

Knickerbocker, F.T. (1973), *Oligopolistic Reaction and Multinational Enterprises*, Boston, MA: Harvard University Press.

Knight, Gary A. and S. Tamer Cavusgil (1996), 'The born global firm', in S. Tamer Cavusgil and Tage Koed Masden (eds), *Advances in International Marketing*, vol. 8, Greenwich: JAI.

Latour, B. (1987), *Science in Action: How to Follow Scientists and Engineers Through Society*, Cambridge, MA: Harvard University Press, p. 265.

Leonidou, Leonidas C. and Constantine S. Katsikeas (1996), 'The export development process', *Journal of International Business Studies*, **27** (3), 517–51.

Lodge, George C. and Ezra F. Vogel (1987), *Ideology and National Competitiveness: An Analysis of Nine Countries*, Boston, MA: Harvard Business School Press.

McClelland, David Clarence (1961), *The Achieving Society*, Princeton, NJ: D. Van Nostrand.

McDougall, Patricia Phillips, Scott Shane and Benjamin Milton Oviatt (1994), 'Explaining the formation of international joint ventures: the limits of theories from international business research', *Journal of Business Venturing*, **9**, 469–87.

McKinsey and Co. (1993), *Emerging Exporters: Australia's High Value-added Manufacturing Exporters*, Melbourne: Australian Manufacturing Council.

Nonaka, I. (1995), 'A theory of organizational knowledge creation', *International Journal of Technology Management*, **11** (7/8), 833–45.

Nonaka, I. and H. Takeuchi (1996), *The Knowledge Creating Company: How Japanese Companies Create the Dynamics of Innovation*, New York: Oxford University Press.

Nelson, R.R. and S.G. Winter (1982), *An Evolutionary Theory of Economic Change*, Cambridge, MA: Belknap Press.

Oviatt, Benjamin Milton and Patricia Phillips McDougall (1994), 'Toward a theory of international new ventures', *Journal of International Business Studies*, **25** (1), 45–64.

Redding, Gordon (1990), *The Spirit of Chinese Capitalism*, Berlin and New York: Walter de Gruyter.

Saxenian, Annalee (1994), *Regional Advantage. Culture and Competition in Silicon Valley and Route 128*, Cambridge and London: Harvard University Press.

Schumpeter, J. (1934), *The Theory of Economic Development: An Inquity into Profits, Capital, Credit, Interest, and the Business Cycle*, translated by Reduers Opie, Cambridge, MA: Harvard University Press.

Teece, D.J., G. Pisano and A. Shuen (1997), 'Dynamic capabilities and strategic management', *Strategic Management Journal*, **18** (7), 509–33.

Williamson, O.E. (1979), 'Transaction cost economics: the governance of contractual relations', *Journal of Law and Economics*, **22**, 3–61.

Williamson, O.E. (1981), 'The economics of organization: the transaction cost approach', *American Journal of Sociology*, **87**, 548–77.

Yoshino, M. and U.S. Rangan (1995), *Strategic Alliances: An Entrepreneurial Approach to Globalization*, Boston, MA: Harvard Business School Press.

PART I

Enterprise–environment interactions and
internationalization

2. The dynamic impact of regional clusters on international growth and competition: some grounded propositions

Hamid Etemad and Hankyu Chu

INTRODUCTION

The economic prosperity of some regions of the world has become the envy of other less developed regions. Increasingly regions are seen as the appropriate unit of analysis, where actual economic and technological interactions take place, amid the failure of the classical paradigms in addressing many of the sociocultural and development problems (Morgan, 1997). De la Mothe and Paquet (2000) argue that 'The most useful perspective point of view is the meso perspective which focuses on development block, technology districts, subnational fora, etc.' (p. 33). They suggest that learning takes place in the regional subsystems and the socioeconomic and technology-centered systems interact for innovation to occur. Similarly, Feldman and Florida (1994) view a region[1] as 'the vessel in which entrepreneurs, venture capitalists, and other agents of innovation, organize infrastructure that brings together the crucial support and resources for innovation process' to flourish (p. 210).

The interest in the region is well reflected in the concept of industrial clusters. While there are many different definitions of clusters, each associated with one of the various theoretical traditions that seek to shed light on this complex phenomenon, the concept may be referred to as 'geographic concentrations of interconnected companies and institutions in a particular field' (Porter, 1998, p. 78). In Porter's conception, clusters also include 'related industries' and 'supporting institutions', including trade associations and educational institutions.

Theoretical richness and the diversity of explanations of what constitutes the essence of a cluster led to what Bergman (1998) called 'conceptual obscurity'. In spite of the diversity, the various schools of thought converge in their conclusion: specialization in interlinked complementary and cooperative activities of firms (in value creation) within the region creates synergies and even symbiosis, introduces innovation, increases productivity, and leads to economic advantage (Steiner, 1998), which in turn contributes to further wealth and value creation in such regions.[2]

Bramanti and Ratti (1997) summarize the convergence of various approaches in the notion of a 'territory' as follows:

> a) the birthplace of technology and innovation – i.e. the progress from given resources allocation processes to a collective build-up of specific resources (Gaffard, 1990);
> b) a place for co-ordinating industrial activities, a link between external territorial economies and organizational and inter-organizational firm trajectories (Veltz, 1993);
> c) a political decision-making unit governing localization, able to create and redistribute resources, and expressing specific governance structures in the relations between actors (Storper and Harrison, 1991); and
> d) a place in which un-traded inter-dependencies (means through which interdependent actors grow technologically and organizationally, and coordinate themselves) form, express themselves, and evolve (Storper, 1995). (Bramanti and Ratti, 1997, p. 4)

Bramanti and Ratti (1997) view the region as the 'relational space' within which most, if not all, of the above relational transactions takes place. However various scholarly inquiries have tried to find out how the relations among agents within a region create synergistic properties which the collection of atomized, unlinked and independent actors cannot replicate on their own outside the region. Thus the discussion of social capital and trust as the basis of cooperative relations has gained currency in the literature of industrial clusters (Cohen and Fields, 1998; Harrison, 1992; Putnam, 1993a, 1993b).

The primary objectives of this chapter are (a) to articulate a relational link from the accumulation of social capital, through innovative capacity, to economic prosperity within a region, (b) to argue in favor of clusters as conducive environments for rapid growth as the relational links can act as springboards for firms within the region, and (c) to suggest that smaller local firms can exploit the catalytic, if not substantive, impact of relational links within the clusters to internationalize eventually beyond the region. This chapter consists of three sections. Following this introductory section, the second presents three substantive elements. The first of these discusses the relationship between proximity and efficient exchange, where trust is seen as the moderating variable; the second examines why trust tends to be localized and looks at a region's characteristics in that regard; the third seeks to explain the dynamics of successful clusters by examining how trust facilitates the efficient exchange of knowledge, leading to increased innovative capacity. Each element concludes its discussion and analysis with a family of related propositions. A synthesis of all the arguments, as well as the implications of this study for internationalization of small and medium-sized enterprises (SMEs), is presented in the concluding section.

THE COMPLEX DYNAMICS OF GEOGRAPHICAL PROXIMITY AND SUCCESS OF INDUSTRIAL CLUSTERS

Proximity, Social Capital and Efficient Exchange

A neoclassical explanation of clustering of firms in an industrial region is derived from Alfred Marshall's (1949) notion of economic vibrancy within localized industrial districts. Marshall established his unique framework for understanding the dynamism within certain localized regions through his conception of 'external scale economies'. To Marshall, economies of scale are not restricted to the internal operations of the individual firm. The concentration of firms in a core location allows for cost reduction to individual firms thanks to the expanding pool of resources in response to the proximity of firms within a region leading to economies that we call 'proximity effects'.

From the supply side, firms in geographic proximity[3] can take advantage of access to the critical mass of specialized suppliers, skilled labor, and other support industries and institutions (Porter, 1998) already in place or attracted to the region,[4] thereby creating an enabling environment for the spill-over of technological knowledge from one firm to another within the region. In addition to the spill-over effects, proximity can minimize costs associated with differences in time and space. Furthermore proximity may also enhance easy access to information and lead to healthy and non-destructive competition.

From the demand side, customers can also benefit from the clustering of firms from three distinct sources: competition, trusting relations within the region and the proximity effects. Customers can, for example, benefit from competition by comparing the rich range of various products' portfolios in one trip to the region. They can also capitalize on trust-based relations among firms in the region. From the firms' perspective, these benefits, in turn, reinforce the advantage of clustering as it attracts buyers and suppliers who value the tradition of trust-based relations and proximity effects within the region.[5] The frequent interaction with customers within the region, for example, enables firms to better identify their needs as compared to competitors outside the region. The combination of access to specialized resources, spill-over possibilities and the ease of interaction with customers and suppliers can give rise to virtuous cycles of healthy and non-destructive competition for higher quality at lower total cost, leading to corporate growth and wealth creation.

The Marshallian agglomeration economies are the cost savings accrued to the firms in a particular place when cost of production decreases because of expansion of common pools of labor, capital and infrastructure, or because of the occurrence of what Scitovsky (1963) later called the 'pecuniary' external economies, stemming from investments made by others within a locality or a region. Scitovsky, as cited in Harrison (1992), identified 'pecuniary external economies' as gains in profitability of the existing operations of the firm when certain other related firms make new 'real' (as distinct from 'portfolio') investments. Such an increased external pool of investments combined with the consequent increased profitability would in turn lead to increased retained earnings for further investment and the further enlarging of the regional scale.

Drawing on Marshallian agglomeration economies, Krugman (1991) proceeds through traditional location theory to the notions of cumulative causation and regional specialization to argue that these external economies tend to be realized more on the local and regional levels than at the national and international levels. Porter (1998), who popularized the concept of clusters, also points to the importance of a region in competition amid the apparent movement toward globalization: 'The enduring competitive advantages in a global economy are often heavily local, arising from concentrations of highly specialized skills and knowledge, institutions, rivals, related business, and sophisticated customers' (p. 90). Borrowing from the transaction cost economic framework, Storper and Scott (1995) argue that geographic proximity reduces the transaction cost of interaction-intensive activities, such as exchange of information and tacit knowledge, as well as goods and services produced in the region.

Although acceleration in geographic concentration of firms and supporting institutions in one region may suggest a movement away from globalization and towards further localization of exchange, globalization may have actually facilitated externalities associated with localization, especially those associated with time-, distance- and location-sensitive aspects of inter-firm relations. Thus the implications of the above are that activities requiring extensive exchange of ideas, information and knowledge among agents, including tacit knowledge and innovation, which we call 'transaction cost-intensive' (or simply transaction-intensive), tend to remain local or to localize further, while relatively fewer transaction-intensive activities, such as mass production, may globalize further. These discussions can, therefore, culminate in the following propositions:

1. Agglomeration of complementary firms in a region with inter-firm interactions gives them efficient access to the critical mass of specialized resources, thus leading to reduced costs.
2. Proximity effects facilitate efficient exchange of ideas, knowledge, goods

and services in the regions, resulting in reduction of production and trans-action costs, leading to further transaction-intensive relations in the region.

3. The lower local costs of relatively high transaction-intensive relations among agents in a regional proximity favor regional concentration of such relations while relatively fewer transaction-intensive relations may spread globally.

4. Complementary inter-firm relations among specialized SMEs exhibit transaction-intensive and trust-seeking characteristics in regional clusters.

5. Specialized SMEs establish more transaction-intensive and trust-seeking inter-firm relations with other specialized SMEs in regional clusters.

6. Increased regional interactions in high transaction-intensive relations, as opposed to relatively low transaction-intensive relations, lead to increased inter-firm trust, especially amongst locally based SMEs, who face greater vulnerability due to their smaller scales.

7. Increases in inter-firm interactions among SMEs in a regional cluster will be more transaction-intensive and trust-seeking than their complementary intra-industry, or inter-cluster, counterparts at the global level.

8. In the inter-firm relations associated with SMEs, specialized functions along their shared value chain will be more trust-seeking within the regional cluster than inter-firm relations outside the regional cluster (which may be more economic efficiency-seeking).

As implied in the above propositions, proximity per se does not necessarily lead to efficient exchange or to developing external economies as the Marshallian industrial district entails. However, proximity appears to be only a necessary condition; and it is not sufficient to predicate efficient exchange among agents in geographic proximity. What distinguishes a successful region from the rest is that there are joint actions among agents in order to accumulate, facilitate and coordinate the collective good(s) within the region. Schmitz and Nadvi (1999, p. 504) confirm that 'it is also agreed, however, that Marshallian external economies are not sufficient to explain cluster development. In addition to external economies, there is a deliberate force at work, namely the *conscious pursuit of joint actions* emerges from research on industrial clusters in advanced and in developing countries' (emphasis added).

Thus we often find a deliberate development of collective efficiency in successful clusters (Nadvi, 1999; Schmitz, 1999; Schmitz and Nadvi, 1999), resulting in 'competitive advantage derived from external economies and joint actions' (Schmitz and Nadvi, 1999, p. 1504). Nadvi and Schmitz's implicit collective efficiency framework distinguishes between passive externalities (referring to the cost benefits of proximity) and active externalities (referring to the collective efficiency gained through joint action) and posits that passive and active externalities should be combined to achieve success in related operations within a region (ibid., pp. 1504–5). The argument of economic efficiency-seeking joint action resonates well with the transaction cost-intensive perspective in regional clusters. When joint action is perceived to reduce relational and transaction costs within a regional cluster, relative to unrelated and independent firms, firms in general, and SMEs in particular, have a strong motive to engage in such efficiency-seeking relations and joint actions as they may lead to economic efficiency as well. Therefore relation building and trust seeking, with the potential of leading to joint action, appear to be the catalytic element, if not the necessary condition, for reducing the expected, or actual, costs of intensive relations within a region.

With the above argument in mind, the question to ask is what circumstances lead to, and what factors facilitate, joint actions among agents in geographic proximity so as to actively promote the synergistic properties of collective goods in order to benefit from both the passive and active externalities within a region. Joint action entails active cooperation, and such cooperation in successful clusters often has a social basis involving affinity, loyalty and trust. Granovetter's (1984) noteworthy contribution to the literature of industrial cluster is his argument of 'embeddedness'. He argues that firms are embedded in networks of social and institutional relations. Harrison (1992) confirms that the concept of embedding has become a distinguishing feature of industrial district theory. Similarly, Piore and Sabel (1984) view economic activities as embedded in a community. They argue that the innovative capacity of a region is achieved by a well-balanced combination of competition and cooperation, suggesting that such a balance can be achieved by the fusion of productivity-oriented activities (entailing competition) with the larger life of the community based mainly on the sense of civic duty and cooperation. Following Granovetter's argument, Saxenian (1994) delineated the differential growth of Silicon Valley and Route 128.[6] Her finding portrays Silicon Valley as an *inter-firm and network-based* industrial system, which promotes learning and mutual adjustment among specialized producers in a complex of related technologies within the region, as opposed to *intra-firm relations* in the Route 128 region, where social relations are only internal to the firms involved. Thus proximity takes an inter-firm character in Silicon Valley, while it is limited to proximity between firms within Route 128, which confirms the role of external, sociocultural factors as suggested by Granovetter and others.

Complementing Granovetter's argument of economic life being embedded in a region's social and cultural relations, the literature from sociology and sociological economics suggests that the accumulation of social capital[7] is the main discriminating factor in successful clusters (Saxenian, 1994; Putnam, 1993a, 1993b). Social capital refers to stocks of norms, networks and social trust, upon which people can draw to solve their common problems (Putnam,

1993a, 1993b). Most importantly, expected common norms in social capital facilitate cooperation and exchange and foster generalized reciprocity in terms of mutual expectations[8] vital to maintaining stable relations within a network. Such norms and expectations also facilitate coordination, communication and cooperation throughout the network. As social capital embodies the history of collaboration in the past – in terms of both successes and failures – it can serve as a template for future collaboration: past successes may serve to produce more successes, and vice versa. Therefore social capital creates rich information channels through which one can know and verify the trustworthiness of other individuals and groups, on the basis of their past social behavior. This mechanism can also reduce the likelihood of opportunistic behavior of agents by establishing implicit, but well-understood, sanctions: opportunistic actors will be restricted as regards future exchange and the benefits associated with the collective goods. Social capital can therefore serve to facilitate mutually beneficial joint actions in a region and discourage opportunistic behaviors, especially those with high opportunity costs.

Trust and Geographic Proximity

At the heart of social capital lies social trust. Trust is the key resource to hold the relations of exchange, which constitute the backbone of social capital. Unless trust in the social relationship amongst the members of a region can be created and maintained, social capital is hard to establish and sustain. Fukuyama (1995) observes that high-trust societies tend to develop greater social capital, and consequently enjoy greater economic growth, particularly in the transition from a traditional to a post-industrial economy. Likewise high-trust groups and cultures can accumulate greater social capital. Thus it is not surprising to find that trust is the foundation of relationships between agents whose collective actions[9] within a regional setting are the key aspect of innovative local economies (Piore and Sabel, 1984).

Contrary to neoclassical views of transaction cost theory, the sociologically oriented arguments suggest that the efficiency of exchange, based on proximity and social capital, may be a secondary issue only if actors question the fairness of exchange (Staber, 1996a). Proximity does not necessarily lead to efficient exchange among agents unless trust becomes embedded in the social relations. Therefore, we may conclude that (a) proximity does not necessarily lead to efficient exchange unless there is trust among individuals in the exchange based on the previously established social capital, and (b) repeated trust, embedded in the relations of exchange among agents in proximity within a region, helps to increase efficiencies of regional exchanges.

When the economic relations are embedded in the social capital and the social life of the region, the neoclassical argument that the geographic proximity itself generates developmental synergies and stimulates innovation in a region appears much less appealing. Staber (1996b) suggests that 'what matters most is not proximity per se but whether or not social relations are such that they lead to trust, loyalty, and tacit understandings, and whether these outcomes enhance firms' willingness to make risky deals to share their resources' (pp. 8–9). In a similar vein, we may argue that, while geographic colocation may be less important because of advances in communication and information technologies, opportunities for social interaction that lead to accumulation of social capital, and social trust, will probably remain local, thus leading to strong tendencies to localize important and even risky economic activities, as considered earlier, even in the face of globalization.

Trust is a relational concept and is embedded in social relations. Granovetter (1984) argues that trust is the basis of social relations. Trust is a product of the history of past relations and of past experiences. Trust between agents can only be earned and accumulated through interactive experiences, directly or indirectly (Putnam, 1993a; Harrison, 1992). One cannot buy trust or sell trust. It has to be earned and accumulated through repeated transactions (Arrow, 1974). Thus, in successful clusters, intensive formal and informal interactions, including face-to-face contacts, social functions and detailed information exchanges, as well as short- and long-term contracts, may lead to accumulation of trust over time. Thus we may conclude that repeated successful exchanges build on the prevailing social norms in the region and transform them into inter-firm codes of conduct based on reciprocity and mutuality of common interests.

In a similar vein, various forms of intense cooperation, quasi-integration and intermediate forms of governance – facilitating material input–output flows and circulation of knowledge embedded in human resources among agents involved in social relations – also tend to create a club-like atmosphere, which is very conducive to the further cultivation of trust.[10] Within this club-like atmosphere, communities of trust are formed in which acceptable norms of business conduct are socialized, leading to the community members' acceptance of formal and informal surveillance (Scott, 1986; Storper and Scott, 1988), which is one of the prerequisites for further accumulation of social capital. From the above discussion, we can therefore restate them formally as follows:

- Trust is embedded in the networks of social relations and can be earned through experience of repeated interaction (especially face-to face interaction).
- Socially embedded norms cultivate accumulation of trust and social capital within a social network and erosion of norms, social capital or trust weakens network-based relations in a region.

- Trust governs interrelations: accumulation of trust increases transaction-intensive inter-firm relations, and opportunistic behavior reduces such interrelations.
- Higher transaction intensity is more likely to lead more to trust-seeking relations than otherwise.
- Specialized SMEs are more likely to seek trust- and social capital-seeking relations within a regional cluster.
- While inter-firm transaction-intensive relations are governed by social embeddedness of actors in the region and beyond firm boundaries, intra-firm transaction-intensive relations are limited to a given firm.

In spite of increasing ease of travel and the universality of communication around the globe, we follow Storper's (1995) and Storper and Scott's (1995) arguments concerning higher opportunities for social interactions and their much greater sensitivity to geographic proximity to articulate two more propositions: first, individuals located in proximity to a regional cluster are more likely to get involved in socially embedded interactions in localized networks and thus in trust-seeking relations than those located in geographically distant regions; second, trust building in a region becomes a virtuous and self-enforcing cycle as the opportunity costs and the costs of social sanctions, in bilateral and multilateral inter-firm relations, increase with time (owing to the increasing size of transactions and number of firms in the communities of practice within the region).

Social Capital, Trust and Innovative Capacity of Clusters

Successful clusters maintain their competitive advantage through continuous innovation (Piore and Sabel, 1984; Porter 1990, 1998). The ideal-type clusters often euphorically use terms such as 'learning region', 'regional innovation system' or 'innovative milieu', revitalizing and developing their economy through continuous innovation and active entrepreneurship: firms pursue far more risky projects in partnership with others in response to expanded and more rewarding activities within the region.

Innovation is not often about increasing the efficiency of doing the same thing. That is the main characteristic of mass production systems.[11] Rather it is about adding new types of work to the old set through the introduction of new products and services so as to create new value. The classical work of Jacobs (1969) vividly highlights the resilience of industrial systems, such as that of Glasgow, through continuous innovation by following the tradition of adding new types of work to the old, as compared to the efficiency-based mass-production system prevailing in Manchester.[12] Jacobs (1969) suggests that a successful region gains its systemic resilience[13] through innovation accompanied by the deepening of the social division of labor[14] (the addition of new types of work to a given economy), which in turn leads to added richness and diversity of the region's economy.

This view accords with Schumpeter's (1943) view of innovation as the driving force of economic development, and the distinction between 'quality competition' and 'ordinary competition'.[15] Quality competition refers to the innovation-driven competition based in part on deployment of a new technology, a new source of supply or a new type of organization, as opposed to the ordinary competition based on price (efficiency-based). This view flows from Schumpeter's (1943) perspective on capitalism as an evolutionary process driven by technological and organizational innovation. We may therefore de-emphasize the efficiency-based argument of classical economics by restating formally the link between innovation and economic development in the context of industrial clusters: economic development of a region is dependent upon the region's capacity to innovate.

The studies of innovation in the past two decades have gained significant advances by making an important transition from a linear view to the more dynamic non-linear view of *process innovation* (Dosi, 1992; Kline and Rosenberg, 1986). Most importantly, innovation is seen as a fundamentally collective process (Hakansson, 1987), the outcome of collective learning (Lundvall, 1992) and not a brainchild of a single individual or the result of a lucky invention. Innovation does not come from a vacuum: it is a cumulative and a creative combination of existing knowledge and ideas. Thus Kogut and Zander (1992) conclude that 'new learning, such as innovations, are products of a firm's combinative capabilities to generate new applications from existing knowledge (p. 391). The idea that innovation is a collective process is further illuminated by the so-called 'network paradigm' of innovation (Hakansson, 1987; Lundvall, 1992). The network paradigm proposes that innovation is a fundamentally interactive process (Rosenberg, 1982; Von Hippel, 1988). Importantly, innovation-seeking interactions involve interactive learning between agents: between functional areas within a firm (characterized as intra-firm relations on page 47), between firms (characterized as inter-firm relations on page 43), between users and producers, and between firms and supporting institutions. Innovation, then, is the outcome of this collective interactive learning (Lundvall, 1992). Complementing Lundvall, Dougherty (1992) points to the lack of links and interaction among agents as an inhibiting factor in the efficient flow of knowledge and ideas and also as the main obstacle to innovation. Therefore we propose that innovation in a region requires efficient exchange of ideas and knowledge among members within and across firms in the region.

Knowledge has been seen recently as one of the most important sources of competitive advantage of firms, nations and industrial regions. While the link between the accumulation of knowledge and competitiveness requires in-depth examination beyond the scope of this chapter, some important gener-alizations about the knowledge itself have emerged. For example, Polanyi's (1969) proposition that knowledge is composed of *tacit* and *codified* (or artic-ulated and explicit) *knowledge* has important implications for our discussion. Referring to tacit knowledge as 'the knowledge of techniques, methods and designs that work in certain circumstances, even when one cannot explain why', Rosenberg (1982, p. 142) identified the importance of tacit knowledge to technological change and to the advancement of science. Senker and Faulkner (1996) argue that tacit knowledge is as important as any other element of knowledge flow for innovation, both internally and externally. They also suggest that the generating of tacit knowledge is also an inevitable advance in both science and technology-enabling innovation. Therefore firms try to acquire such knowledge to support innovation.

The recent view of the firm as a stock of knowledge (Nonaka and Takeuchi, 1995) suggests that knowledge is primarily tacit. This perspective argues that codified knowledge comprises only a fraction of the stock of knowledge while most knowledge remains tacit. Tacit knowledge is heuristic, subjective and contextual. Most importantly, when such knowledge is embodied in individu-als, it cannot be easily codified and therefore cannot be bought or sold as a commodity. Thus Lundvall and Johnson (1994) conclude that 'parts of the know-how can be sold as patents and other parts as turn-key plants, but an important part remains tacit and cannot be removed from its human and social context' (p. 30). For these reasons, many scholars argue that knowledge, and especially the accumulation of it, can be primarily local (Nelson and Winter, 1982; Patel and Pavitt, 1991, 1997). Tacit knowledge is learnt by personal experience, practice and practical examples, and requires much interaction, through communication and experiential learning, for transferring the particu-lar tacit knowledge from one individual to another.

Polanyi points out that tacit knowledge and codified knowledge are not sharply divided. While tacit knowledge is contained by and in its own form, explicit knowledge must rely on an individual's tacit understanding before application. This resonates with Polanyi's (1969) argument that all knowledge is either tacit or rooted in tacit knowledge (p. 114). Thus transfer of knowledge cannot be completed by transferring codified knowledge unless it is accompa-nied by the transfer of corresponding tacit knowledge by personal interaction through apprenticeship, training and other forms of learning. It appears that successful clusters tend to provide a social environment conducive to such transfers. We reformulate the above arguments in order to contextualize them for clusters: as most knowledge is tacit and tends to be local, successful clus-ters tend to facilitate interactions among individuals through rich communica-tions, experiences and other forms of learning required for transfer of knowledge.

As suggested earlier, development of trust, through accumulation of social capital, facilitates efficient exchange among interacting agents. The effective transfer of knowledge in inter-firm relations requires a cooperative context and a high degree of openness (Wathne *et al.*, 1997). The richness of interaction and the channel of communication for effective transfer are positively related to the perceived openness of the social context for such interactions. The role of trust in facilitating exchange of knowledge, especially tacit knowledge, is therefore critical.

Even within the context of a single firm, Dougherty (1992) found that the so-called 'departmental thought worlds'[16] (p. 179) (referring to each department's focus on different aspects of technology-market knowledge) inhibit efficient exchange of ideas within a firm and affect negatively the firm's innovative capacity. The 'departmental thought worlds', coupled with lack of mutual understanding and shared grounds for communication,[17] may inhibit the requisite openness for efficient interdepartmental transfers and consequent synthesis to enable or sustain innovation. Higher degrees of openness are achieved through the establishment of trust (Wathne *et al.*, 1997, p. 61), which is in turn established through prior experience of interaction, as discussed earlier. The effective transfer of knowledge as a basis for a firm's competitiveness, within and beyond a region, would depend on the richness of communication and social interactions based on the prior maintenance and accumulation of social capital resulting in increased trust. We therefore propose that exchange of tacit knowledge through interaction requires trust among individuals involved in the exchange. We may also extend this proposition to further propose that (a) a region where trust among agents is well-established will achieve efficient exchange of ideas within the region, thus leading to higher innovative capacity to achieve higher and faster economic prosperity; (b) for SMEs with relatively high vulnerabilities, relatively high levels of accumulated social capital and trusting relations are necessary for engaging in successful inter-firm transactions; and (c) the high levels of social capital and trust in a region are likely to remove barriers to SMEs' growth through participation in building innovative capacity through transfer and application of knowledge in the region.

CONCLUSION AND IMPLICATIONS

A successful cluster is a distinct place, where Marshallian external economies and Schumpeterian creative destruction take place simultaneously mainly as a result of the efficient exchange of goods, services and ideas among interdependent members of a region. The dynamism that distinguishes a successful cluster from others, however, can be achieved only when the members of the regional cluster deliberately come together to take joint action and create collective goods within the region. Thus the concept of social animation has been proposed, and there is increasing evidence to suggest that public institutions as social animators have played a facilitating, if not catalytic, role in the process of joint action, especially in the formation stages of clusters and in less developed, or in less efficient, regions.

The studies of successful clusters often aptly conclude that the cooperative behavior of a region is culturally specific, without explaining the link from the sociocultural specificity to economic prosperity. This chapter, however, has examined the subject to ascertain the link from social capital, through innovative capacity, to the economic prosperity of a region. It appears that social capital, a distinct manifestation of the sociocultural milieu in a region, facilitates trust-seeking interactions which in turn create conducive conditions for joint action for enhanced efficiency and increased innovative capacity.

This chapter began by identifying the context in which proximity leads to efficient exchange of goods, services and ideas, where members within a region find strong incentives to take joint actions for creating collective goods and efficiency. The establishment of trust, which in turn leads to accumulation of social capital, was proposed as a contextual variable, to enhance and even transform proximity into innovative and efficient exchange.

The chapter went on to deal with trust as a relational concept. Trust can be earned or gained only through experiential social interactions. Even in the face of globalization, the opportunities for social interactions tend to remain local. Thus higher trust is more likely to develop between individuals in geographic proximity than between those separated by both geographical and sociocultural distance. Accumulated trust, mainly due to reduced distance between individuals embedded in the sociocultural life within the region, can then mitigate the perceived costs of transaction-intensive relations, especially when SMEs with elevated levels of vulnerabilities are involved. In such trusting environments, small firms can develop synergistic relations with other members of the regional cluster and contribute to their own growth as well as that of the region without the fear of opportunistic behavior by larger and well-established counterparts.

Finally, this chapter examined how successful clusters achieve higher and faster economic growth than other regions through an effective creation and transfer of knowledge within a region. Knowledge, as an input for innovation, tends to be tacit and requires intensive interaction among individuals for effective transfer and efficient use. A successful region, where trust is embedded in the social relations among the members within the region, facilitates the interaction and exchange of knowledge. Therefore the region tends to exhibit higher capacity for innovation, leading to higher economic prosperity.

This chapter's arguments are formalized in terms of some 26 propositions in three families related to each section. They are theoretically based and deduced logically from the extensive literature covering a wide area of inquiry, including proximity, social capital, trust, knowledge and innovative capacity. Although we have drawn them from the extant theory, they remain untested and should be subjected to empirical testing before they can easily form a solid theoretical base for further theorizing of the subject.

The managerial implications of this chapter are fourfold:

1. trust and social capital are not bought, or sold, and firms cannot rely on others to develop them for them;
2. managers should strive to create social capital, develop trust and accumulate them with a selected list of complementary firms, with sociocultural proximity, embedded in the economic and sociocultural milieu of a region;
3. firms, especially SMEs, should use the geographical and sociocultural proximity prevailing in an industrial region to reduce the perceived and real costs of transactions to enhance their own efficiency as well as that of the region as a whole in relation to others; and
4. the members of the regional cluster should leverage their relations to increase the region's innovative capacity to create wealth and value for all concerned.

As discussed earlier, the social institutions have played a critical role in successful clusters. It has covered a wide range, from passive animation to active and catalytic actions. These institutions can certainly enhance the sociocultural environment and reduce the opportunistic behavior within a region in order to attract innovative firms and individuals as well as progressive buyers, suppliers and other supporting institutions, including knowledge-creating institutions and knowledge-intensive enterprises, together with risk-mitigating institutions and infrastructures.

The empirical testing of the propositions formulated in this chapter may result in a solid theoretical contribution for the better understanding of far more complex interrelations. They may also serve to reorient potentially conflictive relations to mutually supportive and rewarding relations within an industrial region. Naturally such theoretical developments can lead to stronger, synergistic and even symbiotic relations capable of enhancing the growth of all firms, especially SMEs, within the regions and beyond.

NOTES

1. 'Geography' in Feldman and Florida's word.

2. This conclusion, in turn, became the underlying assumption of industry-cluster informed policy, which seeks to leverage the competitive advantage accrued from clustering of firms in geographic proximity.
3. There are various conceptualizations of proximity. Proximity, here, refers to contiguity.
4. An industrial region may begin to form in the proximity of critical support industries and institutions available in a region. Alternatively the prospect of rising demand in a region may bring the critical support institutions to the region. Two examples may help to clarify the point. A shopping mall, which is a dense cluster of stores in a locality, is usually planned around a few megastores which generate the necessary traffic for themselves and complementary goods and services in the mall. These large stores, usually called 'anchors', become instrumental in promoting the locality. Magna International, one of the largest auto part suppliers in the world, locates its parts operations as close as possible to its major buyers. Magna's part plants are sometimes extended into the buyers' plants in order to minimize distance and time.
5. In ancient times suppliers of the same, similar and related goods and services clustered in one location; for example, the kitchen suppliers formed a wing in the household part of the Grand Bazaar.
6. While Silicon Valley is at the heart of the San Francisco Bay area in California, the Route 128 region consists of firms conveniently located along Route 128 in the proximity of Boston in the state of Massachusetts.
7. Putnam's discussion of social capital is based on the study of the Third Italy. Saxenian also used the concept of social capital in her discussion. However it should be noted that the types of social capital found in the two regions differ. For an excellent discussion, see Cohen and Fields (1998).
8. An example of such mutual expectations is that favors given now will have to be returned later.
9. The cooperative side of their joint action leads to more, better or faster innovations in the regions, while the competitive side adds to the rigor and the strength of the region's competitiveness against others and consequently pushes up the basis for competition against which other non-cooperating competitors (that is, not belonging to the social network) must compete.
10. When the Suzuki Motor Cycle plant in Detroit did not have much for its labor force to do, they were offered to the city administration free of charge to help out the city's repair crew instead of being laid off. This created tremendous social capital for both the workers and Suzuki in the years to come.
11. Although process innovations and continuous improvements lead to higher quality and efficiency of a production system, they do not add to the portfolio of goods and services produced in the region and do not serve to create additional wealth through further employment of resources.
12. Glasgow's quality competition is opposed to Manchester's mass-production based ordinary competition.
13. Systemic resilience is one of the main themes of the GREMI (Groupe de Recherche Européan sur le Milieux Innovateurs) approach on innovative regions (see Bramanti and Ratti, 1997).
14. Social division of labor refers to differentiation of tasks between independent firms (Scott, 1986). In the cluster where production is socially divided, economies of scale are presumed to be realized externally in the form of a production complex of firms linked together by market (and quasi-market) transactions. It is not surprising that the social division of labor has become a main theme in the discussion of clusters among economic geographers. The concept has long been one of the major concepts in the explanation of geographic organization of the production system in the discipline, which seeks to understand the territorial organization of social life, patterns in locating social production (understood as the unity of productive forces and relations of production) and human settlement, and the specific ways in which these patterns appear in different countries, areas and localities.
15. In this sense, we may consider the innovator as an integrator of various knowledge sets in existence, who identifies and creates so-called 'windows of opportunity'.

16. The problem associated with departmental thought worlds is similar to Van de Ven's classical problem of management of 'part and whole' in the process of innovation.
17. Creation of information redundancy may be a catalyst for facilitation of mutual understanding and shared grounds for communication among individuals so as to increase openness to each other for building new, or increasing the existing, innovative capacity.

REFERENCES

Arrow, K. (1974), *The Limits of Organization*, New York: Norton.

Bergman, E. (1998) 'Industrial trade clusters in action: seeing regional economies whole', in M. Steiner (ed.), *Clusters and Regional Specialization: On Geography, Technology and Networks*, London: Pion pp. 92–110.

Bramanti, A. and R. Ratti (1997), 'The multi-faced dimensions of local development', in R. Ratti and A. Bramanti (eds), *The Dynamics of Innovative Regions: The GREMI Approach*, Aldershot: Ashgate pp. 3–44.

Cohen, S. and E.J. Fields (1998), 'Social capital and capital gains, or virtual bowling in Silicon Valley', BRIE Working Papers.

De la Mothe, J. and G. Paquet (2000), 'National innovation systems and institutional processes', in Z.J. Acs (ed.), *Regional Innovation, Knowledge and Global Change*, London: Pinter, pp. 27–36.

Dosi, G. (1992), 'Sources, procedures, and macroeconomic effects of innovation', *Journal of Economic Literature*, **26**, 179–202.

Dougherty, D. (1992), 'Interpretive barriers to successful product innovation in large firms', *Organization Science*, **3**, 179–202.

Feldman, M.P. and R. Florida (1994), 'The geographic sources of innovation: technological infrastructure and product innovation in the United States', *Annals of the Association of American Geographers*, **84**, 210–29.

Fukuyama, F. (1995), *The Social Virtues and the Creation of Prosperity*, New York: Free Press.

Gaffard, J.-L., (1990), *Économie Industrielle et de l'Innovation*, Paris: Balloz.

Granovetter, M. (1984), 'Economic action and social structure: the problem of embeddedness', *American Journal of Sociology*, **91**, 481–510.

Hakansson, H. (1987), 'Introduction', in H. Hakansson (ed.), *Industrial Technological Development: A Network Approach*, Worcester: Billing & Sons, pp. 3–25.

Harrison, B. (1992) 'Industrial district: old wine in new bottles?', *Regional Studies*, **26**, 469–83.

Jacobs, J. (1969), *The Economy of Cities*, London: Penguin.

Kline, L. and N. Rosenberg (1986), 'An overview of innovation', in N. Rosenberg (ed.), *The Positive Sum Strategy*, Washington: National Academy Press, pp. 275–305.

Kogut, B. and U. Zander (1992), 'Knowledge of the firm, combinative capabilities, and the replication of technology', *Organization Science*, **3**, 383–397.

Krugman, P. (1991), *Geography and Trade*, Cambridge, MA: MIT Press.

Lundvall, B. (1992), 'Introduction', in B. Lundvall (ed.), *National Systems of Innovation*, London: Pinter, pp. 1–19.

Lundvall, B.-A. and B. Johnson (1994), 'The learning economy', *Journal of Industry Studies*, **1** (2), 23–42.

Marshall, A. (1949), *Principles of Economics*, London: Macmillan.

Morgan, K. (1997), 'The learning region: institutions, innovation and regional renewal', *Regional Studies* **31**, 491–503.

Nadvi, K. (1999), 'Collective efficiency and collective failure: the response of the Sialkot surgical instrument cluster to global quality pressures', *World Development*, **27**, 1605–26.

Nelson, R. and S. Winter (1982), *An Evolutionary Theory of Economic Change*, New York: Oxford University Press.

Nonaka, I. and H. Takeuchi (1995), *How Japanese Companies Create the Dynamics of Innovation*, London: Oxford University Press.

Patel, P. and K. Pavitt (1991), 'Large firms in production of world technology: an important case of non-globalization', *Journal of International Business Studies*, **22**, 1–22.

Patel, P. and K. Pavitt (1997), 'The technological competence of the world's largest firms: complex and path-dependent but not much variety', *Research Policy*, **26**, 141–56.

Piore, M. J. and C.F. Sabel (1984), *The Second Industrial Divide*, New York: Basic Books.

Polanyi, M. (1969), 'The logic of tacit inference', *Knowing and Being*, London: Routledge and Kegan Paul.

Porter, M. (1990), *The Competitive Advantage of Nations*, New York: Free Press.

Porter, M. (1998), 'Clusters and economic competition', *Harvard Business Review*, November–December, 77–90.

Putnam, R. (1993a), *Making Democracy Work*, Princeton: Princeton University Press.

Putnam, R. (1993b), 'The prosperous community', *The American Prospect*, **4** (13), March.

Rosenberg, N. (1982), *Inside the Black Box*, Cambridge, MA: Cambridge University Press.

Saxenian, A. (1994), 'Regional advantage', *Culture and Competition in Silicon Valley and Route 128*, Cambridge, MA: Harvard University Press.

Schmitz, H. (1999), 'Global competition and local cooperation: success and failure in the Sinos Valley, Brazil', *World Development*, **27**, 1627–50.

Schmitz, H. and K. Nadvi (1999), 'Clustering and industrialization: introduction', *World Development*, **27**, 1503–14.

Schumpeter, J. (1943), *Capitalism, Socialism and Democracy*, London: Allen and Unwin.

Scitovsky, T. (1963), 'Two concepts of external economies', in A.N. Agarwala and S.P. Singh (eds), *The Economics of Underdevelopment*, New York: Oxford University Press.

Scott, A.J. (1986), 'Industrial organization and location: division of labor, the firm, and spatial process', *Economic Geography*, 215–31.

Senker, J. and W. Faulkner (1996), 'Networks, tacit knowledge and innovation', in R. Coombs, A. Richards, P.P. Saviotti and V. Walsh (eds), *Technological Collaboration*, Cheltenham, UK, and Brookfield, USA: Edward Elgar Publishing, pp. 76–97.

Staber, U. (1996a), 'The social embeddedness of industrial district networks', in U. Staber (ed.), *Business Networks: Prospects for Regional Development*, Berlin: Walter de Gruyter, pp. 148–74.

Staber, U. (1996b), 'Network and regional development: perspectives and unresolved issues', in U. Staber (ed.), *Business Networks: Prospects for Regional Development*, Berlin: Walter de Gruyter, pp. 1–23.

Steiner, M. (1998), 'The discrete charm of clusters: an introduction', in M. Steiner (ed.), *Clusters and Regional Specialization*, London: Pion pp. 1–17.

Storper, M. (1995), 'The resurgence of economies ten years later: the region as a nexus of untraded interdependencies', *European Urban and Regional Studies*, **5**, 605–44.

Storper, M. and B. Harrison (1991), 'Flexibility, hierarchy and regional development: the chaining structure of industrial production systems and their forms of governance in the 1990s', *Research Policy*, **2**, 407–22.

Storper, M. and A.J. Scott (1988), *The Geographic Foundations and Social Regulation of Flexible Production Complexes*, London: George Allen & Unwin.

Storper, M. and A.J. Scott (1995), 'The wealth of regions', *Futures*, **27**, 505–26.

Veltz, P. (1993), 'D'une géographie des coûts à une géographie de l'organization. Quelques thèses sur l'évolution des rapports entreprises/territoires', *Revue économique*, **4**.

Von Hippel, E. (1988), *The Source of Innovation*, New York: Oxford University Press.

Wathne, K., J. Roos and G. von Krogh (1997), 'Towards a theory of knowledge transfer in co-operative context,' in G. von Krogh and J. Roos (eds), *Managing Knowledge: Perspectives on Co-operation and Competition*, London: Sage Publication, pp. 55–81.

3. Capital structure and the pace of SME internationalization

Rod B. McNaughton and Jim Bell

INTRODUCTION

The pace at which a firm internationalizes is an important characteristic of its international marketing strategy. A set of 'pre-conditions' creates an environment in which early and rapid entry into foreign markets is a strategy that may be pursued successfully by some SMEs (Madsen and Servais, 1997, pp. 565–7). A substantial stream of literature developed over the past decade has contributed to our understanding of when the pace of internationalization is likely to be quick. Influences are summarized in models such as that offered by Kandasaami (1998) and Pedersen and Petersen (1998) in case research focused on international new ventures (McDougall *et al.*, 1994), and in quantitative studies on time to foreign market entry (for example, McNaughton, 1999). Taken as a whole, this literature identifies a large number of possible influences, including the orientation and experience of key decision makers, firm characteristics, domestic market size, quality of the innovation (especially knowledge intensity), industry conditions and other factors.

Absent from the list of influences that have been intensively studied is the capital structure of the firm. The constraints of inadequate 'financial resources' are a frequently cited barrier to internationalization (for example, Bannock and Peacock, 1989) and the influence of 'firm size' is another theme for investigation (for example, Bonaccorsi, 1992; Ali and Camp, 1993). However a well-developed theory of the potential interplay between capital structure and the ability to fund internationalization has yet to emerge. This gap in the extant literature is particularly conspicuous given the importance to international business theory of international investment as a rationale for the existence of multinational enterprises (MNEs), and the stream of literature in international finance that addresses the capital structure of MNEs and the wealth effects of internationalization (for example, Khambata and Reeb, 2000).

The research reported here begins to address this gap. First, the literature on the pace of internationalization and the possible influence of 'financial resources' is reviewed. This is supplemented by the literature on small firm finance that links capital structure to growth and firm strategy. The collection of data from venture capitalists to ground an understanding of the possible interplay between the pace of internationalization and capital structure is then described. The results are discussed, leading to a summary model. Finally the implications for theory development, international marketing practice and export policy are discussed.

LITERATURE REVIEW

A recent theme in the international business literature is the 'challenge' of 'born global' firms to the traditional characterization of internationalization as an incremental process (Oviatt and McDougall, 1997). The notion of incremental internationalization draws from theories that characterize firm internationalization as either a learning sequence (for example, Johanson and Wiedersheim-Paul, 1975; Johanson and Vahlne, 1977) or a series of stages (for example, Bilkey and Tesar, 1977; Reid, 1981). Learning and stage models implicitly assume that firms establish themselves in the domestic market before entering foreign ones, and that internationalization proceeds in a series of steps that represent an escalation of commitment over time (Oesterle, 1997, p. 126). In contrast, 'born global' firms internationalize very quickly, and may be international from inception. The theory that underpins understanding of this phenomenon is closely associated with the work of Oviatt and McDougall (1994), which integrates the international business, entrepreneurship and strategic management literatures to explain the phenomenon of international new ventures.

A consequence of positioning born global firms as a challenge to traditional expectations is that incremental and born global internationalization paths are often treated as dichotomous patterns of internationalization. (See the review by Madsen and Servais, 1997.) However, as Pedersen and Petersen (1998, pp. 483–5) point out, these paths differ more in terms of the *pace* of resource commitment than they do in terms of pattern. Similar views are shared by other researchers such as Kutschker *et al.* (1997, pp. 110–13) who portray the temporal dimension of internationalization as a key strategic variable, which needs to be actively managed in terms of order, timing and speed. In essence, all internationalization reveals some aspects of incrementalism (Pedersen and Petersen, 1998). The key point of differentiation is the speed with which international commitments are made (McNaughton, 1999).

A number of theoretic frameworks suggest influences on the pace of internationalization. These can be categorized as to whether they stress internal resource factors (such as market knowledge and the resource base of the firm) or external factors (such as market volume and the global competitive environment) (Pedersen and Petersen, 1998, pp. 485–90). 'Financial resources' is generally treated as an internal influence, with the implication that capital (like foreign market knowledge) is assumed to accumulate incrementally within the firm (as are the assets that can be used as collateral for debt). The availability of resources is hypothesized to influence both the pace of internationalization and the intensity of commitment (that is, choice of mode). This emphasis on the internal accumulation of capital has led to the frequent use in empirical studies of firm size (or even age) as a proxy for financial resources (for example, Bonaccorsi, 1992; Ali and Camp, 1993). However, statistically significant support for a relationship between size (or age) and foreign market commitment is rare.

One possible explanation for failure to verify this relationship empirically is that firm size or age is not necessarily a good indicator of the availability of free cash to invest in internationalization. A relatively small and young firm could have substantial cash to invest in an internationalization program following an equity injection by a venture capitalist, whereas an older and larger firm could have amassed considerable debt while expanding domestically, making the firm unattractive to equity investors, and limiting the resources that can be directed toward international expansion. Capital structure (the mix and source of short-term and long-term debt, earnings, directors' loans and external equity) more than size or age could clearly influence the financial resources available to invest in internationalization.

The interplay between capital structure, capital availability and the pace of internationalization in smaller firms has not been a major focus of enquiry in the international business literature. However there is a well-developed stream of research in finance that investigates the capital structure of MNEs and the wealth effects of internationalization. (See the recent review and synthesis of this literature by Khambata and Reeb, 2000.) The case of smaller firms that do not have access to public capital markets has attracted less attention, though capital availability is clearly fundamental to implementation of any internationalization strategy. For example, inability to arrange suitable financing, and the possible effect on cash flow of slow, or delinquent, payment by international customers is frequently cited as an important barrier to initiating export activities (for example, Bannock and Peacock, 1989). The potential influence of capital structure on internationalization is also evidenced by the early export activity observed among firms in venture capital portfolios (McNaughton, 1990).

There is a literature concerned with small firm finance, however, which specifically links capital structure to both growth and firm strategy. (See the review in Jordan *et al.*, 1998.) This literature provides some guidance in forming an understanding of the possible link between capital structure and the pace of internationalization. For example, Weston and Brigham's (1981) life cycle model of the use of short-term debt captures a fundamental relationship between capital structure and growth in small firms. They propose that the combination of small size and rapid growth results in a finance gap for firms that do not have access to public capital markets. The cash required for growth outstrips internally generated funds, leading to slower growth or substantial short-term borrowing. The bias in the capital structure of small firms toward financing growth through internally generated funds and then through short-term debt is also reinforced by tax considerations, and a tendency among entrepreneurs to see external equity as expensive and dangerous in terms of interference and potential loss of control (Myers, 1984).

Access to short-term debt can also prove problematic for smaller firms. Myers (1977) posits that the pursuit of growth increases the potential for conflict between internal and external parties, leading to a moral hazard in the form of asset substitution. Agency problems also arise because of information asymmetry between owners and potential lenders (especially in small firms because of unreliable or less sophisticated financial reporting practice), and because of the incentive to take risks created by limited liability. In general, agency problems cause lenders to rely heavily on collateral in advancing debt to small firms, so the amount of debt that can be raised is also often limited (Chittenden *et al.*, 1996).

Extrapolating the insights of this literature suggests that cash demands of early and rapid internationalization could easily outstrip internally generated funds. Further, limited collateral, the risk of foreign receivables and the negative impact on cash flow of debt repayment all constrain the amount of short-term debt that can be raised, creating a financing gap. Unless this gap is filled, the pace of internationalization will have to slow. Thus internationalization funded from internal funds or short-term debt is most likely to be delayed or to proceed at a slower pace. When access to long-term debt is limited, either growth will be slowed or outside equity will be sought. Equity investors may be able to mitigate the problem of information asymmetry through use of convertible preferred stock, investing in rounds, and close monitoring, which may involve a seat on the board.

METHOD

Semi-structured in-person interviews were conducted with directors from five venture capital firms in Sydney, five in Melbourne and two in Brisbane. Venture capitalists were interviewed because they are experienced observers of businesses, and their professional role focuses on the provision of capital and management services to high-growth firms. Such firms are likely to consider entry into international markets.

Most studies of internationalization gather data from managers within the context of a single firm. This viewpoint is limiting. In contrast, venture capitalists are intimately involved in the affairs of several firms in a portfolio, and have reviewed the business plans of tens and possibly hundreds of firms. They are uniquely qualified to compare alternative internationalization paths and to comment on the likely influences and consequences of different capital structures. The directors in the sample all had experience with portfolio firms that had internationalized.

Venture capital firms typically focus their investments in a particular sector and/or investment stage. The directors were chosen so that their experiences would reflect a variety of sectors, stages and the types of deals presented to different sized funds. (The firms represented are described in Table 3.1.) This minimized the likelihood that responses could be attributed to the unique circumstances of a particular industry or type of firm. The directors were selected from a directory of Australian venture capital firms (Bivell, 1999). The directory lists 79 firms in Australia, and reports that those firms have invested $AUS3.1 billion, and that $AUS2.1 billion is available for investment. Initial contact and follow-up was made by e-mail. The typical interview lasted one hour. At one firm a director and an associate were interviewed together.

Data collection during the interview, and subsequent analysis, followed grounded theory-building techniques. The objective was to build inductively a theory of the relationships between capital structure and pace of internationalization. Glaser and Strauss (1967) provide the rationale for a grounded approach. The specific approach followed the techniques described by Miles and Huberman (1984). The interviews were semi-structured and involved questions centred on three issues:

- the motive, pattern and pace of internationalization amongst the firms the venture capitalist had observed,
- the relationship observed between internationalization and the firm value, and
- possible associations observed between the capital structure and the pace of internationalization.

Non-directive probes were used to gain detail, in particular to elicit specific examples, to see if the interviewee could identify an exception to a generalization, to promote comparison or to establish the relative importance of a mentioned relationship or influence. After the first few interviews, a visual organization of the emerging data was formed. This organization was subsequently added to or modified. At the end of the last four interviews the visual model was shown to the subject and they were asked to comment on how well it would fit their own mental model of the illustrated elements and relationships and whether they would suggest any modifications.

FINDINGS

The interviews confirmed that there is significant variability in the pace of internationalization between firms, even within the select portfolios of venture capitalists. The interviewees provided a range of examples from their portfolios and past investments, from domestic-only to rapidly internationalizing firms. These included an investment in medical clinics (domestic only), a manufacturer of prepared packaged foods (that exports to New Zealand), a financial services firm (that had entered the US market) and an Internet firm that started with a global focus. The examples discussed supported the assertion that, as broad categories, the stereotypes of incremental internationalization and born global would have merit.

In tracing through the history of example portfolio firms, respondents were probed to identify key factors that might explain the pace of internationalization. The key influence uncovered by this process was the growth rate of the firm, which would be affected by characteristics of the market and of the entrepreneur. A high growth rate is central to a venture investment as investors are typically seeking to achieve above market returns over a four-to-seven year period. As one investor phrased it: 'The key is to fund firms that have identified a large disorganised and fragmented market, and that have the management who can organise it successfully.'

Given the relatively small size of the Australian population, there are relatively few domestic markets that can sustain rapid growth. Thus many firms are forced to penetrate international markets early on. One respondent illustrated this by characterizing the market size needed to underpin a successful share float. He argued that a successful IPO (initial public offering) would need a valuation of 'at least $20 million'.[1] This valuation would be consistent with a firm that had 'after tax profits of $1–2 million in the year preceding the IPO, and as net profits after tax are rarely over 10 per cent, and more likely near 5 per cent, one needs to be targeting a market around $50 million'. The inference is that there are relatively few unorganized markets of that size in Australia.[2]

In addition to size, other market-related considerations were cited. The case of high-technology firms that need to appropriate quickly benefits from R&D in volatile markets was mentioned several times. One respondent noted that patent searches and registration, when conducted over several major markets,

Table 3.1 Venture capitalists interviewed

Position	Location	Years of experience	Size of fund currently managed (Millions)	Number of firms in current portfolio	Number of divestments	Sector preference of fund	Geographic focus of fund
Director	Sydney	15	$14	5	10	Manf., services, media	Australia, NZ
Principal	Sydney	6	$35	3	0	All except property and mining	Australia, NZ
Chairman	Sydney	8	$20	7	0	Manf., services	NSW and Queensland
Managing director	Sydney	14	$154	14	7	All except property	Australia, NZ
Managing director	Sydney	8	$30	12	4	IT, telecom and biosciences	Australia
Director & senior consultant (interviewed together)	Melbourne	20	$4	7	2	All except mining	Victoria
Director	Melbourne	5	$11	9	0	All except property and resources	Australia
Director/ principal	Melbourne	18	$100	13	47	IT, medical, tourism, business services	Australasia
General manager	Melbourne	20	$800	5	5	High tech, exporters	Asia Pacific
Executive director	Melbourne	5	$35	3	0	IT and telecom	Australia
Investment manager	Brisbane	6	$2	2	1	IT, agribusiness, life sciences	Queensland & northern NSW
Manager	Brisbane	12	$60	10	10	Technology, services	Queensland

become quite costly and can reveal information that is potentially useful to competitors. He concluded that it might be necessary to internationalize quickly to achieve pioneering (or first mover) advantages and appropriate the benefits of R&D investments. Another noted that the involvement of large foreign firms in Australia often leads to internationalization opportunities for indigenous firms. The Australian firm might supply the foreign subsidiary, which then recommends it as a supplier to the parent company or other international subsidiaries. Other firms, particularly in business service industries, may follow domestic clients overseas as they internationalize.

The characteristics of the entrepreneur identified as having an influence on firm growth involve 'vision', 'drive', 'knowing how to make money', 'quality' and 'experience'. Basically the investors suggested that the personal wealth objectives, risk orientation and managerial competencies of the management team had significant influence on both the growth strategy and success of the firm. This appeared to be the case irrespective of whether domestic or international markets were the targets.

To summarize, the venture capitalists interviewed stressed that they sought to fund businesses that addressed a large but as yet poorly organized market, with a management team that was motivated and possessed the competencies to penetrate quickly and to become a significant player in that market. Given the size of the Australian market, it is likely that at least some will have to internationalize quickly to meet high growth objectives, and to provide sufficient return to investors.

When asked whether it followed that business plans that included an internationalization strategy, or evidence that international markets had already been entered, were more attractive or would attract a higher valuation, the answers were equivocal. The relationship appears to be contingent on other factors. As one investor explained, 'We would not look for internationalisation per se, as other avenues of growth might be superior and entail less risk.' Several of the investors commented that managing a rapidly growing business is difficult, and the added problems of internationalization could put even more strain on management. One respondent pointed out that, ideally, ventures should have the potential to enter foreign markets, but that the venture capitalist might try to avoid the risk of funding internationalization if sufficient growth could be achieved otherwise. Another investor commented that in some sectors preparing to internationalize could be a lengthy process because of the need to achieve accreditation, or to meet certain quality standards. Although costly, going through this process can help to build a better business, and thus add value.

A slightly different perspective was offered by an investor who suggested that the question of when to internationalize should be understood in terms of a trade-off between current cash flow and the investment exit value. He stressed that successful internationalization can be both an expensive and a lengthy process. In his experience, this is particularly the case with service firms, which do not have the option of exporting, and must establish offices overseas. The cash 'burn rate' (excess of expenditures over revenues) during the set-up period, and for building brand recognition, can be high. Thus the investor must determine whether the present value of any premium that might be realized at exit, because of expansion into international markets, is greater than the value of maintaining positive cash flow.

Another investor pointed out that, in terms of enhancing firm value, in some cases it is more important to internationalize the equity base of the firm than it is to internationalize the market. The rationale for this assertion is twofold. First, private equity is typically valued higher by overseas investors, especially American investors. In this interview it was pointed out that, 'In Australia five times earnings is a typical valuation, but in the States it is ten. Thus, we can settle at eight and have increased our value, while the American thinks it is a deal.' Overseas investors can also assist in raising subsequent rounds of financing, and can tap larger pools of funds than are available in Australia. In a related vein, an investor commented that venture capitalists were not well positioned to assist with internationalization per se, as they usually do not have the required industry-specific contacts overseas. Instead, they are better placed to facilitate links with overseas investors who can in turn help with local contacts.

The second consideration is that many investments are exited through sale to an MNE. These firms are typically interested in acquiring the technology assets of the Australian firm, and as they have their own international infrastructure are not concerned about the level of internationalization of the acquisition target. Thus greater value might be realized by investing in development of technology rather than in international marketing, although one investor noted that an Australian firm might be brought to the attention of potential purchasers through international activities.

Other investors raised the issue of exiting through a sale to an MNE. A relatively large proportion of Australian investments are exited in this manner. While respondents generally agreed that acquisition by an MNE might be seen as a vehicle for internationalization, their frequent observation was that the result was more likely closure, or poor performance. As MNEs are typically motivated to acquire a specific asset (often a technology), they close the Australian firm, further develop the technology and market it elsewhere, neglect the asset, or have problems integrating the firm into their existing organizational structure. This was not regarded as a necessarily poor outcome for the Australian economy. The investors cited increases in the capital available to invest in new ventures, and releasing experienced managers to start new businesses, as positive aspects of this cycle. One respondent also noted that a sale to an MNE usually takes longer, and involves additional legal considerations. This increases the cost of the acquisition, and creates opportunities to develop international experience amongst local legal and accounting professionals.

Finally the investors were generally in agreement that capital structure could influence the pace of internationalization. In particular the lack of free capital is a significant brake on the rapidity of internationalization, and successive rounds of raising equity can facilitate rapid international expansion. However they were also quick to point out that capital is not the only consideration, and its availability needs to be matched with the speed at which management can scale up the organization, meet quality standards, develop overseas contacts and experience, and build channel relationships. Some respondents also pointed out that the circumstances of building businesses vary by sector, as do capital requirements. For example, firms in 'traditional' industries often need to invest in physical assets to scale up production for international markets, and overseas markets can be served by exporting. As the asset can serve as collateral, taking on debt can fund such scaling up.[3] In comparison, a knowledge-intensive or service firm may need to establish offices overseas and invest in brand building. As this investment is intangible, collateral can be a problem, and new equity must be sought.

The investors felt that many entrepreneurs misunderstand the use of private equity. They see raising equity as a costly way of funding growth and venture capitalists as seeking control and interfering with management sovereignty. This leads entrepreneurs to assume both the business/technology risks of a new venture or expansion and the associated financial risk. The financial risk can be shared with a venture capitalist which, by providing experience in business control, contacts, reputation and synergy with other firms in the portfolio, can also help to mitigate business risk.

One investor noted that the reluctance of entrepreneurs to take on external equity can even be observed among firms in their portfolio, and becomes an issue each time a new round of investment is required. As Australian venture capital funds are relatively small (compared to those in the USA), and fund managers try to diversify investment across several firms, the capital required in subsequent rounds of funding may need to come from other venture capital firms. However entrepreneurs are often reluctant to become involved with additional investors, or to dilute their ownership further. The result is that some firms do not raise as much capital as they could use, and their growth is slowed. The investor cited the relatively low frequency of syndicated investments in Australia as broad evidence of this phenomenon.

The respondents almost universally raised the issue of alliances. They noted that entrepreneurs often see alliances as an alternative to raising equity, and the popularity of this view is reinforced by popular business rhetoric. The basic idea is that an alliance with a larger firm makes additional resources available (for example, an overseas distribution network), without the firm having to make any additional investment. This is appealing to entrepreneurs as it enables expansion without increasing capital costs or having to dilute ownership. The investors noted that in theory this was beneficial to them as well, since it leveraged their investment. However the frequent observation was that alliances perform poorly, retard growth and can cause exit problems for investors. The primary problems relate to 'dependence', and 'unintended business injury'. As one investor put it, 'If you lie down with an elephant it can roll over and squash you without even knowing it has done it.' A problem often observed is that the larger partner does not fully understand the technology involved or does not appreciate its potential, and either miss-sells or poorly services the product, or it becomes buried in a large portfolio of products/services. The result is that less value is realized than if the smaller firm had raised further equity and served the market itself.

Alliances that involve equity investment from the larger firm can have consequences for venture investors. Such deals usually include options to acquire additional equity. These options make the firm less attractive to other outside investors, and increase financial dependence on the alliance partner. Further, if the firm performs well in spite of a lack of attention by the larger alliance partner, the options are likely to be exercised. This can capture value from the entrepreneur and venture investor.

SUMMARY MODEL

Figure 3.1 summarizes the interplay between the influences on pace of internationalization, capital structure and likely market and firm characteristics of both incremental internationalizers and born global firms. The key interaction is between the growth rate of the firm and its capital structure. Rapid growth is most likely when the firm addresses a large market, and when management has the drive and competencies to become a significant player in that market. When the domestic market is small and/or there are other strategic reasons to internationalize (such as pioneering advantages), growth may be expressed as early and rapid internationalization. However, as the investors pointed out, internationalization needs to be compared with other growth options and does not in itself necessarily add value to a firm.

Firms that are unable to grow quickly (because of market characteristics or management inadequacies) are unlikely to attract private equity investors, so their capital structure will necessarily favor debt. Where a firm is able to grow quickly, the capital requirements of rapid expansion, particularly in international markets, can easily outstrip the ability of a firm to fund expansion

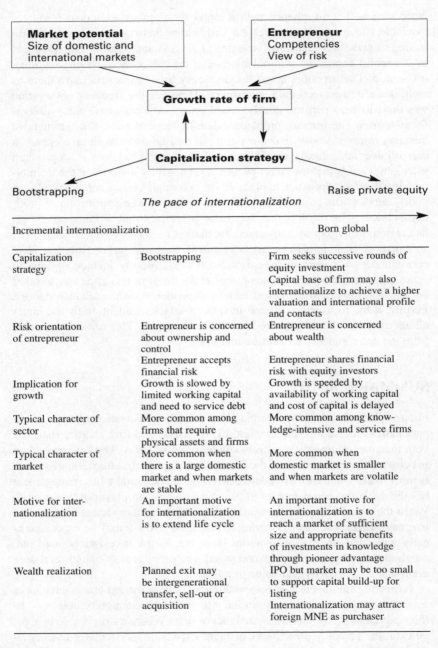

Figure 3.1   Implications of capital structure for pace of internationalization

through either cash flow or debt. This is the case in sectors where asset intensity is low and the firm has little collateral. In these cases, the entrepreneur's attitude toward outside equity and ability to raise funds from private equity investors influence the rate at which growth can be sustained. Entrepreneurs who are concerned about diluting their ownership tend to pursue a bootstrapping financial strategy, and growth is slowed by limited working capital and the need to service debt. Entrepreneurs who are willing and able to raise successive rounds of equity injections are able to expand more quickly as the cost of capital is delayed. Thus decisions about capital structure have an influence on the pace of internationalization.

CONCLUSION

The extant literature on SME internationalization has largely overlooked the influence of capital structure on pace of internationalization, though 'financial resources' are frequently cited as important. The research reported here developed a model of the interplay between capital structure and pace of internationalization in small firms grounded in the experiences of venture capital investors. A contribution to theory is made by the following:

- identifying capital structure and free capital as additional variables that influence the pace of internationalization;
- improving understanding of how different types of capital can facilitate or impede the pace of internationalization;
- emphasizing that internationalization is a growth strategy, the risks and rewards of which are compared with other options by investors.

This research has significant limitations. First, while the interviews provided rich data for theorizing, systematic generalization is not possible from such a small sample. The Australian context also limits the ability to generalize. The Australian economy is relatively small. This means that internationalization is an imperative for many firms as there are few markets that can accommodate rapid growth and high return objectives. Indeed the McKinsey & Company (1993) study that introduced the term 'born global' was conducted in Australia. Second, the venture capital sector is not as mature as in some countries, with smaller funds, fewer syndicated deals and more conservative investment criteria. Finally, the massive flow of funds into Internet start-ups that characterizes current venture capital activity in Silicon Valley is not yet mirrored in Australia. Thus the results are most relevant for Australia and other countries with relatively small domestic markets. However the central contributions listed above are universal. Empirical research needs to be conducted across different countries to verify and quantify the associations identified in the model.

The practical implications of this research are twofold: it emphasizes that entrepreneurs need to consider their international marketing and financial strategies holistically since they are closely intertwined, and export promotion agencies, which typically focus on information provision, can also facilitate internationalization by addressing financial issues: in particular, policies and programs might be considered that improve understanding of the role of private equity and increased access to both equity and debt from sources that are knowledgable about the issues involved in internationalization. Such programs would also need to be sensitive to the differences in firm characteristics and needs associated with the pace of internationalization, and to the requirements of investors.

NOTES

1. The Australian Stock Exchange rules require a minimum capitalization of $1million, but the firm must be much larger to achieve liquidity and attract institutional purchasers.
2. Golis (1998, p. 141) makes a similar argument in his book on Australian venture capital.
3. Such scaling up also has a tax implication.

REFERENCES

Ali, A.J. and R.C. Camp (1993), 'The relevance of firm size and international business experience to market entry strategies', *Journal of Global Marketing*, **6** (4), 91–108.

Bannock, G. and A. Peacock (1989), *Governments and Small Business*, London: Paul Chapman Publishing.

Bilkey, W.J. and G. Tesar (1977), 'The export behavior of smaller-sized Wisconsin manufacturing firms', *Journal of International Business Studies*, Spring/Summer, 93–8.

Bivell, Victor (ed.) (1999), *Australian Venture Capital Guide*, 6th edn, Five Dock, Australia: Pollitecon Publications.

Bonaccorsi, A. (1992), 'On the relationship between firm size and export intensity', *Journal of International Business Studies*, **23**, 605–35.

Chittenden, F., G. Hall and P. Hutchinson (1996), 'Small firm growth, access to capital markets and financial structure: a review of issues and an empirical investigation', *Small Business Economics*, **8**, 59–67.

Glaser, Barney G. and Anselm Strauss (1967), *The Discovery of Grounded Theory: Strategies for Qualitative Research*, New York: Aldine.

Golis, Christopher C. (1998), *Enterprise and Venture Capital: A Business Builders' and Investors' Handbook*, 3rd edn, St. Leonards, Australia: Allen and Unwin.

Johanson, J. and J. Vahlne (1977), 'The internationalization process of the firm: a model of knowledge development and increasing foreign commitments', *Journal of International Business Studies*, Spring/Summer, 23–32.

Johanson, J. and F. Wiedersheim-Paul (1975), 'The internationalization of the firm: four Swedish case studies', *Journal of Management Studies*, October, 305–22.

Jordan, Judith, Julian Lowe and Peter Taylor (1998), 'Strategy and financial policy in UK small firms', *Journal of Business Finance and Accounting*, **25** (1/2), 1–27.

Kandasaami, Selvi (1998), 'Factors influencing the fast-track internationalisation of born-global SMEs: a conceptual model', in S.J. Gray, and S. Nicholas (eds), *Challenges of Globalisation, Proceedings of ANZIBA*, November, Melbourne: Monash University, pp. 13–14.

Khambata, David and David M. Reeb (2000), 'Financial aspects of the multinational firm: a synthesis', *Multinational Business Review*, **8** (1), 74–86.

Kutschker, Michael, Iris Baurle and Stefan Schmid (1997), 'International evolution, international episodes and international epochs – implications for managing internationalization', *Management International Review*, **37** (2), 101–24.

Madsen, Tage Koed and Per Servais (1997), 'The internationalization of born globals: an evolutionary process?', *International Business Review*, **6** (6), 561–83.

McDougall, Patricia Phillips, Scott Shane and Benjamin M. Oviatt (1994), 'Explaining the formation of international new ventures: the limits of theories from international business research', *Journal of Business Venturing*, **9** (6), 469–87.

McKinsey and Co. (1993), *Emerging Exporters: Australia's High Value-added Manufacturing Exporters*, Melbourne: Australian Manufacturing Council.

McNaughton, Rod B. (1990), 'The performance of venture-backed Canadian firms 1980–1987', *Regional Studies*, **24** (2), 109–21.

McNaughton, Rod B. (1999), 'Time-span from start-up to foreign market entry among micro-exporters', *9th ENDEC World Conference on International Entrepreneurship*, 15–18 August, Singapore: National University of Singapore, pp. 1149–57.

Miles, Matthew and Michael Huberman (1984), *Qualitative Data Analysis*, Newbury Park, CA: Sage.

Myers, S.C. (1977), 'Determinants of corporate borrowing', *Journal of Financial Economics*, **5**, 147–75.

Myers, S.C. (1984), 'The capital structure puzzle', *Journal of Finance*, **34** (3), 575–92.

Oesterle, Michael-Jorg (1997), 'Time-span until internationalization: foreign market entry as a built-in mechanism of innovations', *Management International Review*, **37** (2), 125–49.

Oviatt, Benjamin M. and Patricia Phillips McDougall (1994), 'Toward a theory of international new ventures', *Journal of International Business Studies*, **25** (1), 45–64.

Oviatt, Benjamin M. and Patricia Phillips McDougall (1997), 'Challenges for internationalization process theory: the case of international new ventures', *Management International Review*, **37**, 85–99.

Pedersen, Torben and Bent Petersen (1998), 'Explaining gradually increasing resource commitment to a foreign market', *International Business Review*, **7**, 483–501.

Reid, S.D. (1981), 'The decision-maker and export entry and expansion', *Journal of International Business Studies*, **12**, 101–12.

Weston, J.F. and E.F. Brigham (1981), *Managerial Finance*, 7th edn, Hillsdale, NJ: Dryden Press.

4. Academic entrepreneurship and internationalization of technology-based SMEs

Gabriele Beibst and Arndt Lautenschläger

INTRODUCTION: UNIVERSITY-BASED START-UPS AND REGIONAL DEVELOPMENT IN TECHNOLOGY

In a globalized economy, the future of industrialized economies such as Great Britain, Germany and the USA depends on their competence, willingness and freedom to innovate and to build up a knowledge- and technology-based industry. The technologically advanced economies will only compete success-fully on global markets by increasing productivity through process innovation as well as innovation in creating new products and services. This requires a fast transformation of research and development (R&D) results into commercial products.

A glance at successful technology regions shows that innovative business start-ups play a major role in creating a competitive technology-based industry (Röpke, 1998, p. 13). Entrepreneurial firms provide a variety of innovations and technologies to cope with more turbulent dynamics of global competition (ibid., p. 2). Spin-off companies from universities in particular introduce a relatively larger share of commercially-oriented innovations to the market place than others (Abernathy and Utterback, 1978). The experience of successful firms in high-technology regions, including those in the Silicon Valley area and the Boston region in the United States (Saxenian, 1994) and the Oxford and Cambridge regions in the UK (Wicksteed, 1985), highlight several issues: (a) in each of these regions one or more universities have been actively involved in building commercial links with the business community; (b) these universities have become directly involved in establishing companies of their own, staffed by researchers, for marketing scientific insights; and (c) they encourage entrepreneurship among their students and staff in numerous ways. As a result, these regions have increased employment and succeeded in becoming internationally competitive.

Virtually every government in the world seeks to create its own Silicon

Valley. There are 78 names beginning with 'Silicon' in areas outside Silicon Valley in California, including Silicon Triangle in North Carolina, Silicon City in Chicago, Silicon Bog in Ireland and Silicon Wadi in Israel (Dawson, 2000).

The importance of innovative business set-ups by university researchers has been recognized in Germany for some time. The program 'EXIST – university-based start-ups' was launched in 1997 to bring together universities and *Fachhochschulen* (universities of applied sciences) with partners from the scientific world, industry and the government. This program provides students, graduates and scientists with all the services and the stimuli required for starting up their own business. The program is one element in the system of public support for innovative entrepreneurs by the Federal Government of Germany. It seeks to improve the entrepreneurial climate at institutions of higher education and to increase the number of start-up companies originating from academic establishments (Ministry of Education and Research of the Federal Republic of Germany, 2000, pp. 1–15).

Such approaches, however, suffer from their own endemic problems and give rise to a fundamental issue: even if promotional programs succeed in increasing the number of innovative business start-ups, there is no guarantee that a strong technology-based industry will develop. Naturally, not only the quantity of new ventures but also their quality is crucial to meeting the competitive requirements for their survival. Firms that manage to grow and compete successfully in both the domestic and global markets meet the competitive requirements. The fundamental question is, what makes a young innovative/technology-based firm successful and growing?

This chapter focuses on the founders' international orientation among the factors that influence the success of start-up firms originating from universities. In what follows, we would like to examine whether the university researchers who have started new ventures meet the requirements of globally oriented entrepreneurs, that is, both thinking and acting globally, in order to gain competitiveness for survival.

The structure of the chapter is as follows. First, an outline is given to clarify the importance of international business activities for the success of new technology-based firms in the global economy. The hidden champions among firms are those which regard the entire world as their market and act accordingly (Simon, 1996, p. 78). The next section of this chapter will argue that global orientation is especially important to technology-based firms. Because spin-off companies from universities are generally technology-oriented, we emphasize the importance of international orientation to academic entrepreneurs. Such firms frequently face specific problems that hamper their growth, yet the development of international business activities could help them to overcome a host of restrictions.

In the third section we examine whether those academics who act as entrepreneurs are aware of the importance of an international focus to their business. Are they aware of global possibilities and do they make efforts to utilize them? We present the results of a worldwide survey on academic entrepreneurs, responding to our question, to provide fresh insights to problems facing such academic entrepreneurs.

TECHNOLOGY-BASED FIRMS AS GLOBAL PLAYERS

The term 'new technology-based firms' (NTBF) refers to enterprises that operate in new innovative business fields. These firms are generally newly founded and produce and market innovative products (or services) in high-technology sectors, including biotechnology, laser technology and optics, mechanical engineering, information technology, pharmaceuticals and so on. They are characterized by a high level of innovation-oriented activities (Sabisch, 1999, pp. 25f.). As such firms are mostly knowledge-intensive, they are often called 'knowledge-based' firms.

On the one hand, NTBFs face much higher business risks than the average firm. On the other hand, however, they possess higher potentials for sustainable development and business success. Although their novel technological solutions promise competitive advantages and high profits (Baier and Pleschak, 1996, p. 56), the actual attainment, upgrade and maintenance of their competitive advantages depend on their ability and level of efforts in successfully commercializing their innovations. Their success is often adversely affected by numerous difficulties facing them.

Procuring Resource Requirements

NTBFs, and especially firms involved in high-technology products, need large amounts of resources to build up production. The availability of capital is a vital factor when starting up the business because of the necessity of capital investments in high-grade equipment. Moreover the availability of qualified human resources also plays a major role. Although the globalized economy offers numerous novel options to new ventures with limited resources, the actual burden of procuring them is left to the firm. For example, new developments in transportation and telecommunication technologies as well as the liberalization of markets are reducing transaction costs and, as a result, small and growing businesses can easily overcome distance and border restrictions. As capital and human labor are becoming increasingly mobile, new possibilities open up to small firms to procure resources, especially when these are not available in their own home regions. On the procurement side, internationally experienced entrepreneurs can attract potential investors and qualified staff from nearly everywhere around the globe.

Establishing an Efficient Organization for Production and Cost Recovery

As high capital investments in the start-up stages make the economies of scale favorable, NTBFs need sufficient demand for their products in order to control costs and remain in business. However attaining large sales to obtain large-scale economies might be restricted by the limited size of small domestic markets. In such cases, exporting to global markets is one possible option for achieving an efficient production scale.

NTBFs Need to be Customer-oriented

New firms in new technological fields usually face two critical problems: initially, they have no customer base and lack both high reputation and brand recognition; and the novelty and complexity of their products and services require special attention to customer service.

Marketing, communication and distribution activities are essential to NTBFs, as significant information asymmetries can exist in technology-based industries. These asymmetries require special efforts to introduce customers to the benefits of the newly offered technical solutions. Special training, education and even clear instructions are sometimes necessary (for example, for technical aspects in plants) to overcome such difficulties, which may mean substantial training and monitoring costs for sales intermediaries when exporting products. Therefore a local presence with a relatively permanent staff abroad may be necessary to lower the transaction costs, increase the local responsiveness and also improve legitimacy, reputation and brand recognition among their customers.

NTBFs Must Protect their Knowledge Base from Outsiders

The competitive advantage of a firm is related to its unique resources. Knowledge is usually the unique resource of NTBFs. Unfortunately knowledge in some cases portrays aspects of a public good. As knowledge may not remain unique for a long time, NTBFs' earning opportunities decline dramatically with time. Hence it is necessary for them to prevent depletion of their knowledge base through imitation in order to preserve their future innovations, which is not an easy task in the global marketplace. Usually proprietary knowledge can be protected by patents, copyrights, trade secrets or a series of licenses through licensing agreements. Patents and copyrights, however, might be ignored in some countries with lax protection systems. Thus knowledge with potential commercial value is often best protected by concealment and industrial secrets. Alternatively a network-type governance structure may be used to control, even limit, the unauthorized expropriation of the venture's knowledge base. As network structures of alliances, especially those with complementarities, tend to control for the risk of expropriation across national borders, such relationships could be very desirable for NTBFs (Oviatt and McDougall, 1994, p. 57). However the internationalization behavior of the firm is largely influenced by industry-specific factors (McDougall, 1989; Bell, 1995; Boter and Holquist, 1998). Therefore the international activities remain as a very important and substantial factor in the success of firms operating in highly-advanced technological fields, including NTBFs.

Empirical evidence from case studies on the internationalization of start-ups suggests that the phenomenon of international entrepreneurship is particularly pertinent to high-technology industries (Bürgel, 2000, p. 18). The result of a study at the University of Applied Sciences Jena also supports this view. In a study of 71 German NTBFs interviewed, 67.6 per cent confirmed the international character of their business (Reisberg, 2000, p. 118). Furthermore several studies indicate that the founders' international experience facilitates internationalization processes and also leads to a higher degree of internationalization of a firm (Lindqvist, 1991; Bloodgood *et al.*, 1996; Reuber and Fischer, 1996). A case study of four high-technology start-up companies, which challenged incumbent multinational firms successfully, reports that all founders had gained international backgrounds either from education or from previous work experience and also a 'vision' to turn their firms into globally operating businesses (Jolly *et al.*, 1992).

ARE ACADEMIC ENTREPRENEURS INTERNATIONALLY ORIENTED?

We use the term 'academic entrepreneurs' to refer to university researchers who became involved in the process of commercialization of their ideas, and also to those who have implemented their research results through business activities, and consequently became involved with entrepreneurship (Samsom, 1990, p. 11). As they introduce something new by applying science, or a scientific method, their ventures become technology-based and their firms can be considered as NTBFs.

Research Questions and Methods

Following the insights from the previous section, we wanted to know whether university researchers, turned entrepreneurs, are aware of an international focus in their business and also if they meet the requirements of globally thinking and globally acting entrepreneurs. In order to find some evidence to support or refute our concerns, we conducted a five-country-wide survey of academic entrepreneurship, as reported below.

This survey was designed by the University of Applied Sciences Jena in order both to examine and to learn about a number of issues surrounding the entrepreneurial intentions and motivations for starting their own business of researchers in several technology regions. Specifically the survey's objective was to identify effective concepts for motivating and enabling researchers to become successful entrepreneurs, to establish the impact of location-specific factors in the success of innovative business start-ups from universities and to collect information about the intentions of academic entrepreneurs to do business on a global basis in order to improve their simulative effects.

Up to August 2001, we had distributed 10 217 questionnaires to researchers from universities in ten technology regions: Georgia, Chicago, North Carolina, Silicon Valley in California, Austin, Ireland, Scotland, Cambridge, Israel and Munich. Our primary interest was focused on technology regions located in the United States but, eventually, we extended our survey to high-technology regions in four other countries, namely Ireland, Israel, Great Britain and Germany (Munich) to develop further insights and gain information on German researchers as well.

The questionnaire was administered through the Internet. Participants were requested to fill in an online form. The return rate varied between 3 per cent and 25 per cent for the respective universities. We received 993 responses. For the purposes of analysis, we only included responses from researchers under 60 years old, working in a technological field and still engaged in a research activity. After applying these restrictions, there were 895 valid responses. Since the absolute number of researchers in the surveyed universities is not readily known by the authors, it is not possible to report the survey's representativeness. The number of scientists who answered the questionnaire in each country is shown in Table 4.1. Because of sparseness of response from some US regions, all US samples were combined.

Figure 4.1 represents the results of our central question regarding the intention to set up one's own business, showing that there are some regional differences. Altogether, 78 scientists had already set up their own businesses. Some 47 respondents still had detailed plans to do so; while 146 intended to start up their own businesses but had yet to develop detailed plans.

Although we do not focus on the specific reasons for regional differences here, Stankiewicz (1994) has pointed out that the frequency of venture creation can be explained by the technological and R&D strengths of the universities which generate them. Furthermore the presence of an entrepreneurial culture

Table 4.1   University researchers questioned, by region

Region	Scientists questioned	Responses		Valid responses
		n	%	
USA	4 253	300	7.05	259
GB	1 949	193	9.90	182
Israel	1 289	142	11.02	126
Ireland	1 080	89	8.24	75
Munich	1 646	269	16.34	253
Total	*10 217*	*993*	*9.17*	*895*

within the university and its immediate environment and the presence of rich and diversified resources in that environment combine to provide for the technological and economic needs of such start-ups, which are among the crucial success factors (ibid., p. 100).

We asked those university researchers who had plans to set up their own technology-based business ventures, and also those who had already done so, whether they intended to conduct business activities across national borders. We also asked whether they had already developed international business contacts or if doing business in foreign markets was also planned. Because we did not specify a particular kind of international business relationship, all foreign operations (for example, direct exports, subsidiaries, independent representatives) are implicitly included.

Figure 4.2 represents our findings for all responding entrepreneurial researchers. We made a distinction between (a) the researchers who intend to

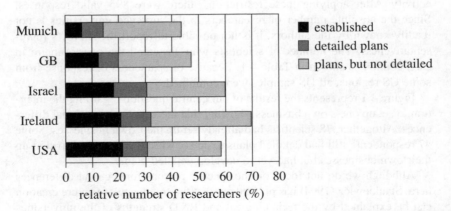

Figure 4.1   Technology-based business set-ups by university researchers

set up a business but do not yet have a detailed plan, (b) researchers who have a detailed plan, and (c) researchers who have already set up a business venture. The absolute number in each category is given by *n*.

Figure 4.2 supplies some interesting insights. The uncertainty of whether or not their technology-based business should act internationally is obviously the greatest among scientists who do not yet have any detailed plans. A large proportion of researchers in this group stated that they had also planned to conduct business in foreign markets. Those researchers who have detailed plans to start a business on the basis of their research intended to establish international business contacts immediately after start-up or at a later time. However there are also a large proportion of researchers who have already set up international connections. Finally, those scientists who have already set up a business venture have, in large part, also established international business contacts. More than 60 per cent of all responding university researchers acting as entrepreneurs in our sample do business across national borders.

Our results support other research that points to the importance of international business contacts for technology-based firms. Additionally we found that the more university researchers know about the business aspects of their venture, including strategies and objectives, the more aware they become of the importance of doing business in international markets. They also use every opportunity to establish international business contacts. These characteristics of technology-based firms make entrepreneurship among university researchers internationally oriented.

As stated in the previous section of this chapter, the local and regional demands for knowledge-based products and services play a major role in the range of business activities offered. Logically the academic entrepreneurs

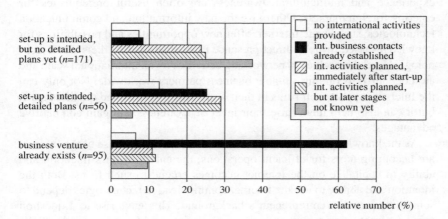

Figure 4.2   International business activities of academic entrepreneurs

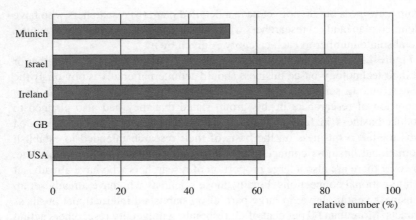

Figure 4.3   Number of internationally oriented academic entrepreneurs

from countries with small domestic markets, such as Ireland and Israel, should be more inclined to do business across national borders than their counterparts in larger domestic markets. If this were true, regional differences in our sample would have been profound. Figure 4.3 shows the relative number of academic entrepreneurs in each region who either want to act internationally or have already done so. It is evident that the relative number of academics who want to do business across national borders is higher in Israel and Ireland. Surprisingly, Munich is lagging far behind, indicating possible deficits in this matter.

The decision to act globally and to have a presence in global markets presupposes a level of willingness and certain special abilities. International experience and multicultural awareness are often useful prerequisites for entering foreign markets. Otherwise the new information and communication technologies, such as the Internet, offer new opportunities and possibilities for knowledge-based firms' indirect presence in international markets. Such technologies lend themselves to networking activities on an international scale and are conducive to finding suitable business partners worldwide. Not only can the Internet support such firms in their search for investors and qualified staff, but it can also help them raise their level of awareness and gain competitive advantages.

As the knowledge of, and experiences with, the effective use of the Internet are becoming tools for efficient operations, the entrepreneur's intention and ability to capitalize on the Internet becomes crucial to such firms. Both the intention and ability to use the Internet communication technologies depend to some extent on the entrepreneur's background. This gave rise to a question about Internet usage behavior in the survey of the university researchers. We distinguished the following categories (or levels) in the use of the Internet: (a)

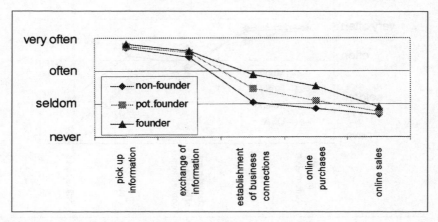

Figure 4.4   Usage of the Internet by university researchers

obtaining information, (b) exchange of information, (c) creating new business contacts, (d) online purchases and (e) online sales. First we focused on the differences in the degree of the Internet utilization between the groups of founders and non-founders.

Figure 4.4 shows that the usage of the Internet differs clearly between those who have already started their own business, those who intend to start a business (potential founders) and those we call non-founders. Generally the researchers that act as entrepreneurs use the Internet more frequently in all the above categories than their colleagues that have fewer, or no, entrepreneurial intentions. The main difference was found in establishing business contacts and online purchases. While non-founders rarely use the Internet for these purposes, academic entrepreneurs often use the Internet to establish new business connections.

Referring to the international orientation of academic entrepreneurs, we also examined the regional differences in the usage of the Internet. Our findings are represented in Figure 4.5, in which the graphs represent an average for each region. While regional differences are smallest for obtaining information on the Internet, there are larger differences in online transactions (purchases and sales) and also in the use of the Internet for establishing business connections. However one has to be cautious in drawing general conclusions on the basis of analysis and their representations in the figures for the reason outlined earlier: representativeness of the regional samples.

To conclude this discussion, we can readily state that the university scientists as entrepreneurs in the regions surveyed are aware of opportunities attributable to the new communication technologies, and they use them in supporting their business.

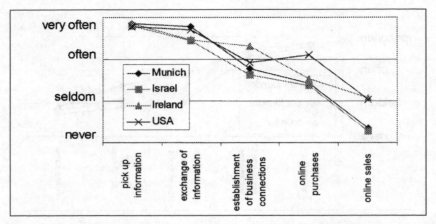

Figure 4.5   Regional differences in the usage of the Internet by academic entrepreneurs

CONCLUSION AND IMPLICATIONS

We have discussed the importance of technology-based industries for indus-trialized economies. As pointed out earlier, innovative business set-ups play a major role in establishing competitive technology-based firms and industries. In the long run, however, the development and success of such firms depend largely on the founders' abilities to develop international business activities. Technology-based firms can gain great advantages when they internationalize.

Empirical evidence indicates consistently that a large proportion of NTBFs operate internationally. This induced us to ask whether university researchers as entrepreneurs also know about the importance of an international focus, and act upon it, in their own business venture. We therefore asked university researchers in ten technology regions about their possible plans to start a busi-ness on the basis of their own research. As discussed earlier, we found that most academic entrepreneurs are in fact aware of the significance of interna-tional activities for their success, and they also took advantage of opportuni-ties derived from globalization.

The results of this study are helpful to both managers of SMEs and start-up firms and policy makers who are involved in creating a successful technology region. We recommend that policy makers establish a culture of entrepreneur-ship at higher education institutions in order to facilitate the creation of successful science and technology regions, but they also should be aware of the international components of technology-based firms.

The comparison of several regions in our study shows that there are differences in the pattern of internationalization behavior of academic entrepreneurs. We suggest that policy makers of upcoming technology regions replicate our survey in their universities and research institutions. In those cases where there are relative deficits, as compared to the regions surveyed in this chapter, efforts have to be undertaken to inform the entrepreneurial community and to train university-based entrepreneurs in order not only to take advantage of the opportunities but also to minimize the risks of global markets.

Networking is central to promoting and to assisting academics in starting their business, but this networking is important not only nationally but also in an international context. And the university can also contribute to building up international networks. In this context we recommend that managers of technology-based SMEs use the resources of universities. This is especially true for academic entrepreneurs. First they should be aware of the importance of an international focus in their entrepreneurial initiatives; second they should make efforts to establish international contacts right from the beginning of their venture. As we have seen, this is already realized in many cases. Managers may check what kind of advantages they can gain when they build up international business contacts. In the case where they are striving for internationalization, the university can assist them in various ways.

Thanks to well-established cooperation between universities and institutions of different countries (such as in common research projects or shared activities in education) in general the following services could be offered by universities for academic entrepreneurs as well as small and medium-sized companies:

- initialization of common research and development projects with universities and industrial partners including an international level;
- common use and reinforcement of existing cooperations and partnerships of the joint institutions in the university regions and identification of further partners in research, science and industry;
- arrangement of contacts with business and industrial institutions abroad;
- support for the establishment of strategic partnerships, for example among small and medium-sized companies in different countries with the target of mutually marketing the products that have been developed on the basis of common research and development.

REFERENCES

Abernathy, W.J. and J.M. Utterback (1978), 'Patterns of industrial innovation', *Technology Review*, **80**, June/July, 41–7.

Baier, Wolfgang and Franz Pleschak (1996), *Marketing und Finanzierung junger Technologieunternehmen*, Wiesbaden: Gabler.
Bell, J. (1995), 'The internationalization of small computer software firms – a further challenge to stage theories', *European Journal of Marketing*, **29** (8), 60–75.
Bloodgood, J., J. Almeida and H. Sapienza (1996), 'The internationalization of new high-potential U.S. ventures: antecedents and outcomes', *Entrepreneurship Theory & Practice* **20**, 61–76.
Boter, H. and C. Holquist (1998), 'Industry characteristics and internationalization processes in small firms', reprinted in A. Haahti, G. Hall and R. Donckels, *The Internationalization of SMEs*, London: Routledge, pp. 19–42.
Bürgel, Oliver (2000), *The Internationalisation of British Start-Up Companies in High-Technology Industries*, ZEW Economic Studies 9, Heidelberg: Physica-Verlag.
Dawson, Keith (2000), *Siliconia* (Internet publication: www.tbtf.com/siliconia.html).
Jolly, V.K., M. Alahuhta and J.P. Jeannet (1992), 'Challenging the incumbent: how high-technology start-ups compete globally', *Journal of Strategic Change*, **1**, 71–82.
Lindqvist, M. (1991), 'Infant multinationals: the internationalizatiom of young technology-based Swedish firms', unpublished doctoral dissertation, Stockholm School of Economics, Institute of International Business.
McDougall, P. (1989), 'International versus domestic entrepreneurship: new venture strategic behavior and industry structure', *Journal of Business Venturing*, **4**, 387–400.
Ministry of Education and Research of the Federal Republic of Germany (2000), 'EXIST-university-based start-ups', information brochure, Bonn.
Oviatt, Benjamin and Patricia McDougall (1994), 'Towards a theory of international new ventures', *Journal of International Business Studies*, **25** (1), 45–64.
Reisberg, Yvonne (2000), 'E-Marketing als Erfolgsfaktor junger Technologieunternehmen', unpublished diploma thesis, University of Applied Sciences, Jena.
Reuber, A.R. and E. Fischer (1996), 'The influence of the management team's international experience on the internationalization behavior of SMEs', *Journal of International Business Studies*, **28** (4), 807–25.
Röpke, Jochen (1998), 'The entrepreneurial university', working paper, Universität Marburg.
Sabisch, Helmut (1999), *Management technologieorientierter Unternehmensgründungen*, Stuttgart: Schäffer-Poeschel.
Samsom, Karel (1990), *Scientists as Entrepreneurs*, Dordrecht: Kluwer.
Saxenian, Annalee (1994), *Regional Advantage. Culture and Competition in Silicon Valley and Route 128*, Cambridge, MA, and London: Harvard University Press.
Simon, Hermann (1996*), Die heimlichen Gewinner. Die Erfolgsstrategien unbekannter Weltmarktführer*, Frankfurt am Main: Campus.
Stankiewicz, Rikard (1994), 'Spin-off companies from universities', *Science and Public Policy*, **21** (2), 99–107.
Wicksteed, Segal Quince (1985), *The Cambridge Phenomenon*, Cambridge: Segal Quince & Partners.

PART II

Entrepreneurial characteristics and
internationalization

5. The international reach of entrepreneurial social networks: the case of James Dyson in the UK

Oswald Jones and Steve Conway

INTRODUCTION: STRATEGIC CHOICE VERSUS ENVIRONMENTAL DETERMINISM

Our objective is to deconstruct the myth of entrepreneurs as 'heroic'[1] individuals solely responsible for the creation and management of new business ventures. We accomplish our goal by drawing on the well-known case of James Dyson, which highlights his invention of the dual cyclone vacuum cleaner (Dyson, 1997). Our argument is the following: networks and networking are central to entrepreneurial creation of new business ventures. It is now accepted that networks add an original dimension to the study of entrepreneurship and innovation (Freeman, 1991; DeBresson and Amesse, 1991). Steward and Conway (1998) suggest that the network approach permits a detailed analysis of dyadic links. Such links provide a framework for exploring the pluralistic patterns of communication and collaboration necessary for the successful development of innovative products and processes. A network can be visualized as a series of dyadic links and relationships between two actors, established for the exchange of ideas, information, goods, power and friendship (Tichy *et al.*, 1979). It is important to look beyond *portfolios* of dyadic links, as networks can be greater than the sum of their interacting parts (DeBresson and Amesse, 1991; Auster, 1990).

Existing theories can be placed on an environment-to-individual continuum, indicating influences on entrepreneurship (Manimala, 1999). At one extreme, economic theories (Kirzner, 1973; Casson, 1982) represent the environmental perspective in which entrepreneurial activity results from disequilibrium in supply and demand. At the other extreme, psychological theories concentrate on individual traits such as risk taking, achievement, autonomy, optimism and self-efficacy (McClelland, 1961). Occupying the middle ground, amid 'strategic choice' and 'environmental determinism', are cultural and sociological theories. Cultural theories (Weber, 1930) focus on the role of particular ideologies, such as the 'Protestant Ethic', while sociological theorists (Hagen, 1962) argue that entrepreneurs emerge in communities that have been displaced or have experienced 'status withdrawal'. For example, Quaker entrepreneurs in the UK founded their own businesses, since they were excluded from other professions (Prior and Kirby, 1998). Perhaps the most widely quoted psychological approach is McClelland's 'need for achievement' trait, even though the concept now 'stands disowned even by its author' (Manimala, 1999, p. 67). Manimala (1999, p. 73) develops his own theoretical model, in which he introduces 'managerial heuristics, policies and strategies' as the intervening variable between 'the entrepreneur in *his* environment and venture performance'. This approach is based on the PI (pioneering innovator) motive, identified by Khandwalla (1985), which has similarities to Maslow's (1954) self-actualization theory.

Van de Ven (1996, p. 39) argues that, while Schumpeter's (1934) dynamic theory of economic growth, based on 'ideal-type' entrepreneurs possessing business vision, investment skills and risk-taking capacities, remains relevant, 'unwittingly or erroneously' the search for 'traits, personalities and individual difference characteristics of entrepreneurs . . . has been almost the exclusive focus of entrepreneurship theories and research'. This focus is attributed to a western cultural bias, which ascribes significant innovations to individuals, whereas, in reality, 'Historical studies clearly show that most innovations are collective achievements of the efforts of many actors working over an extended period of time, often in parallel and independent locations' (Van de Ven, 1996, p. 40).

The population ecology approach (Aldrich, 1979; Hannan and Freeman, 1977) focuses on the birth and death rates of entrepreneurial ventures resulting from selection mechanisms. The ecological approach emphasizes macro influences on business start-ups, including government policies, political events and cultural norms, as well as cooperative relations that affect 'the distribution of resources'. Van de Ven (1996) is critical of the approach, as it does not explain how these macro structures are created, nor does it identify the key elements of the infrastructure. Studying the temporal sequence of events associated with the conversion of scientific knowledge into products and services is the only effective method to understand the interaction between entrepreneur and infrastructure. Such studies, Van de Ven (ibid., p. 42) argues, require a 'social system framework', which contains three components: institutional arrangements, resources endowments and proprietary functions. 'The social system perspective emphasises that any given entrepreneurial firm is but one actor, able to perform only a limited set of roles, and dependent upon many other actors to accomplish all the functions needed for an industry to emerge and survive' (ibid., p. 53).

Data for this chapter are drawn from Dyson's (1997) autobiography, where he describes the difficulties associated with various entrepreneurial ventures. Our interest in Dyson began when we used the case on an MBA entrepreneurship course to illustrate the importance of self-belief and persistence. We gradually recognized that, although Dyson's 'heroic' story confirms the importance of individual traits, other factors contributed to his numerous business successes. In particular, we identified a number of crucial events where Dyson would have failed, had it not been possible for him to draw on extensive social relations (Aldrich and Zimmer, 1986) with the network of family, friends and acquaintances. Therefore we utilize Dyson's story to illustrate the point made by Johannisson (2000), who claims that the concept of networking helps to focus on entrepreneurship as a collective, rather than an individualistic, phenomenon. While acknowledging that our 're-reading' of *Against the Odds* is subjective, rather than objective, we argue that such an approach is legitimate in helping to understand the entrepreneurial process. As Aldrich (2000, p. 14) points out, despite the extensive entrepreneurship literature, few researchers have actually studied the business start-up process. The advantage of first-hand accounts rests in the fact that practitioners can analyze their own intentions and motives; but, at the same time, they may deceive themselves (Hammersley, 1992; Czarniawska-Joerges, 1995). Using biographical material is a legitimate research approach, and is certainly no less valid than other qualitative methodologies, such as in-depth interviews. At the same time, we move beyond description by drawing on the network theory, defined by Oliver and Ebers (1998, p. 575) as focusing on how an actor's position, within their network of relationships, affects opportunities for action (also see Burt, 1992; Powell, 1990). Dyson's story is analyzed in order to identify the entrepreneur's 'social capital': friends, colleagues and contacts through whom the individual actor 'create[s] opportunities to utilise their financial and human capital' (Burt, 2000, p. 282).

The chapter begins with a discussion of the links between social action and the formation of networks. We then briefly review the literature associated with entrepreneurial networks, with a particular emphasis on strong and weak ties (Granovetter, 1973, 1985). To demonstrate the value of the network perspective, we analyze the well-known case of James Dyson, and his invention of the dual cyclone vacuum cleaner. The implications of this case for future studies of entrepreneurs and entrepreneurship are then discussed.

THE 'STRUCTURATION' OF SOCIAL NETWORKS

Individuals writing about networks generally adopt a functionalist perspective, based on a biological metaphor, which emphasizes the structure and functioning of social systems as evolutionary and adaptive (Morgan, 1986). Network scholars can be broadly divided into two categories: those who favor structural explanations, where the social system as a whole (the network) is pre-eminent over individuals (Allen, 1970; Hakansson, 1987; Powell *et al.*, 1996), and those who consider human action to be the key explanatory factor in the formation of networks (Leonard-Barton, 1984; Conway, 1994; Shaw, 1998). All social structures (networks) encompass the enduring pattern of social interrelations, including class, roles, rules and social institutions. Therefore it is necessary to resolve the endemic agency–structure dualism, by emphasizing the way in which knowledgable, reflexive social actors draw on rules and resources in their day-to-day social activities (Giddens, 1995). This recursive activity constantly recreates the 'structural properties' that provide the framework for everyday social practices (Jones, 1997; Jones *et al.*, 2000). Giddens (1995) uses the terms 'system' and 'structuration' to emphasize that the rules and resources drawn on in the (re)production of social action are, at the same time, the means of system reproduction. Social systems do not have structures, but they do exhibit structural properties. In structuration theory, the relationship between agency and structure is similar to the connection between grammar and speech. The rules of grammar are utilized by social actors in their patterns of communication that, in turn, continually recreate the structure of language.

Structuration theory and networks are brought together in Barley's (1990) analysis of new technology. Using the concepts of relational and non-relational roles, he 'explicitly articulates how skills, tasks, and activities influence role relations and how role relations, in turn, affect an organization's and occupation's structure' (ibid., p. 98). In a more recent paper, Barley and Tolbert (1997) develop a more dynamic model, where they categorize the day-to-day interactions by identifying the 'scripts' used by actors. Scripts are the 'observable, recurrent activities and patterns of interaction characteristic of a particular setting' (ibid., p. 98). This implies that networks cannot be studied as objective social structures that are independent of human agents. As Roberts and Grabowski (1996, p. 418) point out: 'organizational researchers are now more explicit in acknowledging that social activity is embedded in social networks which include family, friends and co-workers as well as broader factors such as religion, gender and ethnicity'.

Our interest in the topic relates to the role networks play in helping entrepreneurs acquire the necessary resources to establish and maintain viable businesses (Jones *et al.*, 2001). In other words, we are interested in examining a range of stages, from idea conceptualization to the institutionalization of a new business venture. Entrepreneurial networks may focus either on the analysis of social interaction within organizations or on external linkages, including joint ventures and strategic alliances. In either case, the research interest could be formal linkages, defined by organizational structures and contractual agreements, or the informal relationships associated with the 'grapevine'. Both formal and informal linkages contribute to entrepreneurship by providing access to additional skills, knowledge, information and technologies. This does not imply that we adopt a managerial approach, where networking is seen as a way of improving the effectiveness to acquire and utilize knowledge. Rather we are attempting to further our understanding of the process(es) entrepreneurs undertake to create new products and services.

In his literature review, Freeman (1991) discusses various definitions of the term 'innovation network'. They range from the 'basic institutional arrangements to cope with systemic innovation' (Imai and Baba, 1989) to the linkages which are 'of a mainly informal and tacit nature' (Camagni, 1991). Our own definition emphasizes the idea of networks as a way of understanding the embeddedness of entrepreneurial activity (Jones *et al.*, 2001, p. 13): a network is a conceptualization of the entrepreneurial process as a complex and pluralistic pattern of interactions, exchanges and relationships between actors participating in that process.

Thus entrepreneurial networks incorporate both formal and informal linkages. They are established within and across organizational boundaries as a means of capturing codified knowledge, represented in specifications, reports and software, as well as tacit knowledge, which can effectively be communicated by direct social interaction (see Nonaka and Takeuchi, 1995).

ENTREPRENEURSHIP AND SOCIAL EMBEDDEDNESS

Key writers on innovation stress the importance of external links or networks in gaining access to new technologies (Coombs *et al.*, 1987; Twiss, 1992). Research focusing on entrepreneurship and SMEs acknowledges the significance of networks (Leonard-Barton, 1984; Birley *et al.*, 1990; Lawton-Smith *et al.*, 1991; Rothwell and Dodgson, 1991). Until SMEs are well established, and relatively sophisticated organizational structures are adopted, entrepreneurs tend to take sole responsibility for creating and maintaining networks. These personal networks can fulfill a number of roles by providing social support, extending the strategic competences, identifying opportunities and threats, and supplementing internal resources to resolve acute internal problems (Johannisson and Peterson, 1984; Birley *et al.*, 1990; Conway, 1997; Conway and Shaw, 1999). Thus, it is argued, entrepreneurship is both constrained and facilitated by linkages between the resources and opportunities that are created via the entrepreneur's social network. In fact, Johannisson and Peterson (1984, p. 1) point to the apparent paradox that, on one hand, entrepreneurship 'personifies individualism and independence' while, on the other hand, individuals are 'dependent on ties of trust and cooperation'.

Leonard-Barton (1984, p. 113) suggests, 'entrepreneurs who, for geographic, cultural or social reasons, lack access to *free* information through personal networks, operate with less capital than do their well-connected peers'. Equally it is recognized that effective personal networks 'must become as complex and as heterogeneous as the daily activities of the venture' (Johannisson and Peterson, 1984, p. 4). Therefore nurturing an extensive and diverse network is essential (Leonard-Barton, 1984; Aldrich and Zimmer, 1986). In a recent entrepreneurship study, Jones and associates (Jones *et al.*, 1997) highlighted the importance of managerial education in encouraging the creation of networks. A lack of higher education implies that entrepreneurs have neither the personal contacts, which are a source of information, nor any real understanding of the expertise available through the university links. To a large extent, this work is based on Granovetter's (1973) concept of weak ties, which are an important potential source of knowledge and information (see Fletcher, 1998; Shaw, 1998). Strong ties restrain access to innovative ideas and knowledge sources, whereas weak ties open up networks to provide access to new areas of expertise.

Networks are interconnected, dyadic relationships where various ties can be analyzed in terms of their content. First, information ties provide business information; second, exchange ties extend access to resources; finally, influencial ties legitimate the entrepreneur's activities, and help to create barriers to entry (Johannisson, 2000, p. 370). These three factors are heavily interdependent, which emphasizes the social embeddedness of all entrepreneurial activities. 'Embeddedness refers to the fact that economic action and outcomes, like all social actions and outcomes, are affected by actors' dyadic (pairwise) relations and by the structure of the overall network of relations' (Granovetter, 1992, p. 33).

The networking perspective 'invites the image of *entrepreneurship as a collective phenomenon*, i.e., not primarily associated with resourceful individuals . . . the new venture represents a collective effort possibly orchestrated by a single person' (Johannisson, 2000, p. 375). At the same time, all start-ups need an 'organizing context' that will help structure the exchanges with the broader environment. This context helps the entrepreneur cope with ambiguity, provides a shelter against uncertainty and eases reactions to unexpected changes in the marketplace (ibid., p. 379).

THE GEOGRAPHICAL REACH OF ENTREPRENEURIAL NETWORKS

The important features of entrepreneurial networks have been highlighted by a number of researchers. The diversity of membership and actors within a network allows the entrepreneur to draw upon a broader range of external sources that supplement scarce internal resources. The external sources provide social support, finance and additional information. Furthermore, these studies have identified the predominance of informal linkages that span 'structural holes' (Burt, 1992) and create a range of dynamic opportunities for entrepreneurial firms (Birley and Cromie, 1988; Birley *et al.*, 1990; Conway, 1997; Baaijens, 1998; Shaw, 1998).

Other studies have also identified factors that influence the geographical 'reach' of entrepreneurial networks: the entrepreneur's previous experience, educational level, firm size and the firm's growth orientation. Birley and associates note that

> entrepreneurs, at an early stage of enterprise development, rely heavily on an informal network of friends, family members and social contacts from the local neighbourhood to gather relevant data. At a later stage, entrepreneurs rely increasingly on professional bankers, accountants, lawyers, suppliers, government agencies, etc. to gain access to requisite business information'. (Birley *et al.*, 1990, p. 59)

Interestingly entrepreneurs tend not to include other small-firm owner–managers in their personal network (Birley *et al.*, 1990). In their study about the impact of entrepreneurial characteristics and network structure, Donckels and Lambrecht (1997) found that highly educated entrepreneurs were more likely to have wider networks, which in turn allowed them to obtain additional advice and judgments from their wider networks, besides the family and friends. Furthermore the study found that bias towards local contacts in the network was lower for businesses of more than ten employees and growth-oriented small firms. The majority of those interested in small-firm and entrepreneurial networks (Aldrich and Zimmer, 1986; Birley and Cromie, 1988; Johannisson and Peterson, 1984; Leonard-Barton, 1984) tend to concentrate on informal linkages; but there is now an increasing emphasis on the importance of more formal networks. In a recent research survey, addressing strategic alliances as mechanisms for international growth, Weaver (2000, p. 387) argues: 'Faced with rapidly changing markets, technology, governance and increased risks of independent action, SMEs are adopting alternative organizational models based on cooperation.'

While the extension of the entrepreneur's network across national boundaries is important for the internationalization of smaller firms, it must be viewed in terms of resource constraints and the intensity of cross-border network building. Over the past decade, this issue has been addressed by regional, national and European agencies. For example, policies have emerged and evolved at both the nation-state and European Union levels (see De, 2000; Storey, 2000). The UK government has established a number of institutions designed to aid the internationalization of smaller firms. The Export Credits Guarantee Department (ECGD) is the UK's official export credit agency, which directly reports to the

Secretary of State for Trade and Industry. Support for exporters is provided by setting up finance facilities and credit insurance for contracts ranging from approximately £20 000 to hundreds of millions of pounds. Export credit insurance can be used to cover three basic risks: buyer default, buyer insolvency and country risk. This helps smaller firms to improve their global competitiveness and, at the same time, reduce the risk of non-payment.[2]

JAMES DYSON: A CASE STUDY IN ENTREPRENEURSHIP

For a number of reasons, the Dyson case is extremely important in the study of entrepreneurship. First, all of Dyson's entrepreneurial ventures (the 'Sea Truck', 'Ballbarrow' and 'dual cyclone') illustrate that creative thinkers can identify exceptional opportunities in mature markets. Second, Dyson is, in some respects, a modern reincarnation of the traditional inventor–entrepreneur. He could be compared to Richard Arkwright, Robert Stephenson, James Watt and Isambard Kingdom Brunel, who represent the UK's economic history (Mathias, 1969). Third, the case highlights the importance of self-belief, persistence and sheer hard work in the creation of new businesses. Finally, and perhaps most importantly, the case illustrates the role played by informal or social networks in providing support, information and knowledge for one of the most outstanding entrepreneurs.

Dyson studied humanities at 'A' level (non-technical subjects), which is a noteworthy point, as he had few engineering skills when he began his career as an inventor. After leaving school, he studied at an art school in London, and even though he never obtained a first degree, he managed to get accepted on a master's program in design at the Royal College of Art (RCA). He was particularly inspired by Buckminster Fuller, the American engineer dismissed by many as a 'dreamer', and the great Victorian engineer Isambard Kingdom Brunel, who was responsible for many of the railways, steamships and bridges symbolizing the UK's industrial power. Dyson sums up the inspirational qualities that encouraged him in his own ventures:

> There was in Brunel's determination, a level of conditioning. His father had been an engineer of almost gargantuan vision, building the first tunnel under the Thames and planning one under the Channel. For Isambard, there was that double-edged Oedipal desire both to impress and outdo his father. It was what the literary critic Harold Bloom calls the Anxiety of Influence, and the need for a figure to be slain was paramount in the creation of originality and genius. (Dyson, 1997, p. 40)

Dyson's father died when he was young, and he believes this contributed to his self-sufficiency and identification with 'external figures', who inspired him to be 'the Brunel of the modern ages'. While studying at the RCA, he began working for Jeremy Fry, an entrepreneur who manufactured motorized valve actuators for pipelines. Fry encouraged him to adopt a 'hands-on' approach to design, rather than one purely based on theory. Shortly after beginning to work, Dyson had an innovative idea for a 'Sea Truck', and subsequently built a prototype in about eight months. He patented his idea, and Fry set up a subsidiary (Rotork) to manufacture the product. Dyson began to feel he had been 'away from the drawing board for too long' (ibid., p. 70), even though the Sea Truck was extremely popular and experienced a high turnover rate.

While working for Rotork, Dyson and his family moved from London to a 300-year-old farmhouse in the Cotswolds. Undertaking most of the rebuilding himself, Dyson became familiar with the traditional wheelbarrow's failings: unstable when fully laden, tyres prone to puncture, sinking into soft ground and a steel body that damaged doorjambs and human limbs. He considered the problem for twelve months and, having reinvented the wheel as a ball, he decided to set up his own manufacturing company. Dyson's company launched the 'Ballbarrow', even though he had little experience in selling consumer products: 'I had not drawn up a business plan, this was a real seat-of-the-pants, kamikaze approach' (ibid., p. 82). Despite the lack of preparation, the Ballbarrow was such a success that the idea was stolen by a US company. Rotork, however, lost the case against the American company, which induced tension between the company's board members. As a result, Dyson's business associates voted him out of the company.

Following this event, Dyson turned his attention to another product: the 'Hoover' vacuum cleaner. His mission: to investigate why the performance of the family 'Hoover' declined so rapidly after installing a new dust bag. He discovered that, once a thin layer of dust formed inside the bag, it clogged the pores, which reduced performance to 'an enfeebled suck' (ibid., p. 103). The concept for creating a cyclone vacuum cleaner stemmed from his familiarity with the Hoover. Using an old Hoover, cardboard and industrial tape, Dyson spent one evening building a complete working model of the world's first bagless vacuum cleaner, known as the 'dual cyclone'.

After two years trying to convince British and European companies of the dual cyclone's potential, Dyson decided to turn his attention to a larger, more competitive market: the USA. Acknowledging that consumer spending power was much higher there, Dyson believed his invention could obtain the recognition it deserved, but unfortunately no company was willing to manufacture the dual cyclone.

In November 1984, after five years of trying to interest European and American manufacturers, Dyson was informally approached by a Japanese company, Apex, who rapidly agreed to produce the 'G-Force' (as the dual cyclone was known in Japan). With funds from this contract, he once again turned to the US market, and eventually set up an agreement with Iona, a Canadian-owned company. As the 'Drytech' (US name for the dual cyclone) was about to be launched, Dyson discovered that Amway, a US-based company that had rejected the dual cyclone several years before, had unlawfully marketed their own version. Once again, Dyson found himself involved in a long-running and extremely expensive legal battle with a US company. Suddenly, in 1991, after almost five years of litigation, Amway came to an agreement over their patent infringement, and the haemorrhage of legal fees came to an end. On 1 July 1993, 15 years after creating his product, the very first 'DC01', built in the UK, came off the assembly line.

DYSON'S ENTREPRENEURIAL NETWORK

Dyson's most significant and influential contact was Jeremy Fry, who inspired and supported his early ventures. During his RCA studies, Dyson met Joan Littlewood, a theatre and film impresario, who encouraged him to design a new theatre she was developing. As a result of the influence of Buckminster Fuller, Dyson created a 'mushroom-shaped' auditorium made of aluminium. He then sought financial support from British Aluminium, but the senior managers were unimpressed, although one did suggest that he contact Jeremy Fry: 'I had shown Fry my model of the proposed theatre, and I think he rather liked it, if not enough to cover me with gold. What he *did* offer me, however, was to prove far more useful in the long run: work, and the first of many collaborations' (Dyson, 1997, p. 47).

Dyson eventually left Rotork to set up his own company, to manufacture and market the Ballbarrow. Although he had made a considerable amount of money from the Sea Truck, he needed support to establish a manufacturing company. Not surprisingly, as with most entrepreneurs, he turned to his family:

> I went to see a lawyer friend of my brother-in-law . . . Andrew Phillips not only helped with the formation of the company, but fell in love with the Ballbarrow and persuaded said brother-in-law (Stuart Kirkwood) to invest in it. Stuart was the son of one Lord Kirkwood, former chairman of the mining company RTZ. He and his brother . . . as a result, inherited some family money. Which is always nice. (Ibid., pp. 79–80)

These contacts were fundamental to the founding of Kirk-Dyson, as they provided legal advice and funding to develop the Ballbarrow and the investments for plastic molding equipment. Even with this support, events did not progress smoothly, and the new entrepreneurs had considerable difficulty in finding a market for their revolutionary barrow. However, help was at hand:

I had a friend called Gill Taylor whom I had met in Badminton and just so happened to have been Miss Great Britain in 1964. She was blond, attractive, curvaceous and a typical 'travel around the world and help people' beauty queen. She was also at a loose end and quite prepared to tour the garden centres of the West Country touting Ballbarrows. (Ibid., p. 82)

Gradually the partners managed to make the Ballbarrow a success, and began considering ways in which they could expand the business. They wanted to increase the output by acquiring a 'proper' factory, as well as investing in injection-molding equipment. George Jackson, a local property developer, acquired a third share in the company. Dyson does not explain how this particular contact was made, or why he was judged to be an appropriate member of the board (other than having the required £100,000). His social network was important in providing industrial expertise:

I brought in an old friend of my father's, Robert Beldam, to have a bit of moral support on the board. He was chairman of the CBI [Confederation of British Industry] small companies section, and though his presence created a little, never expressed, resentment on the board, having him there made me feel somewhat better. (Ibid., p. 87)

Tension mounted between the board members, which subsequently led to Dyson being voted out of the Ballbarrow company. Following this event, Dyson chose to concentrate his efforts on developing the dual cyclone. He sought a partner to finance the development of the Air Power Vacuum Cleaner Company:

Fry . . . was always likely to be my best hope. And so it proved. With £25,000 from Jeremy, and £25,000 from me, £18,000 of which I raised by selling the vegetable garden at Sycamore House and the rest borrowed with my home as security . . . I was in the vacuum cleaner business'. (Ibid., p. 120)

Dyson built over 5000 prototypes in three years, and by 1982 had a totally efficient dual cyclone, and debts in excess of £80,000. He had spent a considerable amount of time trying to persuade various European companies, including Hoover, Hotpoint, Electrolux, AEG and Zanussi, to manufacture his vacuum cleaner. Once again, the Fry connection proved to be extremely useful. Fry persuaded Rotork's chief executive, Tom Essie, to provide further funding for Dyson's invention:

Together we drew up a business plan for the production of an upright dual cyclone vacuum cleaner, and the Rotork board of directors, swayed presumably by Jeremy's dual involvement, approved it. We thrashed out an agreement that paid me £20,000 and gave me a 5 per cent royalty, and I went off to develop the vacuum cleaner. (Ibid., p. 138)

Ultimately, Essie was replaced by what Dyson describes as a 'money man', and Rotork did not proceed with the manufacture of the dual cyclone. Fry's company did, however, provide Dyson with financial support at a crucial time in the development of the dual cyclone. Not only was Fry's extensive social network of value to Dyson, but serendipity also played an important role. A key element in the ultimate success of the dual cyclone was the deal he established with a Canadian company, which assumed responsibility for the North American market. The company was headed by an Englishman, Jeffery Pike:

> with whom I had become friendly quite by chance after we sat next to each other on an aeroplane in May 1986, and both turned out to be reading the same novel by Fay Weldon. Having flunked English A Level all those years before, my fortune looked as if it was about to be made by a novel. (Ibid., p. 175)

In 1991, while Dyson was involved in a major legal battle with Amway for infringement of his dual cyclone patent, he decided to set up production in the UK himself. Once again he was hampered by the lack of capital. As usual, in times of crisis, he turned to his extensive network and was able to resolve the problem:

> When I started with the Ballbarrow I had approached a man called David Williams, whose plastics company, WCB, built all our tooling and then recouped the money in instalments as we began to sell . . . He was now running a company called Linpak which, quite handily for me, was Britain's biggest plastic producer. (Ibid., p. 186)

As plans for the manufacture of the dual cyclone in the UK progressed, Dyson was keen that the product embody the latest technological developments. By this time he had a healthy stream of royalties from Japan and the USA, and could therefore afford to hire designers from his Alma Mater: 'The team consisted of four design engineers straight out of the RCA – Simeon Jupp, Peter Gammack, Gareth Jones and Mark Bickenstaffe – all in their twenties, a marvellous bunch, whose presence made me feel as if I was freshly sprogged from the Royal College myself' (Ibid., p. 192).

Even when Dyson's business venture was well-established, he still retained links with the RCA, which exemplifies the importance of exploiting long-standing social networks: 'Round about the time I was planning the DC-02, I was at the RCA degree show – for I had since become an internal examiner on their product design course – and I went around offering one or two of the graduates jobs, as is my habitual wont' (ibid., p. 239). The RCA connection continued to be of value to Dyson once the company became highly successful. By 1995, growing demand implied moving to a larger factory, since the current one had a limited capacity of 30 000 units per week:

> A fantastic new factory was designed for us by my old tutor Tony Hunt, and a whizz-kid architect called Chris Wilkinson, but we expanded so fast that we had outgrown it before it was even built . . . Wilkinson and Hunt were back though in the Autumn of 1996, drawing up plans to treble the 90,000 square foot factory space by extending over more of our twenty-acre site. (Ibid., p. 246)

In 1996, Dyson was considering ways to expand into the increasingly global market. After considering Germany and France as future expansion sites, he settled on Australia. As usual, the reason for choosing the Antipodes was strongly linked to his social network:

> I got a call from a man called Ross Cameron. Cameron was an Australian who had seen a presentation of mine at Johnson-Wax in Racine, Wisconsin. 'Why not start up in Australia?' I asked. A couple of days later Ross rang back to say 'OK'. He was that sort of man, not one to mess about. (Ibid., pp. 252–3)

A further issue to bear in mind is the role played by Dyson's immediate family, particularly his wife Deidre. He makes passing reference to the support of his wife in overcoming problems, such as promoting the Sea Truck: 'Deidre designed a brochure, and they began to sell. And it all seemed so obvious: you simply cannot mix your messages when selling something new' (ibid., p. 62).[3] He later acknowledges that Deidre provided him with a considerable amount of support when he first left Rotork: 'I still marvel at Deidre's encouragement of me at that time. It could have meant losing everything. But she was always philosophical, and insisted that if everything failed she could paint pictures for money and I could make furniture' (ibid., p. 78).

The Dyson case demonstrates that persistence, hard work and self-belief contributed to his success. At the same time, it is important to recognize that, at crucial points, his extensive social network provided considerable financial, legal, business and emotional support. Without these networks it is unlikely that he would have overcome the formidable odds.[4]

EXTENDING THE ENTREPRENEUR'S GEOGRAPHICAL REACH

A 're-reading' of *Against the Odds* suggests that the creation of Dyson's various business ventures was heavily dependent on both family and friends (strong ties) and acquaintances (weak ties), as well as serendipitous meetings with 'strangers' (Aldrich *et al.*, 1997, p. 3). Dyson's family and friends provided him with financial and knowledge-based resources, which encouraged him to transform his ideas into successful business ventures. Evidently not every potential entrepreneur will be fortunate enough to call on an ex-Miss Great Britain to sell their products or a senior member of the CBI to provide business expertise. Perhaps what distinguishes entrepreneurs is their ability to make use of strong ties, as well as their effectiveness in mobilizing weak ties. As the case illustrates, contacts made on aeroplanes, in business meetings and in seminars can be the key elements in business success. In other words, neither strategic choice nor environmental determinism adequately explains why some entrepreneurial ventures succeed and others fail.

Van de Ven (1996, p. 42) argues that it is necessary to examine an entrepreneur's proprietary functions, institutional arrangements and resource endowments. Proprietary functions, in Dyson's case, included the appropriation of basic knowledge through his development of the dual cyclone, the establishment of manufacturing facilities and the reconstruction of a mature market. Institutional arrangements that aided (and restricted) his entrepreneurial venture consisted of various government regulations, including the patent system that enabled Dyson to appropriate and protect the knowledge associated with the dual cyclone. Resource endowments, such as basic scientific research, financing mechanisms and skilled human resources, are fundamental to the emergence of entrepreneurial ventures. Dyson and his extensive social network were certainly responsible for some of these activities. However, at the same time, public organizations were also essential in 'creating and providing these public goods' (ibid., 44).

The case study highlights the important contributions made by Dyson's personal network in terms of providing finance, legal advice, emotional support, marketing and public relations skills, as well as direct access to talented young design engineers. At the same time, the case study reveals that much of this network was based in the UK. It appears that the geographical reach of Dyson's personal network extended across international borders rather slowly and serendipitously. For example, the Japanese company, Apex, which produced the first version of the dual cyclone, initially approached Dyson in an informal manner. Other casual relationships, such as those developed with Ross Cameron from Australia and Jeffery Pike from Canada, became important beach-heads for Dyson into these international markets. Dyson's exploitation of such weak ties could be viewed as both a personal strength and a weakness in his approach to doing business internationally.

Research on the growth of small firms (McGhee *et al.*, 1995) emphasizes the importance of entrepreneurial teams which 'expand the organization's network of contacts and provide the balance of expertise required to profit from certain types of cooperative activity' (Birley and Stockley, 2000, p. 289). This illustrates the main weakness of Dyson's ad hoc approach in which, according to his own account, he was solely responsible for establishing all important network linkages associated with his business activities. In other words, Dyson behaved as a traditional entrepreneur by demonstrating his unwillingness to delegate any element of control or responsibility to others within the organization (Levie and Hay, 2000, p. 257). Even though Dyson's business is certainly an example of a fast-growing company, there is no mention of the other members in the 'entrepreneurial team'. Hence it might be concluded that the growth of Dyson's company was very much 'against the odds', in the sense that he failed to recognize the limits of a proprietor's control.

CONCLUSIONS

There are few doubts that Dyson is an example of a successful entrepreneur, who created a new business by challenging incumbents in an extremely mature market. In the early stages of his entrepreneurial activities, he recognized the importance of entering international markets with the Sea Truck. While attempting to interest reputable companies in the dual cyclone, he rapidly moved beyond the UK to establish contacts with major manufacturers in Europe (Electrolux and Zanussi) and North America (Amway and Iona). As the case study illustrates, he was extremely effective in making use of weak ties as a means of promoting his various business ventures. However we have also shown that the creation of his international networks lacked strategic dimension (Jarillo, 1988). It appears that Dyson was unwilling to give up control to an 'entrepreneurial team', through which he could have expanded competences within the organization. The team could have also helped to establish a broader network, which would be particularly important for international ventures (Birley and Stockley, 2000).

Johannisson (2000) argues that the concept of networking helps us move away from the traditional view of entrepreneurs as resourceful individualists to an image of entrepreneurship as a collective phenomenon. We are not suggesting that the motivation of individual entrepreneurs can be discounted in explaining the creation of new business ventures. Rather we agree with Wickham's (2001, p. 39) characteristics of successful entrepreneurs, which include hard work, self-starting, goal setting, resilience, confidence, assertiveness and comfort with power. James Dyson certainly demonstrated all these characteristics over a considerable amount of time. At the same time, we argue that Dyson's activities were heavily embedded in an extensive network of family, friends and casual acquaintances. Clearly this network would not have developed in the way it did without Dyson's ability (agency) to utilize existing strong ties, while developing a range of weaker ties at the same time.

We have drawn on Granovetter's work (1973, 1985) to illustrate the centrality of social embeddedness in entrepreneurial activity. We believe it is important to extend the study of entrepreneurship beyond the psychological approaches, which emphasize the sources of individual motivation (McClelland, 1961; Manimala, 1999), or economic theories that concentrate on the economic rationality of those starting their own businesses (Casson, 1982, 1990). Entrepreneurial networks are created through a process of social interaction where various resources, necessary to establish and maintain a viable business, are accessible. This is a 'structuration' approach in which the ability of individual entrepreneurs helps mobilize various networks, in order to transform business ideas into new ventures. Such a perspective is summarized by Van de Ven (1996, p. 53): 'The social system perspective emphasises that any given entrepreneurial firm is but one actor, able to perform only a limited set of roles, and dependent upon many other actors to accomplish all the functions needed for an industry to emerge and survive.'

Therefore we suggest that individuals researching entrepreneurial activities and start-ups should place less emphasis on psychological attributes and, instead, highlight the broader institutional context which can be attained as a result of individuals mobilizing their strong and weak network ties. Furthermore entrepreneurs should consider formal, as well as informal, approaches to network building. This, as illustrated by the Dyson case, is particularly important for individual entrepreneurs attempting to establish international entrepreneurial ventures.

NOTES

1. The IPR (2000) reports that the UK government recently recruited a number of entrepreneurial 'heroes' such as Branson and Dyson to tour schools and colleges urging students to start their own businesses (see heroes@enterprising-britain.com).
2. In November 2000, Richard Caborn, British Minister for Trade, announced a new export credit package for SMEs seeking to exploit export markets outside Western Europe and North America (www.tradepartners.gov.uk; www.ecgd.gov.uk).
3. Early in his story, Dyson describes his mistakes in attempting to market the Sea Truck, by conveying a message that was too complicated for potential buyers.
4. Overall, Deidre, Dyson's wife, plays a minor role in the Dyson story and is certainly not credited with anything other than that of the supportive wife responsible for child-rearing and housekeeping. The point of these examples is not to suggest that Dyson is a chauvinist nor that he overemphasizes the importance of his own contribution to the success of his various business ventures. Rather what we are trying to illustrate is that it is all too easy to attribute the success of entrepreneurial ventures to the efforts of the man or woman responsible for founding a new business.

REFERENCES

Aldrich, H. (1979), *Organizations and Environments*, Englewood Cliff, NJ: Prentice-Hall.

Aldrich, H. (2000), 'Learning together: national differences in entrepreneurial research', in D. Sexton and H. Landstrom (eds), *The Blackwell Handbook of Entrepreneurship*, Oxford: Blackwell.

Aldrich, H. and C. Zimmer (1986), 'Entrepreneurship through social networks', in D. Sexton and R. Smilor (eds), *Art and Science of Entrepreneurship*, Cambridge, MA: Ballinger.

Aldrich, H., A.B. Elam and P.R. Reese (1997), 'Strong ties, weak ties and strangers: do women owners differ from men in their use of networking to obtain assistance?' in S. Birley and I. Macmillan (eds), *Entrepreneurship in a Global Context*, London: Routledge.

Allen, T. (1970) 'Communication networks in R&D laboratories', *R&D Management*, **1** (1), 14–21.

Auster, E. (1990), 'The interorganizational environment: network theory, tools and applications', in F. Williams and D. Gibson (eds), *Technology Transfer: A Communication Perspective*, London: Sage, pp. 63–89.

Baaijens, R. (1998), 'Explanatory meta-analysis for the comparison and transfer of regional tourist income multipliers', *Regional Studies*, **32** (9), 839–50.

Barley, S. (1990), 'The alignment of technology and structure through roles and networks', *Administrative Science Quarterly*, **35**, 61–103.

Barley, S. and P. Tolbert (1997), 'Institutionalization and structuration: studying the links between action and institution', *Organization Studies*, **18** (1), 93–117.

Birley, S. and S. Cromie (1988), 'Social networks and entrepreneurship in Northern Ireland', Enterprise in Action Conference, Belfast.

Birley, S. and S. Stockley (2000), 'Entrepreneurial teams and venture growth', in D. Sexton and H. Landstrom (eds), *The Blackwell Handbook of Entrepreneurship*, Oxford: Blackwell.

Birley, S., S. Cromie and A. Myers (1990), 'Entrepreneurial networks: their emergence in Ireland and overseas', *International Small Business Journal*, **9** (4), 56–74.

Burt, R.S. (1992), *Structural Holes: The Social Structure of Competitiveness*, Cambridge, MA: Harvard University Press.

Burt, R.S. (2000), 'The network entrepreneur', in R. Swedberg (ed.), *Entrepreneurship: The Social Science View*, Oxford: Oxford University Press.

Camagni, R. (1991), 'Introduction: from the local milieu to innovation through cooperation networks', in R. Camagni (ed.), *Innovation Networks: Spatial Perspectives*, London: Belhaven.

Casson, M. (1982), *The Entrepreneurs: An Economic Theory*, Oxford: Martin Robertson.

Casson, M. (1990), *Entrepreneurship*, Aldershot, UK, and Brookfield, US: Edward Elgar.

Conway, S. (1994), 'Informal boundary-spanning links and networks in successful technological innovation', unpublished PhD dissertation, Aston Business School, Birmingham.

Conway, S. (1997), 'Informal networks of relationships in successful small firm innovation', in D. Jones-Evans and M. Klofsten (eds), *Technology, Innovation and Enterprise: The European Experience*, London: Macmillan, pp. 236–73.

Conway, S. and E. Shaw (1999), 'Networking and the small firm', in S. Carter and D. Jones-Evans (eds), *Enterprise and Small Business: Principles, Policy and Practice*, Reading, MA: Addison-Wesley Longman.

Coombs, R., P. Saviotti and V. Walsh (1987), *Economics and Technological Change*, Basingstoke: Macmillan.

Czarniawska-Joerges, B. (1995), 'Narration or science? Collapsing the division in organization studies', *Organization*, **2** (1), 11–34.

De, D. (2000), 'SME Policy in Europe', in D. Sexton and H. Landstrom (eds), *The Blackwell Handbook of Entrepreneurship*, Oxford: Blackwell.

DeBresson, C. and F. Amesse (1991), 'Networks of innovators: a review and introduction to the issues', *Research Policy (Special Issue)*, **20** (5), 363–79.

Donckels, R. and J. Lambrecht (1997), 'The network position of small businesses: an explanatory model', *Journal of Small Business Management*, April.

Dyson, J. (1997), *Against the Odds: An Autobiography*, London: Orion Business Books.

Fletcher, D, (1998) 'Swimming around in their own ponds: the weakness of strong ties in developing innovative practices', *International Journal of Innovation Management*, **2** (2), 137–60.

Freeman, C. (1991), 'Networks of innovators: a synthesis of research issues', *Research Policy*, **20** (5), 499–514.

Giddens, A. (1995), *The Constitution of Society: Outline of the Theory of Structuration*, Cambridge: Polity (1st edn 1984).

Granovetter, M. (1973), 'The strength of weak ties', *American Journal of Sociology*, **78** (6), 1360–80.

Granovetter, M. (1985), 'Economic action and social structure: the problem of embeddedness', *American Journal of Sociology*, **91** (3), 481–510.

Granovetter, M. (1992), 'Problems of explanation in economic sociology', in N. Nohria and R.G. Eccles (eds), *Networks and Organizations: Structure, Form and Action*, Boston: Harvard Business School Press.

Hagen, E. (1962), *On the Theory of Economic Change: How Economic Growth Begins*, Homewood, IL: Dorsey.

Hakansson, H. (1987), 'Product development in networks', in H. Hakansson (ed.), *Industrial Technological Development: A Network Approach*, London: Croom Helm.

Hammersley, M. (1992), *What's Wrong with Ethnography? Methodological Explanations*, London: Routledge.

Hannan. M. and J. Freeman (1977), 'The Population Ecology of Organizations', *American Journal of Sociology*, **82** (5), 929–64.

Imai, K. and Y. Baba (1989), 'Systemic innovation and cross-border networks: transcending markets and hierarchies', OECD Conference on Science, Technology and Economic Growth, Paris.

IPR (2000), 'Entrepreneurs of the future', *Innovation Policy Review*, **1** (1), 12.

Jarillo, J.C. (1988), 'On Strategic Networks', *Strategic Management Journal*, **9**, 31–41.

Johannisson, B. (2000), 'Networking and entrepreneurial growth', in D. Sexton and H. Landstrom (eds), *The Blackwell Handbook of Entrepreneurship*, Oxford: Blackwell.

Johannisson, B. and R. Peterson (1984), 'The personal networks of entrepreneurs', *Third Canadian Conference, International Council for Small Business*, Toronto, 23–5 May.

Jones, O. (1997), 'Structuration theory and technology transfer: towards a social theory of innovation', Aston Business School research paper, RP9704.

Jones, O., C. Cardoso and M. Beckinsale (1997), 'Mature SMEs and technological innovation: entrepreneurial networks in the UK and Portugal', *International Journal of Innovation Management*, **1** (3), 201–27.

Jones, O., S. Conway and F. Steward (2001), 'Introduction: social interaction and organization change', in O. Jones, S. Conway and F. Steward (eds), *Social Interaction and Organisational Change: Aston Perspectives on Innovation Networks*, London: Imperial College Press.

Jones, O., T. Edwards and M. Beckinsale (2000), 'Technology management in a mature firm: structuration theory and the innovation process', *Technology Analysis and Strategic Management*, **12** (2), 161–77.

Khandwalla, P. (1985) 'Pioneering innovative management: an Indian excellence', *Organization Studies*, **6** (2), 161–83.

Kirzner, I. (1973), *Competition and Entrepreneurship*, Chicago: University of Chicago Press.

Lawton-Smith, H., K. Dickson and S. Smith (1991), 'There are two sides to every

story: innovation and collaboration within networks of large and small firms',
Research Policy, **20**, 457–68.

Leonard-Barton, D. (1984), 'Interpersonal communication patterns among Swedish
and Boston-area entrepreneurs', *Research Policy*, **13** (2), 101–14.

Levie, J. and M. Hay (2000), 'Life beyond the "kitchen" culture', in S. Birley and
D. Muzyka (eds), *Mastering Entrepreneurship*, London: Financial Times.

Manimala, M. (1999), *Entrepreneurial Policies and Strategies: The Innovator's
Choice*, New Delhi: Sage.

Maslow, A. (1954), *Motivation and Personality*, New York: Harper & Row.

Mathias, P. (1969), *The First Industrial Revolution: An Economic History of Britain
1700–1914*, London: Methuen.

McClelland, D.C. (1961), *The Achieving Society*, Princeton, NJ: Van Nostrand.

McGhee, J.E., M.J. Dowling and W.L. Meggison (1995), 'Co-operative strategy and
new venture performance: the role of business strategy and managerial experience', *Strategic Management Journal*, **16**, 563–80.

Morgan, G. (1986), *Images of Organization*, Beverly Hills: Sage.

Nonaka, I. and H. Takeuchi (1995), *The Knowledge Creating Company: How
Japanese Companies Create the Dynamics of Innovation*, Oxford: Oxford
University Press.

Oliver, A.L. and M. Ebers (1998), 'Networking network studies: an analysis of
conceptual configurations in the study of inter-organizational relationships',
Organization Studies, **19** (4), 549–83.

Powell, W.W. (1990), 'Neither market nor hierarchy: network forms of organization',
Research in Organizational Behavior, **12**, 295–336.

Powell, W.W., K. Koput and L. Smith-Doerr (1996), 'Interorganizational collaboration and the locus of innovation: networks of learning in biotechnology',
Administrative Science Quarterly, **41** (1), 116–45.

Prior, A. and M. Kirby (1998), 'The Society of Friends and business culture,
1700–1830' in D. Jeremy (ed.), *Religion, Business and Wealth in Modern Britain*,
London: Routledge, pp. 115–36.

Roberts, K. and M. Grabowski (1996), 'Organizations, technology and structuring',
in S. Clegg, C. Hardy and W. Nord (eds), *Handbook of Organization Studies*,
London: Sage.

Rothwell, R. and M. Dodgson (1991) 'External linkages and innovation in small and
medium-sized enterprises', *R&D Management*, **21** (2), 125–37.

Schumpeter, J. (1934) *The Theory of Economic Development*, Cambridge, MA:
Harvard University Press.

Shaw, E. (1998), 'Social networks: their impact on the innovative behaviour of small
service firms', *International Journal of Innovation Management*, **2** (2), 201–22.

Steward, F. and S. Conway (1998), 'Situating discourse in environmental innovation
networks', *Organization*, **5** (4), 479–502.

Storey, D. (2000), 'Six steps to heaven: evaluating the impact of public policy to
support small business in developed economies', in D. Sexton and H. Landstrom
(eds), *The Blackwell Handbook of Entrepreneurship*, Oxford: Blackwell.

Tichy, N., M. Tushman and C. Fombrun (1979), 'Social network analysis for organizations', *Academy of Management Review*, **4** (4), 507–19.

Twiss, B. (1992), *Managing Technological Innovation*, 4th edn, London: Pitman.

Van de Ven, A.H. (1996), 'The development of an infrastructure for entrepreneurship' in I. Bull, H. Thomas and G. Willard (eds), *Entrepreneurship: Perspectives
on Theory Building*, Oxford: Pergamon.

Weaver, M. (2000), 'Strategic alliances as vehicles for international growth', in D. Sexton and H. Landstrom (eds), *The Blackwell Handbook of Entrepreneurship*, Oxford: Blackwell.
Weber, M. (1930), *The Protestant Ethic and the Spirit of Capitalism*, New York: Scribner.
Wickham, P. (2001), *Strategic Entrepreneurship*, 2nd edn, London: Pitman.

6. Cultural effects on delegation in the small business life cycle

Supara Kapasuwan and Jerman Rose

The importance of small business and new ventures has been thoroughly examined in academic research and literature. Many researchers have proposed stages-of-development models, most of which, differing in number of stages, usually follow a linear process, from start-up, rapid growth and investment expansion to a period of stability or maturity (Churchill and Lewis, 1983; Scott and Bruce, 1987; Dodge and Robbins, 1992). Frequently researchers suggest that a small firm that grows rapidly will outpace the founder–manager's managerial capabilities at some point during its development. If the firm's growth is to be maintained, the founder–manager should be replaced by 'professional managers' (Tashakori, 1980; Churchill and Lewis, 1983; Flamholtz, 1986; Baird and Meshoulam, 1988; Fuller-Love and Scapens, 1997).

Other researchers have examined whether founder–managers of small firms have sufficient capabilities and skills to manage high-growth firms. They found no significant differences between the performance of founder-managed and professionally-managed firms (Willard et al., 1992; Daily and Dalton, 1992). However, as a firm develops, changes in managerial requirements play an important role.

We define delegation as the willingness of a founder–manager to yield the authority of an important management function to others. The founder–manager's willingness to delegate several functions can be crucial for success (Rubenson and Gupta, 1996). The significance of delegation has been widely discussed in small business literature (Cuba and Milbourn, 1982; Davidsson, 1989; Gilmore and Kazanjian, 1989; Mount et al., 1993; Fuller-Love and Scapens, 1997). Churchill and Lewis (1983) suggested that 'the level of delegation should increase' for firm growth to occur, and operational and strategic planning should involve other managers and, therefore, 'the owner and the business should become reasonably separate' (p. 40). By contrast, a recent study by Ardichvili et al. (1998) provides evidence that strategic planning is the function least likely to be relinquished by the founders, since they remain interested in contemplating and determining the future directions of their businesses.

While small firms may not conform to the stages-of-development theories, since the impact of delegation varies, the question of what determines the likelihood that the founder–manager will delegate his or her power base to subordinates remains interesting and significant. It is interesting as it reflects the nature of entrepreneurial management, and it is significant because, while mixed, there is evidence that delegation has an impact on firm performance.

In practice, successful organizations have different managerial styles. The need to delegate functions depends on the characteristics of the entrepreneur, founder–manager, as well as the complexity of management practices, which are influenced by diverse social institutions and cultures. Therefore the objective of this study is to explore whether cultural differences, between Western and Asian cultures, have an effect on management practices and delegation patterns of small firms.

A case study method is employed to gather information on two selected enterprises in Thailand. By focusing on cultural effects in the Asian business environment, this chapter will provide insight into (a) how the enterprises operated and developed through different stages of growth, (b) the founder–manager's role, which is crucial for economic success, (c) how the founder–manager or the owner managed firm growth and (d) the extent to which delegation or professional management is deemed essential for growth.

LITERATURE REVIEW

Theorists of small business growth suggest that firms progress through a predictable set of stages (Steinmetz, 1969; Churchill and Lewis, 1983; Scott and Bruce, 1987; Dodge and Robbins, 1992). Although the number of stages may vary across small business growth models, there are three common phases: the start-up period, where the development of a viable enterprise occurs, followed by a rapid growth stage and, finally, the maturity phase. However firms may progress through different stages, at different times and in different sequences (Birley and Westhead, 1990).

When a small firm grows through each development stage, it faces different sets of internal and external environmental variables (Dodge and Robbins, 1992). The internal environment includes the managerial skills and leadership characteristics of the founder–manager, his or her educational and occupational background, and personal values and attitudes towards growth. The external environment consists of the market conditions and competition, as well as social, legal and political conditions (Birley and Westhead, 1990). In order to be successful, a small firm must be able to manage the balance of both internal and external environmental variables. External environmental problems are usually more important in the early stages, including inception and survival, whereas the internal problems become more critical as the small business progresses through the rapid growth and expansion stages (Dodge and Robbins, 1992; Jones-Evans, 1996).

In small business growth models, much of the emphasis falls upon the internal environmental factors of an organization: specifically, the role and characteristics of the founder–manager, which strongly influence the size and growth of the business (Barkham, 1994). It is notable that the internal organizational characteristics of successful early-stage firms differ from those of successful mature firms (Gilmore and Kazanjian, 1989). In their conceptualization of the development stages of the small-business life cycle, Churchill and Lewis (1983) emphasized the organizational changes small businesses experience as they grow. They described five management factors that influence small business growth: managerial style, organizational structure, the extent of formal systems, major strategic goals and the owner's involvement in the business. The framework of small business growth proposed by Churchill and Lewis (1983) influenced subsequent small business research, and provided a useful foundation for other stages-of-development theories (Scott and Bruce, 1987; Dodge and Robbins, 1992; Mount *et al.*, 1993).

According to Churchill and Lewis (1983), knowing specific growth factors for each stage should enable the founder–manager to anticipate organizational requirements, especially the need for delegation and changes in the managerial roles as the business grows larger. The transition from entrepreneurial to managerial work is addressed between Stage III – Success (Growth) – and Stage IV – Take-off. It should be noted that, during Stage IV, 'often the entrepreneur who founded the company and brought it to the Success Stage is replaced either voluntarily or involuntarily by the company's investors or creditors' (ibid., p. 40). The separation of the founder–manager from the company is expected to occur after the Success (Growth) stage. However, in many cases, the founder–manager may not be willing to delegate his or her work. In addition, the founder–manager may overlook the necessity to delegate and decentralize management and decision making, even though he/she may still be capable of managing the firm's growth as it becomes larger.

The entrepreneur, considered in this discussion as the founder–manager of a small business, plays an important role in determining the ultimate success or failure of the firm. Churchill and Lewis (1983) discussed four elements related to the founder–manager which influence small business development: the owner's goals, operational abilities, strategic vision and willingness to delegate. The role of the founder–manager of a small firm cannot be overemphasized, since he or she plays a central role in the small business (Smith and Miner, 1983). More often than not, the values and goals of a small firm are identical to those of the founder–manager who founded the business. The size and growth of a small firm are dependent upon his or her entrepreneurial skills and knowledge, including communication skills, imagination, practical knowledge and foresight (Barkham, 1994). Ardichvili *et al.* (1998) described the major functions performed by the founder–manager during the small firm's early stages of development. They consist of financial and strategic planning, new product development, marketing, operations management, personnel, finance, accounting, sales and purchasing. As a small business grows, the founder–manager cannot perform all functions, thus subordinates must be hired to assist with some of the above activities. Accounting is usually the first function to be delegated during the development of a small business, while strategic planning is the function least likely to be passed on to other employees (Ardichvili *et al.*, 1998).

A number of researchers have suggested that, as a firm becomes larger, in terms of operations, the founder–manager should shift his or her focus, from the role of 'doing' towards 'managing' (Churchill and Lewis, 1983; Scott and Bruce, 1987; Jones-Evans, 1996; Atkins and Lowe, 1997). However it is quite difficult for the founder–manager of a small firm to delegate his responsibilities, for a number of reasons. First, autonomy is believed to be of great importance for small business founder–managers, hence he or she may be unwilling to delegate for fear of losing control of the firm's direction (Cuba and Milbourn, 1982; Davidsson, 1989; Gilmore and Kazanjian, 1989; Mount *et al.*, 1993; Jones-Evans, 1996). Second, the founder–manager may have doubts concerning employees' judgment and leadership skills (Rubenson and Gupta, 1996; Cuba and Milbourn, 1982). Given that managers behave differently from the founder–manager, their stakes, as well as interest in the business, are not as intense (Daily and Dalton, 1992). Lastly, the manager–owner may enjoy performing all activities and, therefore, not delegate any responsibilities (Cuba and Milbourn, 1982).

If the founder–manager does not delegate some of his or her responsibilities, including marketing and or strategic planning, to subordinates, will he or she be able to lead the venture through rapid growth? Baird and Meshoulam (1988) pointed out that high growth may create changes that require considerable shifts in critical skills, such that new leadership, or a 'professional' manager, would eventually replace the founder–manager. However we need to recognize that adaptability, motivation and long-term focus of the founder–manager influence the growth of a small business. According to Scott and Bruce (1987), the survival or growth of small businesses is due either to the nature of the industry in which the firms operate or to the personal motives and ambitions of the founder–manager. A study by Rubenson and Gupta (1996) provides a thoughtful conceptualization regarding the connection between the specific characteristics of a founder or founder–manager and the growing enterprise. They proposed that specific individual characteristics of the founder–manager, such as their educational level, managerial experience, diversity of functional experience and market experience, play an important role in adapting his or her ability to respond to changing organizational needs resulting from rapid growth of the business. Thus the founder–manager who is well educated and possesses a considerable amount of experience in marketing and management tends to lead high-growth firms successfully. In addition, it is safe to assume that the founder–manager who demonstrates high motivation and exemplifies the 'opportunistic' type would most likely be able to manage the firm efficiently through rapid growth. This argument is supported by Davidsson (1989), who found that the need for achievement and increased dependence could have a positive effect on the growth of a small firm.

DELEGATION ISSUES

Stages-of-development models and much of the small business/entrepreneurship literature have suggested that, the faster a small firm grows, the higher the level of delegation needed (Churchill and Lewis, 1983; Scott and Bruce, 1987; Dodge and Robbins, 1992). Other studies suggest that the emerging complexity of the organization and decision making, under high growth, outpaces the founder–manager's capabilities. Therefore the performance of the growing firm will deteriorate, unless a new professional manager is hired to replace the founder–manager (Tashakori, 1980; Flamholtz, 1986).

Notwithstanding there are some limitations in the small business growth conceptual framework's emphasis on the need for additional delegation in operational and strategic planning, and the separation of the owner or founder–manager from the business to sustain the performance of a high-growth small firm. As discussed earlier, the extent of delegation depends on the founder–manager, his or her perception of delegation and the particular type of organizational needs. In addition we believe the need for delegation and professional management is subject to specific business environments, which are influenced by different cultures and social institutions. As a first step, we propose an assessment of the differences in delegation patterns between Western and Asian small firms.

CULTURAL EFFECTS ON MANAGEMENT PRACTICES AND DELEGATION ISSUES

Different institutional contexts and values affect management practices (Whitley, 1992; Hodder, 1996). Given that culture affects managerial practices, we believe no specific standardized formula exists for the success of small businesses worldwide. Should we then expect diverse delegation patterns due to the differences in business institutions and cultures?

Diverse economies constitute distinctive business systems, which are dominated and developed by different types of business and market organizations. These business systems are made up of specific management techniques, which reflect successful patterns of business behavior (Whitley, 1992). A variety of studies, conducted in East and Southeast Asia, seek to explain the differences between small firm management in the West and those in the Asian business environment (Skinner, 1957; Cunningham, 1995; Whitley, 1992; Redding, 1980, 1990; Redding and Wong, 1986; Limlingan, 1986; Hodder, 1996).

Given their overwhelming power in the regional economic development, we intend to focus on the management practices of small businesses in Southeast Asia (Clad, 1989; Whitley, 1992; Hodder, 1996). Many Southeast Asian economies are dominated by Chinese family businesses (Limlingan 1986; Redding, 1990). The number of 'Overseas Chinese' in the region is approximately 43 to 50 million (Hodder, 1996). In Indonesia, 'Overseas Chinese' account for about 3 per cent of the population, yet about three-quarters of private domestic capital and more than half of the national trade lies in their hands (ibid.). Nearly all the economic elite in Thailand consist of 'Overseas Chinese' traders and financiers, and most prominent businesses are run by Thai Chinese families (Skinner, 1957; Clad, 1989). A glance at the list of international billionaires in Southeast Asia reveals how dominant the 'Overseas Chinese' are, as well as the level of prosperity they are able to generate.

The Chinese family businesses in Southeast Asia are initially small in size. They subsequently expand into large corporations, under the leadership of the founder–manager. These businesses represent a particular management practice and organizational form that is extremely different from the characteristics of Western-style management (Kirkbride and Tang, 1992). Cunningham (1995) performed exploratory research on success in corporate and entrepreneurial organizations in Singapore. He discovered that Asian organizations tend to have unique characteristics which Western organizations do not possess and, therefore, the Western management practices may not be appropriate under Asian business systems. The management practices of the 'Overseas Chinese' in Southeast Asia are generally highly centralized, in terms of the decision-making process, which appears to be flexible and responsive to environmental change (Whitley, 1992; Hodder, 1996). As opposed to the Western management style, where decentralization is the norm, centralized management in Southeast Asia is effective, owing to the common view of the moral superiority of the leader in Chinese society (Whitley, 1992), as well as the high reliance on the founder–manager to achieve economic success (Kirkbride and Tang, 1992).

According to Redding (1990), the founder–manager maintains autonomy in making decisions concerning financial, marketing and personnel management issues. While some delegation of control over production activities might occur, planning decisions usually remain centralized through all stages of development, until the small firm stabilizes and reaches maturity. The autonomy of the 'Overseas Chinese' founder–managers in small Southeast Asian firms is reinforced by the fact that inter-firm connections, market organization, trust and cooperation between kinship groups have strong influences on the internal organization and management practices of the firms (Whitley, 1992).

Since the success of small firms in Southeast Asia depends on their ability to establish connections and to seek the best market information, it is difficult for the founder–managers to step away from the companies they founded. Given the role of personal relationships and the founder–manager's social networks, the importance of delegation, for small business growth, is diminished. The founder–manager and his social capital are essential at every stage of small business development. Therefore his or her control over strategic planning might not be a growth deterrent but a crucial factor for success.

Drawing on distinct institutional contexts and cultures that have fostered a rich discussion pertaining to the differences between Western and Asian management practices, our goal is to investigate the validity of the stages-of-development framework conceptualized by Churchill and Lewis (1983). The authors' propositions are that (a) under specific circumstances characterized by various cultural and institutional contexts, during the stage of rapid growth and expansion, the founder–manager does not need to be separated from his/her business operationally and strategically, and (b) a high degree of centralization with a limited degree of delegation might be important growth factors in some business systems.

RESEARCH METHOD

We performed exploratory research by drawing on firms in the canned fish industry in Thailand, in order to gain insight into the way cultural factors and values affect the role of the founder–manager of a small firm, as well as the delegation patterns employed for business success. The reasons for choosing the canned fish industry are as follows: first, the industry processes Thailand's natural resource, and could be considered as one of the high-priority industrial sectors (Akrasanee *et al.*, 1996); second, the firms in this industry are usually typical family businesses, which start small and expand into large companies once they have achieved economic success ('Canned seafood industry', 1994); finally, being labor-intensive in nature, the canned fish industry should provide relevant insights on the division of work, as well as the extent of delegation.

A case study approach was considered an appropriate methodology for this research, since an in-depth investigation covered not only the phenomenon and the underlying issues but also the specific contextual conditions needed (Yin, 1993). In selecting relevant cases, we employed Churchill and Lewis's (1983) conceptual framework to set the boundaries. The selection criteria for the organizations to be studied were progress in terms of economic growth from Stage I to Stage IV and a current move towards Stage V, based on Churchill and Lewis's conceptualization, as shown in Figure 6.1. Note that Stage III – Disengagement was not considered in this study, since the focus was on the role of the founder–manager and delegation patterns of a small firm that reached Stage IV.

In Thailand, a small manufacturing firm possesses no more than 50 million Thai Baht in total permanent assets (Ministry of Industry, Thailand, 2000). Given that most companies' permanent asset figures were kept confidential, the registered capital figures were used as a determinant of size. The change in value of the Thai Baht currency was taken into consideration, which helped us in selecting typical small firms that were founded with initial registered capital of no more than 20 million Baht. Measures of company growth included the increase in registered capital and the expansion of business locations. Finally, the last criterion for selecting cases was the specific condition that the founder–managers of such small firms would be fully involved in the day-to-day operations and strategic planning of the business.

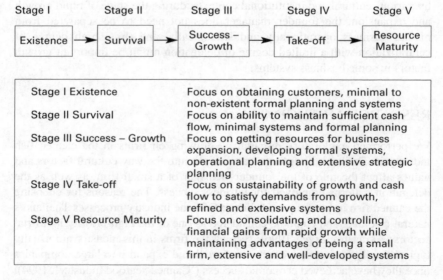

Figure 6.1   Characteristics of the development of organizations in selected case studies

According to the predetermined design and procedures, two canned fish companies, Hi-Q Food Products Co., Ltd and Kuang Pei San Food Products Public Co., Ltd fitted the criteria. Both firms were among the top players in the industry: each held approximately a 30 per cent market share in the industry. They provide preliminary insights into specific management practices and key success factors of the canned fish industry in Thailand. In gathering information, we relied on multiple sources of data such as documentation, public archival records from the Ministry of Commerce, Thailand, as well as interviews. The semi-structured interviews were conducted with some members of the Wangpatanamongkol family, who own Hi-Q Food Products Co., Ltd. In the case of Kuang Pei San Food Products Public Co., Ltd, we used secondary sources such as articles from magazines and newspapers, and recorded interviews from television programs.

On the one hand, the implementation of a case-study method for this exploratory study provided us with a main advantage in performing an in-depth investigation of the issues at hand, and gaining insights into specific contextual conditions (Yin, 1993; Tellis, 1997). On the other hand, limitations do exist, specifically because of the absence of a cross-case analysis approach (Miles and Huberman, 1994) and the lack of triangulation (Yin, 1993), which can be useful in an effort to enhance generalizability. Our primary goal, however, was not generalizability; rather the major purpose of this study was to determine whether cultural differences would affect management practices and delegation patterns within an accessible context.

We next address the background information of each company. We then explore various issues concerning the owner of each company, including his role in the firm, his characteristics, the growth of each firm and how the owner manages growth, his views on professionalism and, finally, the importance of personal relationships and networks as a key success factor in the canned fish industry.

Hi-Q Food Products Co., Ltd: Background Information

Mr Pramitr Wangpatanamongkol founded Hi-Q Food Products in 1986 after leaving Roza Food Products, a family-owned business, where he played a key role in the development of the company's brand of canned sardines. A Japanese company buying from Roza Food Products contacted him to produce pet food, which may have been the cause of his departure. Following Mr Wangpatanamongkol's departure, Roza was faced with a major problem: no one in the company had sufficient knowledge and/or competence to manage or create an effective business deal. Consequently the company filed for bankruptcy ('Premier group offers Baht 10 million to buy Roza brand', 1996).

Initially Mr Wangpatanamongkol wanted to produce only canned pet food for export and never intended to produce canned sardines so long as Roza Food Products was still in business. Hi-Q was founded with 13 million Baht in capital (Larpadisorn, 2000). A major portion of the investment came from his in-laws, as well as his own savings. In addition, he was well supported by his friend, Mr Boonsong Phuangsombat, who was the major supplier of raw fish for the company, and eventually became one of its major shareholders.

Hi-Q started to manufacture canned pet food, and exported all of its products to Japan. Mr Wangpatanamongkol started producing canned fish again once Roza Food Products Co., Ltd. went bankrupt, and the Roza brand fell into the hands of Premier Canning Industry Co., Ltd. It was now more difficult to compete for a share of the market, because of the intensity of competition. Armed with an innovative mind, Mr Wangpatanamongkol attacked the Thai market with a new easy-to-open packaging for canned fish, which led to Hi-Q's rapid sales growth of approximately 30–40 per cent in 1990. The company subsequently introduced new products to the canned fish market and invested a considerable amount of money in advertising to build consumer brand loyalty.

In 1996, Hi-Q bought back the Roza brand. Major products include tomato sauce, chili sauce, canned sardines in tomato sauce and in chili sauce, canned flavored sardines and various types of canned flavored tuna. The company now employs 820 workers in its factories in Samutprakarn and Pattani provinces (Department of Industrial Works, Thailand, 2000). It also has a factory in Nongkhai province that produces tomato paste for canned fish production.

Kuang Pei San Food Products Public Co., Ltd: Background Information

Kuang Pei San Food Products Public Co., Ltd. (Kuang Pei San) was established when Mr Surin Tohtubtiang noticed that the canned fish products he ordered from a manufacturer for his trading business were of low quality. Rather than ordering products from other manufacturers, Mr Tohtubtiang and his older brother, Mr Sutham Tohtubtiang, acquired a canned fish factory in Trang province to manufacture products of standard quality (Wishu-Lada, 1989). Founded in 1979, with 2 million Baht in capital, Kuang Pei San had a production capacity of one million cans per year (Kuang Pei San Food Products Public Co., Ltd. Annual Report, 1999). The geographical location of its Trang factory, which is close to the Andaman Sea, provides an advantage in terms of supplying fresh raw fish.

In 1980, Kuang Pei San expanded its production capacity to 12 million cans per year (ibid.). Besides offering good quality, Kuang Pei San's canned flavored fish became a legendary success for two reasons. First, 'Pum Pui' and the new brand, 'Pla Yim', were heavily advertised on provincial radio networks, reaching a vast pool of targeted consumers in provincial areas. Second, the Tohtubtiangs had a close personal relationship with one of the most famous tasters in Thailand, M.R. Thanadsri Sawasdiwat, who guaranteed the quality and delicious taste of 'Pum Pui' and 'Pla Yim' products. In 1982, the Tohtubtiangs founded a separate trading company, Bangkok Acme Co., Ltd, to handle the trading and exporting of the 'Pum Pui' and 'Pla Yim' products. In 1984, they began exporting to Malaysia, Singapore and Brunei. Over the next decade, they developed a number of successful new products (Kuang Pei San Food Products Public Co., Ltd Annual Report, 1999). Today its main factory, in Trang province, employs 880 workers (Department of Industrial Works, Thailand, 2000).

The Role of the Owners

In typical entrepreneurial fashion, the owners of both companies had worked very hard since the establishment of their businesses (Rattanamon, 1989; Larpadisorn, 2000). They began by training the workers themselves, teaching them how to cut fish properly, and how to operate machines effectively. Moreover they engaged in all of the day-to-day activities, from sweeping the floor to mechanical engineering, sales and marketing, and budget planning (Rattanamon, 1989; Larpadisorn, 2000).

Once both businesses expanded, they each adopted a division of labor (Wishu-Lada, 1989; Rattanamon, 1989; Larpadisorn, 2000), whereby additional subordinates were hired to help relieve the owners' burdens (Wishu-Lada, 1989; Larpadisorn, 2000). As a result, the owners gradually shifted from 'doing' to 'managing'. However subordinates would usually receive orders from the owner and would perform their jobs as they were told (Larpadisorn, 2000). Although operational activities are delegated to a large extent, strategic planning is still tightly controlled by the owners, since they have more personal connections and superior market information (Larpadisorn, 2000; 'Surin Tohtubtiang, owner of Pum Pui – his remarkable strategies and his role as the hero in Trang province').

Given that the quality of products is the most important factor for success, the owners closely watch over the manufacturing process and sample their products on a daily basis to ensure maximum quality (Larpadisorn, 2000; Tohtubtiang, 2000). It should also be noted that accounting and finance are functions performed, or closely monitored, by the owners. For instance, Mr Wangpatanamongkol's wife is responsible for controlling the finance and the accounting functions for Hi-Q (Larpadisorn, 2000), while, for Kuang Pei San, the fourth sister of the Tohtubtiang family manages both functions (Kuang Pei San Public Co., Ltd Annual Report, 1999).

The Characteristics and Philosophy of the Owners

Mr Wangpatanamongkol and Mr Tohtubtiang differ in their educational backgrounds. Mr Wangpatanamongkol gained a professional diploma in accounting from Penang, Malaysia (Larpadisorn, 2000), while Mr Tohtubtiang did not finish high school, since he had to earn a living in order to support his family (Tohtubtiang, 2000). However they share the following common characteristics: high level of discipline, hard-working personality, patience, risk taking, sincerity, loyalty and trustworthiness, and flexibility to adapt to changes (Larpadisorn, 2000; 'Surin Tohtubtiang, owner of Pum Pui – his remarkable strategies and his role as the hero in Trang province'.

Growth and How the Owners Manage Growth

As discussed earlier, the degree of delegation influences a company's growth. In order to understand this issue in the Thai context, the growth of both studied companies is outlined in Tables 6.1 and 6.2 below. The growth of Hi-Q Food Products Co., Ltd is shown in Table 6.1. The firm experienced rapid growth between 1990 and 1992, as a result of the development of the easy-to-open packaging strategy. In 1996, Mr Wangpatanamongkol did not hesitate to buy back his original 'Roza' brand and then he invested a large sum in expanding production capacity (Larpadisorn, 2000). He also established two new factories close to the source of raw material production, hired more assistants and engaged in the division of labor (ibid.).

Table 6.1   History of Hi-Q Food Products

Year	Major changes
1986	Company founded with 13 million Baht registered capital; produced canned pet food for export only
1987–8	Launched canned sardines in Thailand; market share 7%, export/domestic sales 90/10%
1990	Introduced new packaging; sales growth 30–40%, market share to 20%; expanded production capacity
1992	Registered capital rose to 70 million Baht
1993	Export/domestic sales were 80/20%
1996	Bought Roza brand name for 92 million Baht, founded Hi-Q Canning in Pattani province
1997	Established Roza Agri-Industrial Co., Ltd in Nongkhai province

Source: Wangpatanamongkol (2000).

Mr Wangpatanamongkol played a major role in all operational and strategic activities and was responsible for final decision making during Hi-Q's rapid growth phase (ibid). This worked well for two main reasons: first, he was the only individual who was familiar with all aspects of the canned fish business; second, he had good connections with suppliers and other business partners (ibid.). With regard to strategic planning, investment policy and management, Mr Wangpatanamongkol is extremely cautious, and watches over every single detail, because of the disastrous experience he encountered with his old family firm; he does not want to fail again (ibid.).

By comparison, Kuang Pei San seemed more willing to take greater risks in expanding its business, and the construction of its new factory led to the change of its status from a limited company to a public company in 1994 (Kuang Pei San Annual Report, 1999). The growth of the company can be observed from its 1996 and 1999 annual reports summarized in Table 6.2.

Between 1981 and 1983, Kuang Pei San rapidly expanded its production, as suggested by the increase in production capacity by 6.5 times. To manage the company's rapid growth, Mr Tohtubtiang raised his registered capital, in order gradually to expand his factory (Kuang Pei San Annual Report, 1999). He admitted he was tired of running the business alone and, therefore, hired additional subordinates to help with some operational activities (Rattanamon, 1989). Because of the need for a large capital investment in Kuang Pei San's new factory in Trang province, he decided to float his company on Thailand's Stock Exchange in 1994. However his family's holding company, Kuang

Table 6.2   History of Kuang Pei San

Year	Major changes
1979	Company founded with 2 million Baht registered capital; capacity of one million cans per year; export/domestic sales were 0/100%
1980	Production capacity expanded to 12 million cans per year
1981–2	Rapid sales growth
1983	Production capacity expanded to 90 million cans per year
1984	Began exporting to Malaysia, Singapore and Brunei; export/domestic sales were 5/95%
1989	Registered capital rose to 20 million Baht; export/domestic sales were 20/80%
1992	Registered capital rose to 50 million Baht
1993	Registered capital rose to 100 million Baht
1994	Status changed from limited company to public company and registered capital rose to 135 million Baht
1996	Production capacity rose to 130 million cans per year

Holding Co., Ltd, owns a large portion of the shares (Kuang Pei San Annual Report, 1999).

The Owners' Attitudes towards Professional Management

Hi-Q hired a professional manager to supervise its factory in order to relieve Mr Wangpatanamongkol's workload (Larpadisorn, 2000). In 1997, Mr Wangpatanamongkol hired a professional manager with 20 years' experience in the canned food business. They provided him with a high salary, as well as other incentives, and waited to see if the manager could push the business forward (ibid.). The final decisions were still under Mr Wangpatanamongkol's control because he could not 'trust' an outsider. However he tried to let someone else do most of his functions in the factory. The company were disappointed with the manager, whom they perceived to lack initiative, motivation for success and long-term focus (ibid.). The manager might not be determined to work hard enough as his stake in Hi-Q was insignificant compared to Mr Wangpatanamongkol's share.

The failure of Hi-Q's attempt to delegate to a professional manager exemplifies key features of the Thai business culture, a force the chosen manager, though Thai, was unable to overcome. As with the Japanese and Chinese cultures, hierarchy and seniority are important (Promyu, 1983; Wangpatanamongkol, 2000). It is not unusual for the founder–manager to be well respected by all employees simply because he or she owns the business, and is at the center of their well-being. However, when a 'professional' manager is hired to alleviate the owner's responsibilities, issues of hierarchy and seniority need to be carefully taken into consideration, or a lack of cooperation from subordinates, as well as business partners, could manifest itself. While it is still possible for a junior employee to rise within the organization, it will most likely occur on the basis of a reciprocal relationship of loyalty and trust with senior mentors, and it will also depend on performance and competence (Wannawibul, 1995; Thiemthanorm, 2000). Loyalty and trust are extremely important values in Thailand (Promyu, 1983; Adulyanont, 2000; Thiemthanorm, 2000; Larpadisorn, 2000; Tohtubtiang, 2000). These values are significant in relationships among employers and employees, friends and business partners (Larpadisorn, 2000). In fact they are probably the most important reason why the founder–manager cannot leave the business in other people's hands.

According to the available information, we assume that Mr Tohtubtiang does not see the need to hire a professional manager, outside his family, to run Kuang Pei San. His vast experience in the industry is significant for the company's success (Wishu-Lada, 1989). Moreover, his ability to establish connections in the industry could not be easily surpassed ('Building brand loyalty – Pum Pui and Pla Yim's success as ready-to-eat Thai food', 2000). Finally, he works well with his brothers and sisters, and they have been able to manage the company's high growth successfully (ibid., 2000). This could reflect the paternalism inherent in the Thai management style.

The Importance of Personal Relationships

Hi-Q indicated that, in the Thai business system, personal relationships play an important role in business success (Larpadisorn, 2000). Mr Wangpatanamongkol maintains a close relationship and establishes loyalty and trust with his business partners. The importance of establishing a good relationship with suppliers is emphasized (Wangpatanamongkol, 2000; Kuang Pei San Annual Report, 1999). For example, one of Mr Wangpatanamongkol's suppliers, Mr Boonsong Phuangsombat, finally became a Hi-Q shareholder (Hi-Q Food Products Co., Ltd Annual Report, 1998; Wangpatanamongkol, 2000). Kuang Pei San also stated in its 1999 Annual Report that 'the continuous supply of raw fish is significant for our business success and our close relationship with the suppliers for more than ten years could guarantee us the supply of fresh, good quality of raw materials.'

For Kuang Pei San, the use of personal relationships has brought the company tremendous success. Mr Tohtubtiang's brother-in-law had a reliable connection in the local radio network, making it easy for 'Pum Pui' and 'Pla Yim' products to reach the target consumers directly and successfully in provincial areas outside Bangkok ('Canned fish market attractive for giant consumer product company', 1987). In addition, his older brother knows M.R. Sawasdiwat personally, and their relationship has led to new recipes for canned flavored fish, which resulted in a 95 per cent market share in the canned flavored fish segment ('Canned fish market attractive for giant consumer product company', 1987; Rattanamon, 1989; Kuang Pei San Annual Report, 1996). Furthermore Mr Tohtubtiang's powerful position as the chairman of the Trang Thai Chamber of Commerce for six years has made him extremely popular and widely known in both the government and private sectors (Rattanamon, 1989). His position in the organization helps strengthen existing business relations, and could provide a lead to potential informal credit systems.

The importance of the owner's ability to use personal relationships in creating business opportunities, and thus attaining economic success, has been observed in both case studies. Friends and partners are absolutely essential in the Thai society and business system. Unsurprisingly, the success of both Hi-Q and Kuang Pei San relies on the owners' personal relationships with several groups of people, especially their suppliers. These personal relationships are, most of the time, based on loyalty, trust and connections between kinship groups, which take a substantial amount of time to build up and are exclusively reserved for a close-knit group of businessmen. If the owner leaves the firm and hires a professional manager from outside to replace him, it will be quite difficult for the professional manager to receive the same level of trust and special treatment from the owner's existing business partners.

IMPLICATIONS OF THE STUDY

Managers should expect different management practices, and thus diverse delegation patterns, to emerge from various business systems. It is important for managers to be aware of the cultural differences that affect specific management practices in each distinct business system. Management practices performed in one business system might not be applicable in others. Successful managers are those who can adapt to specific organizational needs and institutional contexts.

Moreover the findings of this study should provide some insights for entrepreneurs or owners of small businesses. In addition to being innovative, hardworking and flexible to change, an entrepreneur should realize that certain circumstances demand that entrepreneurs learn specific business norms and values, establish social networks and take advantage of personal relationships and informal systems for business to develop further. Specifically entrepreneurs of Western firms, conducting business in Southeast Asia, should keep in mind that, in the Asian business context, relationships are valued more than objective business criteria.

CONCLUDING REMARKS

Both cases highlight typical Southeast Asian small firms that have been successfully managed by the founder–managers through their rapid growth stages. Although the findings of this study pose some limitations with regard to generalizability, they point out that some cultural factors affect delegation patterns in distinct business systems. After comparing our findings with Churchill and Lewis's (1983) conceptualization of small-firm growth, we noticed that small firms are likely to conform to different stages of development in terms of economic success, from start-up to rapid growth, as stated in the growth model. However the level of delegation needed for growth might not be similar across all types of business systems. The study shows that small firms can develop successfully through rapid growth with the tight control of the owner–manager still present. It should be noted that, in some cultures and business contexts, the impact of personal relationships and networks is critical for the success of a firm. Under such circumstances, it is quite difficult for the owners of small firms to delegate responsibilities, given that the owners establish personal connections and receive mutual assistance and trust from their business partners. On one hand, limited delegation of the owners' responsibilities, such as strategic planning and decision making, may not be a major obstacle for small business growth. On the other hand, the significance of the owner's ability to take advantage of personal relationships for success creates a suitable setting for centralization of management in the Thai business context, since the firm can be more responsive and adaptive to changes in highly competitive business environments.

Any business system that relies upon personal relationships renders delegation very difficult. In a world where entrepreneurs rely heavily on networks, there is a possibility that this Southeast Asian model will have greater applicability. Differences in technical skills, which require delegation of responsibility to outside professional managers, may be less important to the small business founder–manager.

The question we propose for future research is the following: should the founder–manager of a small firm be separated from the business, both operationally and strategically, when the firm grows and develops rapidly? The importance of cultural differences cannot be overlooked in an effort to propose a widely applicable growth model for small business. We suggest that an in-depth, comparative study of the significance of delegation across different business systems should be performed. As a result, the validity and applicability of the stages-of-development framework for small business growth in a global context would be ensured.

REFERENCES

Adulyanont, Sorakol, (2000), *The Philosophy of Thai Businessmen – Secrets for Success*. Bangkok: Matichon Publishing House.

Akrasanee, Narongchai, Mingsarn Kaosa-Art, Warapatr Todhanakasem, Supachai Manusphaibool, Surasak Nananukool and Supachai Panitchpakdi (1996), *Essays on Business Management in Thailand*, Bangkok: The Industrial Finance Corporation of Thailand.

Ardichvili, Alexander, Brian Harmon, Richard N. Cardozo, Paul D. Reynolds and Mary L. Williams (1998), 'The new venture growth: functional differentiation and the need for human resource development interventions'. *Human Resource Development Quarterly*, **9**(1), 55–70.

Atkins, M.H. and J.F. Lowe (1997), 'Sizing up the small firm: UK and Australian experience', *International Small Business Journal*, **15**(3), 42–55.

Baird, Lloyd and Ilan Meshoulam (1988), 'Managing two fits of strategic human resource management', *Academy of Management Review*, **13**(1), 116–28.

Barkham, R.J. (1994), 'Entrepreneurial characteristics and the size of the new firm: a model and an econometric test', *Small Business Economics*, **6**, 117–25.

Birley, Sue and Paul Westhead (1990), 'Growth and performance contrasts between "types" of small firms', *Strategic Management Journal*, **11**, 535–57.

'Building brand loyalty – Pum Pui and Pla Yim's success as ready-to-eat Thai food' (2000), *Than Sethakit*, 18–21 June, 48.

'Canned fish market attractive for giant consumer product company' (1987), *Khukhaeng Journal*, **8**, November, 26–39.

'Canned seafood industry – an analysis' (1994), *Phujadkarn Daily*, 6 August.

Churchill, Neil C. and Virginia L. Lewis (1983), 'The five stages of small business growth', *Harvard Business Review*, May–June, **61**(3), 30–50.

Clad, James (1989), *Behind the Myth: Business, Money and Power in Southeast Asia*, Cambridge: Cambridge University Press.

Cuba, Richard C. and Gene Milbourn, Jr (1982), 'Delegating for small business success', *Entrepreneurship Theory and Practice*, **7**(2), 33–41.

Cunningham, J. Barton (1995), 'Success in corporate and entrepreneurial organizations in Singapore', *Journal of Small Business Management*, **33**(4), 80–86.

Daily, Catherine M. and Dan R. Dalton (1992), 'Financial performance of founder-managed versus professionally managed small corporations', *Journal of Small Business Management*, **30**(2), 25–34.

Davidsson, Per (1989), 'Entrepreneurship – and after? A study of growth willingness in small firms', *Journal of Business Venturing*, **4**(3), 211–26.

Department of Industrial Works, Thailand (2000), 'Factory information', retrieved on 24 July (http://www.diw.go.th/scripts/results.asp).

Dodge, H. Robert and John E. Robbins (1992), 'An empirical investigation of the organizational life cycle model for small business development and survival', *Journal of Small Business Management*, **30**(1), pp. 27–37.

Flamholtz, E.G. (1986), *How to Make the Transition from an Entrepreneurship to a Professionally Managed Firm*, San Francisco: Jossey-Bass.

Fuller-Love, Nerys and R.W. Scapens (1997), 'Performance related pay: a case study of a small business', *International Small Business Journal*, **15**(4), 48–63.

Gilmore, Thomas N. and Robert K. Kazanjian (1989), 'Clarifying decision making in high-growth ventures: the use of responsibility charting', *Journal of Business Venturing*, **4**(1), 69–83.

Hi-Q Food Products Co., Ltd. Annual Report (1998).

Hodder, Rupert (1996), *Merchant Princes of the East: Cultural Delusions, Economic Success and the Overseas Chinese in Southeast Asia*, Chichester: John Wiley & Sons Ltd.

Jones-Evans, Dylan (1996), 'Technical entrepreneurship, strategy and experience', *International Small Business Journal*, **14**(3), 15–31.

Kirkbride, Paul S. and Sara F.Y. Tang (1992), 'Management development in the Nanyang Chinese societies of South-east Asia', *Journal of Management Development*, **11**(2), 54–66.

Kuang Pei San Food Products Public Co., Ltd Annual Report, 1996.

Kuang Pei San Food Products Public Co., Ltd Annual Report, 1999.

Larpadisorn, Patthanee (2000), A personal interview on Monday 17 July.

Limlingan, V.S. (1986), *The Overseas Chinese in ASEAN: Business Strategies and Management Practices*, Pasig, Metro Manila: Vita Development Corporation.

Miles, Matthew B. and Michael A. Huberman (1994), *Qualitative Data Analysis: An Expanded Sourcebook*, 2nd edn, Thousand Oaks, CA: SAGE Publications.

Ministry of Industry, Thailand (2000), 'Definition of SMEs'.

Mount, Joan, J. Terence Zinger and George R. Forsyth (1993), 'Organizing for development in the small business', *Long Range Planning*, **26**(5), 111–20.

'Premier group offers Baht 10 million to buy Roza brand' (1996), *Krungthep Dhurakij*, 22 May, 8.

Promyu, Jaran (1983), *Understanding of Thai Society*, Bangkok: Odien Store Publishing House.

Rattanamon (1989), 'Surin Tohtubtiang – chairman of the Trang Chamber of Commerce', *Sakul Thai*, **1819**, August, 66–7, 90.

Redding, S.G. (1980), 'Cognition as an aspect of culture and its relation to management processes: an exploratory view of the Chinese case', *The Journal of Management Studies*, **17**, 127–48.

Redding, S.G. (1990), *The Spirit of Chinese Capitalism*, Berlin: de Gruyter.

Redding, S.G. and G.Y.Y. Wong (1986), 'The psychology of Chinese organisational behaviour', in M.H. Bond (ed.), *The Psychology of the Chinese People*, Hong Kong: Oxford University Press, pp. 267–95.

Rubenson, George C. and Anil K. Gupta (1996), 'The initial succession: a contingency model of founder tenure', *Entrepreneurship Theory and Practice*, **21**(2), 21–35.

Scott, Mel and Richard Bruce (1987), 'Five stages of growth in small business', *Long Range Planning*, **20**(3), 45–52.

Skinner, George W. (1957), *Chinese Society in Thailand: an Analytical History*, New York: Cornell University Press.

Smith, Norman R. and John B. Miner (1983), 'Type of entrepreneur, type of firm and managerial motivation: implications for organizational life cycle theory', *Strategic Management Journal*, **4**(4), 325–40.

Steinmetz, L.L. (1969), 'Critical stages of small business growth', *Business Horizons*, **12**, 29–34.

Tashakori, M. (1980), *Management Succession: From the Owner–Manager to the Professional Manager*, New York: Praeger.

Tellis, Winston (1997), 'Application of a case study methodology', *The Qualitative Report*, **3**(3).

Thiemthanorm, Sanyalak (2000), *The Secrets of Success – Mr. Thiem Chokewatana*, Bangkok: Mitimai Publishing House.

Tohtubtiang, Surin (2000), An interview in 'Game Gae Jon' television show on Sunday 30 July.

Wangpatanamongkol, Navanuch (2000), A personal interview on Thursday 3 August.

Wannawibul, Witit (1995), *Arts and Science of Organization and Management – The East and the West*, Bangkok: Europa Press Co., Ltd.

Whitley, Richard (1992), *Business Systems in East Asia: Firms, Markets and Societies*, London: SAGE Publications.

Willard, Gary E.; David A. Krueger and Henry R. Feeser (1992), 'In order to grow, must the founder go: a comparison of performance between founder and non-founder managed high-growth manufacturing firms', *Journal of Business Venturing*, **7**, 191–4.

Wishu-Lada. (1989), 'Surin Tohtubtiang', *Naka*, 54, October, 89–95.

Yin, Robert K. (1993), *Applications of Case Study Research*, Newbury Park, CA: SAGE Publications.

7. An international examination of potential future entrepreneurs' self-efficacy

Kent E. Neupert, Norris Krueger and Bee-Leng Chua

INTRODUCTION

The 'heart' of entrepreneurship, as Stevenson and Jarillo (1990) remind us, is an orientation toward seeking opportunities. Before one can act on an opportunity, the opportunity needs to be perceived by someone. In addition, we know that two critical antecedents drive perceptions of opportunity and intention. These are perceptions of desirability and feasibility (Krueger and Brazeal, 1994; Shapero, 1982). Perceived feasibility is often the more critical element in predicting whether a prospective opportunity is credible (Krueger and Reilly, 2000). Although an outcome may be highly desired, the perceived likelihood that the outcome can be achieved may determine whether the necessary actions are ever taken.

Entrepreneurial self-efficacy (ESE) is a construct that measures a person's belief in their own abilities to perform the various skills required to pursue a new venture creation (DeNoble et al., 1999; Krueger and Reilly, 2000). What causes someone to have such a strong belief in one's abilities to justify taking the risk of creating a new business venture? Is such a strong self-belief related to a systematic preparation for and rehearsal of the necessary actions? It is plausible that an individual's perception of opportunities for new ventures becomes increasingly credible through the process of formal business planning. In particular, is the process of preparing and presenting an intense, in-depth business plan associated with perceptions of competence to perform critical entrepreneurial tasks?

This study extends the findings of two groups of researchers interested in Bandura's (1986) powerful construct of self-efficacy and its application to entrepreneurial activities. Self-efficacy, as a construct, is based on a well-received theory and on consistent empirical results, making self-efficacy highly attractive. As Gartner (1989) suggested, entrepreneurship studies need to use explicit theory, preferably when strongly supported.

Two research groups have developed similar ways of assessing ESE. DeNoble *et al.* (1999) developed a measure of entrepreneurial self-efficacy that specifically addressed entrepreneurial tasks (as distinct from managerial tasks). This measure increases the potential explanatory power of entrepreneurial phenomena. Similarly, Krueger and Reilly (2000) have shown that self-efficacy is a critical antecedent of entrepreneurial intent. Through their application and refinement in the context of entrepreneurship, these researchers have extended Bandura's original (1986) theory.

The purpose of this study is to extend these prior findings on ESE by testing the developed measures in new settings. We do this in three stages. First, we try to replicate DeNoble *et al.*'s (1999) investigation of the relationship between ESE and entrepreneurial intention by drawing on a sample of non-US and international respondents. Second, we test the two related measures to determine whether the ESE relationships found by DeNoble *et al.* (1999), and Krueger and Reilly (2000) are applicable to participants in business plan competitions. Lastly, we examine the relationships between ESE and entrepreneurship education programs.

This study introduces two aspects that differentiate it from prior research. First, it focuses on Master of Business Administration (MBA) students participating in business plan competitions. We expect the intense and in-depth process of preparing a business plan for competition to do the following: it should enhance participants' perceptions that their venture is highly feasible, and that they possess the requisite entrepreneurial skills to launch the venture. In a sense, participating in a business plan competition can be an important first step towards creating a new business. Actually many students use these business plans, developed for the competition, to start their own businesses. By observing these competitors, we believe that these students are one step closer to becoming entrepreneurs.

The second differentiating aspect of this study is that it draws on an international sample of students to investigate the above relationships. To date, most ESE research has mainly focused on US-based samples. However this study draws on two international samples: Asian MBA students involved in an international business plan competition, and MBA students in Hong Kong. By introducing an international dimension, we hope to determine the measure's extent of applicability.

LITERATURE REVIEW

Self-efficacy

Self-efficacy is better described as perceived self-efficacy. Bandura (1986) conceived the theory as one's judgment about one's ability to execute a target behavior. The individual gradually develops his self-efficacy through prior cognitive, social and physical experiences (Gist, 1987). Therefore a successful performance of a task can alter expectations, and help to strengthen one's self-efficacy (DeNoble *et al.*, 1999), resulting in a higher level of self-efficacy, which can help an individual maintain their efforts until their initial goals are met (Gist, 1987).

Later research has shown that self-efficacy is a conceptually sound, empirically robust predictor of initiating and persisting in a wide variety of goal-directed behaviors. For example, Krueger and Dickson (1994) found that increasing self-efficacy promoted strategic risk taking by increasing the perception of opportunity (and decreasing the perception of threat). Self-efficacy judgments vary across both persons and situations, arguing that one tailors measurements to the appropriate level of specificity. In addition, research studies have differentiated between entrepreneurs and non-entrepreneurs in regard to ESE (Chen *et al.*, 1998; Golden and Cooke, 1998).

Sources of Self-efficacy

The primary source of change in self-efficacy is achieved through gaining hands-on experience. Consequently, any successful experience pertaining to high-level business planning should translate into increased self-efficacy. Alternatively, a pre-existing high level of self-efficacy may be necessary for competitors to engage in the competition. Bandura (1995) offers empirical evidence for a 'virtuous cycle': that both conditions are likely to be true, as increasing self-efficacy leads to initiating and achieving higher goals, which then leads to higher self-efficacy. Nevertheless the experience of developing and presenting a business plan could have either an encouraging or a reinforcing effect. This relationship has been conceptualized as a self-fulfilling prophecy, also known as the Pygmalion effect (Eden, 1992).

Individual differences play a role in self-efficacy judgments. For example, optimistic causal attributions encourage increases in self-efficacy (Krueger and Reilly, 2000). Previous experiences often anchor judgments of self-efficacy, thus entrepreneurial training and experiences can strongly influence such judgments (Krueger, 1993). Therefore individuals may already possess strong levels of self-efficacy, thanks to their prior experience in creating new business ventures.

Hamel and Prahalad (1994) argue that, for organizations to identify viable new opportunities, senior managers must consider potential developments both outside the organization and beyond the present. Moreover they argue that an increased awareness of external and future possibilities enhances management's perceptions of viable opportunities.

This raises one final important issue for this research. Business planning for the purpose of a business plan competition, just as with non-student (that is, senior management) planners, is a team-based process. Two measures of self-efficacy should be considered. Individual efficacy should be important, but Bandura would caution that the research should also consider perceptions of collective efficacy (Bandura, 1986, 1995; Krueger and Brazeal, 1994). Similarly team climate could prove important to both types of self-efficacy.

Measurement Issues

Self-efficacy is situation-specific. While one could argue for a more global measure of 'entrepreneurial' self-efficacy that includes managerial tasks, we strictly focus on the entrepreneurial aspects. DeNoble *et al.* (1999) developed a measure of ESE that distinguished six dimensions of entrepreneurial skills: risk and uncertainty management; innovation and product development; interpersonal and networking management; opportunity recognition; procurement and allocation of critical resources; and development and maintenance of an innovative work environment. Through confirmatory factor analyses and subsequent testing, they determined a positive and significant relationship between entrepreneurial intention and preparation for starting a business. In this study, we extend DeNoble *et al.*'s (1999) instrument to two international (non-US) samples of would-be entrepreneurs. By doing this, we hope to extend the ability to generalize the six dimensions. Moreover we hope to test the applicability of the entrepreneurial self-efficacy measure to business plan competition participants.

In testing formal models of entrepreneurial intentions, Krueger and Reilly (2000) found that self-efficacy is a critical antecedent of intentions. That is, intentions are predicted, not just explained, by perceptions that the prospective course of action (for example, a venture) is desirable and feasible. In turn, perceptions of feasibility were primarily determined by self-efficacy, as predicted by the theory (Shapero, 1982; Krueger and Brazeal, 1994).

Finally, as with any process phenomenon, intentions should be studied prospectively (pre-behavior) not retrospectively. Retrospective accounts (especially of causality) are potentially subject to hindsight and other biases. Researchers should, therefore, draw on subjects who are facing imminent business decisions (for example, 'Should we launch this venture?').

METHODOLOGY

Participants

Two sets of participants were involved in the study. One group comprised participants in a business plan competition, and the other group was made up of Master of Business Administration (MBA) students.

Business plan competitors

Asia Moot Corp© is an international business plan competition held each year in Hong Kong since 1998. Participants are invited from 13 to 15 different universities across Asia. As part of the competition, student teams present their business plans before panels of judges. The business plans developed by the students are for new business start-ups. The plans are fully developed, including documents that describe the product or service, the management team and the funding requirements for launching the business venture. The judges in Asia Moot Corp© represent international venture capitalists, international entrepreneurs and senior business managers. In most case the teams present at the competition have already competed in their university for the privilege of competing in the pan-Asia competition. They represent many countries, including China, India, Japan, Korea, the Philippines, Singapore, Taiwan and Thailand.

A total of 52 participants, representing 13 universities in eight Asian countries, participated in the study. As mentioned above, all participants were competing in the international business plan competition, held in March 2000. Of the participants, 88 per cent were MBA students, while 7.8 per cent were undergraduates and 3.9 per cent were 'others'. The mean age of the participants was 27.8 years, with the standard deviation being 3.9 years. As for gender, 59 per cent of the participants were male, and 41 per cent were female.

For the participants, the mean number of years of full-time work experience was 4.7. Approximately 35 per cent had experience in marketing, 18.4 per cent in systems design and development, 15.8 per cent in administration, 10.5 per cent in production and the remaining 20.3 per cent had experience in other areas. While 80.4 per cent lived in the country where they were born, 52.9 per cent had lived in another country for more than three months and 45.1 per cent had worked in a country other than where they were born.

MBA students

Our second sample was drawn from MBA students in a Hong Kong university. The university's MBA program is AACSB/IAME accredited, and consistently ranks in the top five MBA programs in Asia. The university does not have an entrepreneurship major for MBA students; however, it offers related courses.

A total of 53 MBA students participated in the study. The mean age of the participants was 28.2 years, with a standard deviation of 3.2 years. Of the respondents, 60 per cent were male, 40 per cent female. Overall their mean amount of full-time work experience was 5.7 years. Slightly more than 32 per cent had work experience in administration, 13.3 per cent in systems design and development, 11.3 per cent in marketing, 9.3 per cent in sales, 5.7 per cent in human resources, 3.8 per cent in product design and development, 1.9 per cent in production, and the remaining had work experience in 'other' fields. Over 90 per cent lived and worked in the country in which they were born, more than 41 per cent had lived in another country for more than three months, and almost 38 per cent had worked in a foreign country.

Measures

This study draws on the entrepreneurial self-efficacy measure developed by DeNoble *et al.* (1999). This measure utilizes 35 items, which are rated on a five-point scale, ranging from 'strongly disagree' to 'strongly agree', and are based on the general question, 'How capable do you believe you are in performing each of the following tasks?' All the measures have been successfully applied in previous studies, including DeNoble *et al.* (1999).

In addition, we measured the participants' intentions to start their own business by using a three-item scale developed by Krueger and Reilly (2000). These items are the following questions: 'To what extent have you considered starting your own business?', 'To what extent have you prepared to start your own business?', and 'How likely is it that you are going to start your own business in the next five years?' All three items are measured on a five-point scale, ranging from 'extremely unlikely' to 'extremely likely'. The participants were also asked how many hours per week they had spent on activities related to starting their own business. Additionally we asked the participants several questions regarding the amount of time they would typically spend thinking about various issues and time frames. Lastly we inquired about their previous experience in starting their own business, and whether anyone in their family had their own business.

Given that we were interested in the role of participation in the business plan competition, we asked the participants several questions concerning their universities' entrepreneurship programs, the support they received and their business plan training (that is, writing). We also asked several questions regarding the membership of the business plan teams, as well as members' backgrounds, such as their previous work experience and international exposure.

Methodology

T-tests in the SAS system were employed to assess differences between competitors and non-competitors. Correlation analysis was employed to assess the association between ESE and the other variables of interest.

RESULTS AND FINDINGS

Entrepreneurial Self-efficacy

As stated earlier, one of our goals was to extend the ESE measures developed by DeNoble *et al.* (1999) and Krueger and Reilly (2000) by testing each of them with two different samples: one sample consisting of non-US MBA students and the other sample made up of MBA students participating in an international business plan competition. DeNoble *et al.* (1999) reported that their ESE measures had six dimensions: risk and uncertainty management; innovation and product development; interpersonal and networking management; opportunity recognition; procurement and allocation of critical resources; and development and maintenance of an innovative work environment. This six-factor structure was supported through confirmatory factor analysis.

When we tested the DeNoble *et al.* (1999) ESE measure, we were unable to identify the above six factors. In contrast, the results of our study indicate that the ESE is a unidimensional measure. However, while the measure did not exhibit multiple distinct factors, the overall measure was highly reliable, with an overall Cronbach's alpha of 0.93. (The business plan competition sample had a Cronbach's alpha of 0.94, while the MBA students had a Cronbach's alpha of 0.92.) This proved to be an encouraging result as it demonstrated that the ESE concept would hold in different domains. The differences between the sample of students participating in the business plan competition and the non-competing MBA students were also noted in our results, and are discussed below.

The T-tests conducted yielded several interesting differences between the sample of students in the business plan competition and the sample of MBAs not involved in the competition. We found a significant difference (at $p < 0.005$) between these two groups' ESEs. Students participating in business plan competitions averaged an overall self-efficacy score of 136.7, while non-participating MBAs averaged an overall score of 128.2. It should not be surprising that business plan competition participants have a higher level of self-efficacy than those who do not compete. However, our goal here is not to determine whether the higher self-efficacy score is the cause or the result of the participation in a business plan competition. Longitudinal analysis would be useful in exploring this issue further.

The two groups provided significantly different (at $p < 0.05$) responses when asked about their individual beliefs concerning their ability to perform certain tasks. The tasks included the ability to

- originate new ideas,
- foresee new market opportunities for new products and services,

- recruit and train key employees,
- discover new ways to improve existing products,
- develop relationships with key people, such as those with ties to capital sources,
- react quickly to take advantage of business opportunities,
- create an autonomous work environment,
- develop a well-conceived plan for presentation to investors,
- convince others to join me in pursuit of my vision.

Arguably these tasks are important to an entrepreneur's success. The above results may help to distinguish entrepreneurs from non-entrepreneurs. This suggests that it might be useful to explore item analyses further.

Furthermore we discovered a difference between the groups' intentions in starting their own business. Our findings show that business plan competitors had higher scores than non-competitors ($p < 0.0001$). In addition, we created a composite measure of intent and, once again, the business plan competitors had higher scores (at $p < 0.0001$). Although we do not know the chain of causal relations, a pertinent question must be raised: does being involved in a business result in a higher level of intent to start one's own business, or do those who intend to start a business use the competition as a way to perfect their business plan and presentation?

As one might expect, higher ESE was positively correlated with two variables: age and greater work experience. The average age of the respondents was 27.8 years and the average working experience was 4.72 years. Also the extent of internationalization of the team's planned markets was positively correlated with the extent of the participants' international backgrounds. In other words, the more international experience the participants possessed, the more inclined they were to aim at international markets. However ESE was not associated with the extent of internationalization of a student's background. Thus more (or less) international experience did not influence self-efficacy. We have no reason to expect such an association, since there are no ESE items that address global ventures. Similarly self-efficacy was not associated with the extent of internationalization of the venture's anticipated markets. Combined, these findings suggest we should consider developing items or a separate measure of ESE for global ventures.

Aspects of Entrepreneurship Education

Other issues we explored were the characteristics of the various MBA programs being undertaken by the students who participated in the competition. The programs were examined in order to assess the breadth of each university's entrepreneurship education program. The programs contained all or some of the following features: formal coursework, seminars and workshops, project supervision by faculty members, a specific course and project in business plan writing, interaction and information sharing with successful entrepreneurs and experienced venture capitalists, and financial support to take part in the business plan competition. We were interested in knowing whether any, or all, of these provisions had an impact on the respondents' ESEs.

The aspects of the programs that were found to be significant included contact with entrepreneurs (at $p < 0.08$), the originator of the product or service being the leader of the team (at $p < 0.04$), the originator of the product or service being a key member of the team (at $p < 0.08$) and the originator of the product or service being an active member of the team (at $p < 0.003$).

DISCUSSION

Entrepreneurial Self-efficacy

As part of the competition, the students created business plans for new start-up ventures and presented them before a panel of judges, made up of entrepreneurs, venture capital providers and other business managers. The process simulates the experiences of entrepreneurs who develop business plans and seek funding for their ideas. While we were not able to confirm the six factors noted by DeNoble *et al.* (1999), we did find the unidimensional ESE instrument reliable for use with this sample of 'budding entrepreneurs'.

Overall we were able to accomplish the goals of the study, one of which was to extend the ESE measures developed by DeNoble *et al.* (1999) and Krueger and Reilly (2000), by testing them in different settings. In particular, we chose a sample of non-US MBA students to see whether the measures could be applied in an international setting. We found the instrument to be highly reliable for the non-US sample. As in DeNoble *et al.* (1999) and Krueger and Reilly's (2000) results, we discovered that students' involvement in academic entrepreneurial training was positively associated with higher levels of perceived self-efficacy than those without the academic experience. As mentioned earlier, we do not know which comes first, the training or the ESE. However we know this relationship seems to hold for students, regardless of their geographic location.

In applying the ESE measures developed by Krueger and Reilly (2000) in this non-US setting, we were able to confirm that the same relationships that distinguished entrepreneurial self-efficacy in the USA would also be present in Asia. This reinforces the appropriateness of using ESE as a measure of entrepreneurial orientation. Therefore we were able to accomplish our goal of extending the ESE measures to entrepreneurs in different national or geographic settings.

We also tested the ESE measures by drawing on an international sample of business plan competitors, with the intention of extending the earlier work on entrepreneurship students.[1] This is, however, the first study to employ ESE measures in a business plan competition setting. Our results indicate that the measure is applicable in such settings. Competitions, such as the one we examined, are key components of many well-regarded entrepreneurship programs. Competitions such as those offered by the University of Texas-Austin, MIT, the University of Oregon, San Diego State University and others provide high-visibility arenas for entrepreneurship students to showcase their new venture start-up skills and fund their business ideas. In essence, they are 'real-life' new venture experiences for students.

The Role of Entrepreneurship Education

Among the education program questions, the amount of contact that entrepreneurs or venture capitalists had with the program was significantly correlated with high ESE among the respondents. This finding strongly suggests that programs which provided the students with opportunities to meet and interact with entrepreneurs and venture capitalists greatly contributed to the students' level of confidence and determination to act on their entrepreneurial goals. During the contact periods, entrepreneurs usually shared their experiences of starting their business, their successes and failures, as well as how they had dealt with adversity and difficulties. The exposure to entrepreneurs who had experienced failures, but ultimately succeeded, seems to provide powerful examples for nascent entrepreneurs. Through the sharing of information and answering of questions, students are able to gain awareness and an understanding of what they would have to go through to become an entrepreneur. Venture capitalists provide the students with useful information, such as what they look for in a business plan in order to fund it, and the entrepreneurial qualities and skills they regard as valuable. In seeking funds for their venture, students learn about what investors expect of them. In effect, this information enables them to prepare a business plan that contains relevant information for the investors to make a sound decision.

In addition we found that ESE was significantly correlated with the originator of the venture occupying a key role in the business plan team. This finding suggests that universities which provide entrepreneurship education also stimulate individuals to conceive original business venture ideas. As a result, these individuals would play a lead role in the entrepreneurial teams.

We also wanted to know if there were any differences in ESE between the teams who developed the venture idea themselves and teams who were helping a third party commercialize its idea or technology. (Teams usually develop the idea for their business plan in one of two ways: either the team conceives the idea and builds the plan around it, or they use someone else's idea and seek to commercialize it.) In the former case, the idea originator is actively involved in the development of the business plan and the related team activities; in the latter case, the idea initiator may or may not join the team, and may not actively participate in developing the business plan.

In our study, respondents who were part of teams actively involving the venture idea originators were found to be more confident in their ability to implement their business plan successfully. This suggests that, while entrepreneurship education programs should allow students to employ different start-up models, it is important to create an environment that encourages students to be the innovators of their venture ideas. This in turn helps build a higher sense of entrepreneurial self-efficacy in the students.

High levels of ESE were correlated with respondents reporting a large amount of time spent on activities that prepared them to start their own business. The intensity of work involved in preparing their business plans contributed to their sense of ESE. This is consistent with earlier findings that effort spent on an activity contributed to one's perceived self-efficacy regarding the activity.

High ESE was also significantly correlated with items that gauged the time within which respondents intend to start their own business. The highest significant level was found in the response item 'likely to start own business in next five years'. This is quite plausible, as the respondents were currently enrolled in an MBA program and many had full-time jobs. Five years would be an adequate time frame for individuals to complete their studies, as well as gain additional business experience or even prepare themselves to resign from their current occupations before setting out as entrepreneurs.

IMPLICATIONS

Implications for Management Researchers

This study has shown that the entrepreneurial self-efficacy measures developed by DeNoble *et al.* (1999) and Krueger and Reilly (2000) have applicability in geographic settings beyond the USA. Our findings provide an early step in developing a potentially universal measure of ESE. In particular, we found strong evidence for the reliability and validity of the DeNoble *et al.* (1999) instrument as a measure of entrepreneurial self-efficacy. The scale exhibited a Cronbach's alpha from 0.92 to 0.94, suggesting clear evidence of scale reliability. It also supports the scale being unidimensional, despite the original authors finding some evidence for subscales.

The significantly higher ESE scores for business plan competitors (relative to non-competitors), along with the significant correlations between ESE and preparations for and the intentions to start a business, as well as prior exposure to entrepreneurial activity (for example, parental self-employment, personal self-employment), all suggest the validity of the ESE instrument in this domain and for these samples in this study. These findings support the earlier work of Krueger and Reilly (2000). Taken as a whole, this study should enable management researchers to build on earlier research by applying these measures in different contexts. As advocated by Gartner (1989), entrepreneurship research needs to use robustly supported explicit theory. We hope that this study contributes to further development of entrepreneurship theory.

Implications for Educators

This study has several implications for those involved in entrepreneurship education. First, a strong relationship exists between students' perceived capability for new venture success and their experience in business plan competitions. While most entrepreneurship programs provide training in marketing, accounting, management and finance, in the context of starting a new venture, the results of this study indicate that developing a business plan, and having it evaluated by experienced outsiders, is an extremely valuable tool for entrepreneurship students in creating and stimulating an attitude for success. The process of working in a team, to get the new business idea to a fundable state, takes the students through the typical steps carried out by real-world entrepreneurs. In essence, it creates a learning process close to the 'real thing', without actually starting the business. Not surprisingly many teams who prepare for and compete in business plan competitions go on to start their own new ventures, regardless of whether they win the competition or not. Therefore educators should, whenever possible, encourage their students to enter business plan competitions. Institutional support of competition participation can be very useful in helping students to develop their entrepreneurial skills.

This study also noted a significant relationship between ESE and having contact with entrepreneurs and venture capital providers. Indications are as follows: the more interaction students have with entrepreneurs and other industry players, the stronger their belief in their skills and capabilities as entrepreneurs. If an academic program's goal is to create successful entrepreneurs, it is in the best interest of the educators to reach out to the local business community and bring their experience into the classroom. This study confirms that students benefit from exposure to various experiences brought into the classroom.

Regarding team dynamics, we found evidence to suggest that teams which actively include the venture idea originator have higher levels of ESE than those that do not. This suggests we should consider having new venture teams work directly with the idea originator as part of the business plan team, rather than taking an idea off the shelf and attempting to commercialize it. Several universities try to create a tie between business and engineering students, as a way to cross-fertilize. This study suggests it may be worthwhile to do so, especially if the idea generator is actively involved in the project.

Implications for Entrepreneurship Students

It may be fair to assume that students pursue entrepreneurship studies in order to become successful entrepreneurs. If so, they should seek programs which provide the highest value added, in order to prepare for the trials and tribulations of entrepreneurship. Developing a strong belief in one's ability to become successful can be a valuable asset to an entrepreneur. Participating in programs that enable the development of such a belief may help students to become successful entrepreneurs.

This study suggests there are several features that can enhance an academic program to encourage self-belief and the development of the necessary skills and capabilities to be a successful entrepreneur, such as participating in business plan competitions. Exploiting the competition process can be a valuable tool for launching a new business venture. By executing the idea generation process, market analysis, trademark and patent searches, and financial analysis, which ultimately results in creating a comprehensive business plan, students obtain the necessary hands-on experience for launching their own business. In fact most of the contending business plans are fully capable of becoming viable new ventures, as long as the right management team exists to take the idea forward. Therefore students should participate in business plan competitions and, in turn, entrepreneurship programs should encourage and support this effort.

An additional suggestion, which would enhance an entrepreneurship program, is the inclusion of entrepreneurs and venture capital industry participants in the program. Granting students the opportunity to communicate with such individuals can provide valuable examples of what it entails to be a successful entrepreneur. By sharing their experiences and advice with the students, entrepreneurs can provide students with an in-depth look at their way of life. This opportunity should allow students to develop a realistic view, which would in turn better prepare them for the development of their new venture.

DIRECTIONS FOR THE FUTURE

Measurement Issues

This study is a first step in extending current ESE to new areas and settings. Additional comparative data could be collected from business plan competitors in the USA and other countries, as well as data for non-business plan competition students in the USA and Asia. This will permit us to compare and contrast across countries of origin, as well as between business plan competitors and non-competitors.

Also comparative data should be gathered from non-student samples (for example, adults in NxLevel™ classes and so on) to test the ESE measures outside an academic setting. While research on intentions should be prospective (not retrospective) in nature, age and other factors may confound findings and interpretations. Yet, purposively sampling subjects who face career decisions (including the possible choice of self-employment) can provide additional understanding of the topic.

Longitudinal analysis would provide further insight into the way self-efficacy judgments change throughout the entire process, from planning and preparation to the actual competition. Collecting data at various points, such as at the beginning, during and at the end of the competition, could provide added insight into the process of developing self-efficacy in entrepreneurial activities.

Other cognitive phenomena, such as scripts, schemata and cognitive maps, could also be compared. Similarly other predictors of opportunity perception, such as future orientation, should be tested. Furthermore, in keeping with the cross-national nature of this study, it would make sense eventually to develop self-efficacy items specifically dealing with international issues. Such items could address the factors that foster an international orientation in entrepreneurs.

Team Dynamics

Team dynamics could prove to be a significant aspect of this research stream. Since most business plan competitions are performed in teams, understanding the interactions between team members can provide further insight into what distinguishes successful teams from unsuccessful teams. Accordingly team performance data should add further evidence to support (or disconfirm) the relationships identified above. In particular, a significant positive correlation between ESE and performance would provide additional evidence for the scale's reliability. Similarly, as the business plans are team-oriented, we should explore measures of collective efficacy and of team climate.

Other key implications suggest other avenues to pursue for future research. For example, the significant positive correlation between the perceived centrality of the team's idea originator and ESE is most intriguing. If replicated, it would suggest that team members' self-efficacy would be enhanced by the presence of the idea generator. By extension, involving lead entrepreneurs with student teams should enhance their ESE. This could have important implications for both team management and team performance.

CONCLUSION

Entrepreneurial self-efficacy (ESE) is a construct that measures a person's belief in their own abilities to perform the various skills required to pursue the creation of a new venture (DeNoble *et al.*, 1999; Krueger and Reilly, 2000). Research indicates that one's perception of opportunities for new ventures can become increasingly credible through the process of formal business planning. In this study we extend the findings of earlier researchers, including Bandura's construct of self-efficacy, and its application, to entrepreneurial activities.

We set out to extend prior research on ESE by testing developed measures in new settings and contexts. We tried to replicate DeNoble *et al.*'s (1999) study regarding the relationship between ESE and entrepreneurial intention by drawing on a sample of non-US and international respondents. Our findings supported those of earlier researchers. Moreover we tested DeNoble *et al.* (1999), and Krueger and Reilly's (2000) ESE measures for their applicability to participants in business plan competitions and found them to be generally appropriate. In addition we examined the relationship between ESE and entrepreneurship education programs.

In summary, this study introduced two differentiating aspects. One aspect involved MBA students participating in business plan competitions. This was the first study to address the role of ESE in business plan competitions, and we found that entering such events led to a stronger belief in one's entrepreneurial abilities. The other aspect is that we used an international sample of students to investigate these relationships. Previous studies relied on domestic samples. By introducing an international dimension, we hoped to extend the applicability of ESE measures to international settings.

NOTES

1. DeNoble *et al.* (1999) and Krueger and Reilly (2000) have tested ESE by drawing on entrepreneurship students.

REFERENCES

Bandura, A. (1986), 'The social foundations of thought & action', reprinted in A. Bandura (ed.), *The Social Foundations of Thought & Action*, Englewood Cliffs, NJ: Prentice-Hall.

Bandura, A. (1995), 'Exercise of personal and collective efficacy in changing societies', reprinted in A. Bandura (ed.), *Self-Efficacy in Changing Societies*, New York: Cambridge University Press.

Begley, T.M. and D.P. Boyd (1987), 'Psychological characteristics associated with performance in entrepreneurial firms and smaller businesses', *Journal of Business Venturing*, **2**, 79–93.

Chen, C., P. Greene and A. Crick (1998), 'Does entrepreneurial self-efficacy distinguish entrepreneurs from managers?', *Journal of Business Venturing*, **13** (4), 295–316.

DeNoble, A., D. Jung and S. Ehrlich (1999), 'Initiating new ventures: the role of entrepreneurial self-efficacy', paper presented at the Babson Research Conference, Babson College, Boston, MA.

Eden, D. (1992), 'Leadership and expectations', *Leadership Quarterly*, **3**, 271–305.

Gartner, W.B. (1989), 'Some suggestions for research on entrepreneurial traits and characteristics', *Entrepreneurship Theory and Practice*, **14** (3), 27–37.

Gist, M. (1987), 'Self-efficacy: implications for organizational behavior and human resource management', *Academy of Management Journal*, **12**, 472–85.

Golden, P. and D. Cooke (1998), '*Entrepreneurial self-efficacy: some antecedents and outcomes*', paper presented at the National Academy of Management meeting, San Diego, CA, August.

Hamel, G. and C.K. Prahalad (1994), *Competing for the Future*, Boston: Harvard Press.

Krueger, N.F. (1993), 'The impact of prior entrepreneurial exposure on perceptions of new venture feasibility and desirability', *Entrepreneurship: Theory and Practice*, **18** (1), 5–21.

Krueger, N.F. and D. Brazeal (1994), 'Entrepreneurial potential and potential entrepreneurs', *Entrepreneurship: Theory and Practice*, **18** (3), 91–104.

Krueger, N.F. and P. Dickson (1994), 'How believing in ourselves: increases risk-taking: perceived self-efficacy and opportunity recognition', *Decision Sciences*, **25** (3), 385–401.

Krueger, N.F. and M.D. Reilly, (2000), 'Competing models of entrepreneurial self-efficacy', *Journal of Business Venturing*, **15** (5/6), 411–33.

Shapero, A. (1982), 'Some social dimensions of entrepreneurship', paper presented at the Babson Research Conference, Baylor University, Waco, TX, June.

Spence, J.T. (1985), 'Achievement U.S. style: the rewards and costs of individualism', *American Psychologist*, **40**, 1285–95.

Stevenson, H. and J.C. Jarillo (1990), 'A paradigm of entrepreneurship', *Strategic Management Journal*, **11**, 17–27.

PART III

High technology and strategy

8. The Internet and SME exporting: Canadian success stories

Philip Rosson

Despite all the attention that Internet companies get these days, it's just a transitory phase, because in five years time there won't be any Internet companies – they'll all be Internet companies. (Andy Groves, Intel chairman)

While every ecommerce Website can make its offerings globally accessible, very few sites know how to serve foreign customers well. In a recent study, Forrester Research found that 46 percent of all orders placed by people living outside the United States went unfilled due to process failures. (Business 2.0)

These two quotations provide the logic for this chapter. Although the Internet has become accepted as a tool of business, relatively few companies have thought carefully about how it might be used to capture export business. The chapter focuses on this matter and describes how ten small and medium-sized businesses (SMEs) in Canada have successfully employed Internet technology to expand their international reach. Company profiles are provided, as well as a summary of the lessons drawn from their experiences. First, however, we present background material on Internet usage by SMEs, and on the Internet and exporting.

INTRODUCTION

The Internet has experienced extraordinary growth in a few years. One measure is that the number of computer hosts increased from 4.9 million in January 1995 to over 43 million four years later (Hanson, 2000). Forecasts about Internet growth continue to be bullish. Forrester Research (2000) estimates that e-commerce will account for 8.6 per cent of worldwide sales of goods and services in 2004 (approaching US$5 trillion), with a dramatic shift of both 'business to business' (B2B) and 'business to consumer' (B2C) business to the Internet. Much of the early development and growth of Internet-based business took place in the United States. Other nations are poised to experience fast growth in e-commerce: Canada lags the USA by about 18 months, with the UK and Germany (24 months) and Japan, France and Italy (48 months) further behind. Just as certain nations have made early headway in e-commerce, the same is true for industries. Computing and electronics were the first to embrace the potential offered by the Internet. Other industries with high Internet penetration levels are aerospace, telecommunications and automobiles (*The Economist*, 1999).The extent to which companies are Internet-enabled varies within, as well as across, industries. Much depends on the competitive situation facing each company but, as the above quotations suggest, no company can afford to ignore the emerging competitive and economic space facilitated by the Internet.

The majority of business owners and managers recognize that e-commerce is not a passing fad. A survey of 250 large and medium-sized US companies, for example, revealed that 58 per cent of corporate decision makers considered the World Wide Web (WWW) to be important or very important to their business strategy. A large majority reported that marketing and the generation of sales were key objectives for their websites, with somewhat fewer endorsing the goal of cost cutting. However a revealing statistic is that the websites of three-quarters of those surveyed did not support online transactions or tie-in to customer or supplier databases (ibid.). Clearly, most large companies and SMEs have some way to go before they will be able to fully exploit e-commerce opportunities.

THE INTERNET AND SMEs

The Internet is seen as creating significant opportunities for SMEs but, at the same time, presenting a set of fresh challenges. E-commerce gives a chance for SMEs to offset their traditional weaknesses in areas such as gaining access to new markets, undertaking research and promoting themselves internationally. At the same time, the fixed cost of adopting new technologies is a bigger burden for SMEs than for others. Further, SMEs are probably more susceptible to security and liability problems that might arise out of e-commerce (OECD, 1998). A number of research studies provide a snapshot of where SMEs currently stand in relation to e-commerce.

In the USA, a useful review of adoption and use of the Internet by SMEs is found in a 1999 report of the Office of Advocacy, US Small Business Administration. Although the statistics vary across the studies cited, the overall picture is clear. The number of SMEs with access to the Internet is growing quite rapidly, with e-mail, research and the provision of company/product/service information dominant. When SMEs operate a website (20–35 per cent of cases), the overwhelming reason for this is the ability to reach new and potential customers (SBA, July 1999). Relatively few SMEs carry out business transactions from their websites. This results from uncertainty, limited resources and a general lack of information technology expertise among smaller firms. The emergence of a new category of company – e-business service providers – will help overcome these problems and push SMEs' e-commerce involvement to 50 per cent by 2004 (Pastore, 2000).

Canadian Federation of Independent Business research shows that SMEs in Canada have keenly embraced the Internet as a business tool. In the first half of 1999, 61 per cent of business owners were connected to the Internet, which is almost double the number from two years before. SMEs principally use the Internet for e-mail and obtaining business information (more than 80 per cent each). More sophisticated usage of the Internet is at a lower level: 18 per cent of SMEs report employing a website for outbound marketing and communications, whereas financial transactions are conducted via the Internet by 24 to 31 per cent of SMEs, with larger companies more active (CFIB, 1999).[1] A second Canadian study reports higher levels of website operation (52 per cent) among SMEs. However, consistent with other research, websites were found primarily to be informational in nature, with product and service information, product/service catalogues and search engines as the most common features. The level of e-commerce activity reported by SMEs parallels that elsewhere. In the prior six months, 28 per cent of SMEs had purchased, and 15 per cent sold, products or services over the Internet (International Data Corporation, 1999).

Research on SMEs' adoption and usage of the Internet in the UK and Asia–Pacific nations both confirms and extends other studies. In the UK, for example, SMEs state that the largest current and planned use of the Internet is for communicating with customers, followed by marketing, market research, communicating with suppliers and sourcing products/services. Security continues to be a concern for SMEs in the UK, as is potential competition from new entrants, price visibility and transparency. Emerging concerns for some companies include tax and legal issues, and multiple currencies exposure (KPMG, 1999b).

An Asia Pacific Economic Cooperation (APEC) study, based on fieldwork conducted in the 21 member nations of this organization, provides a broader sense of e-commerce and SMEs. The most significant potential benefits of e-commerce arising out of the research were the following:

- improved customer service and information exchange, which is of greatest importance for SMEs;
- enhancing the company image and improving its competitive position, which is very important;
- using e-commerce to reach international markets, important for some but not all firms;

- increasing revenue and reducing costs through e-commerce channels, of moderate overall importance.

The most significant barriers to the adoption of e-commerce by SMEs in APEC nations were as follows:

- low use of e-commerce by customers and suppliers;
- concerns about security aspects of e-commerce;
- concerns about legal and liability issues;
- high costs of computer and networking technologies;
- limited knowledge of e-business models and technologies;
- uncertainty about the benefits of e-commerce for the company;
- uncertain quality of telecommunications services for e-commerce.

(PriceWaterhouseCoopers, 1999)

Several models of Internet technology capability have been proposed. These reflect an expectation that companies will move from relatively simple use of the Internet to higher levels of e-commerce capability and activity (Yankee Group, 1998; von Goeler, 1998; Ng *et al.*, 1998). A typical model is described below:

Level 1   SMEs with very basic or no online capabilities,
Level 2   SMEs with a website but no advanced capabilities,
Level 3   SMEs able to take orders and provide customer service on their website,
Level 4   SMEs able to complete transactions and receive payments on their website.   (PricewaterhouseCoopers, 1999)

E-commerce is advancing so rapidly that inclusion of a Level 5 is probably justified. This would reflect the fact that some companies are now fully automated, with customer purchases linked into back-end systems, including procurement and inventory control. However most companies, large, medium and small, have yet to progress beyond Level 3 (KPMG, 1999a).

THE INTERNET AND EXPORTING

Although much is made of the market expansion possibilities provided by the Internet, and many companies are realizing international sales in this manner, the literature dealing with Internet-based exporting is very limited (Hamill and Gregory, 1997). Despite this situation, a number of important topics are reviewed in this section and links are made to relevant works. The discussion covers Internet export fundamentals, exporter type and decisions, localization efforts and global e-business developments. Before we turn to these topics, three important general points are noted (Samiee, 1998).

First, it is noteworthy that the sustainable competitive advantage of a company cannot be derived simply from its connection to the Internet or the presence of a website. The competitive advantage of a company usually results from its product, service or process know-how, and its ability to satisfy the needs of chosen customer groups. The skillful deployment of technology often enhances competitive advantage but does not create advantage in its own right. This is true for both domestic and export marketing activities.

Second, non-exporters cannot expect to become exporters overnight because of a website. However, once the appropriate export infrastructure is in place, and a strategy has been developed, a website can certainly prove helpful. Third, some export markets will not yield much business for exporters in the near term, since structural impediments to the use of Internet technology, such as telecommunications systems, computer usage levels and government regulations, will restrict access and usage by intermediate and final users.

Internet Export Fundamentals

SMEs can use the Internet to support their export operations in three main ways:[2] (a) as a global marketing tool, (b) as a cost-efficient transaction medium, and (c) as a customer care tool. One advantage of the Internet, as a marketing tool, is its availability for 24 hours a day in all time zones, which gives companies an uninterrupted global presence. At the same time, through the adaptation of information to local visitor needs (see below), it provides an opportunity for the exporter to be local in many markets. The Internet is a medium for communication, and website visitors interact with the information provided. This provides many opportunities for the exporter to learn more about the interests of visitors, to collect specific information directly and to involve the visitor in a continuing dialogue. Websites are an efficient and low-cost way for disseminating substantial amounts of information that is up-to-date and easy-to-use material. Such comprehensive information will attract the interest of competitors, as well as prospective buyers, but access to some areas of the site can be password restricted.

The Internet is also a medium for carrying out transactions. Critical questions to be dealt with here include ordering procedures (direct or through resellers), pricing transparency, delivery options, electronic payment methods and security. E-commerce provides for and encourages direct interaction between sellers and buyers, which can cause channel conflict when intermediaries have historically been involved in marketing. Intermediaries, such as foreign agents and distributors, retain their position in marketing channels when they provide services that are valued. In some instances, they offer a local servicing capability, whereas, in other cases, they help gain access to difficult-to-reach buyers. The advent of the Internet is likely to challenge the position of some intermediaries but it would be wrong to assume that e-commerce marks the end of all resellers (or disintermediation). Price information is found on many websites, which makes it easier for competitors to collect intelligence. In addition it creates a more difficult situation for exporters whose prices vary significantly on a market-by-market or customer-by-customer basis. Password protected areas, once again, provide a vehicle for individual pricing arrangements.

The fulfillment and delivery of orders is another question meriting serious attention. Internet technology permits SMEs to offer their products and services on a world stage. A downside of such exposure is the creation of more interest than can be satisfied, as well as receipt of inquiries from locations the company cannot effectively supply. Exporters should, therefore, decide which markets they can realistically pursue, and supply these either directly or through a third-party fulfillment company. Tracking and tracing of orders is increasingly a feature demanded by customers. Export transactions run the gamut from orders that must be pre-paid, through sales on letter of credit, to sales on account. Companies that are new to exporting tend to be understandably nervous about extending credit to unknown buyers in distant places. Most B2B export transactions involve electronic forms of payment. B2C transactions are also moving in this direction, although many websites still do not permit purchases to be consummated on-line. To some degree, this is a result of lingering doubts many buyers have about providing credit and personal information over the Internet, as well as a lack of familiarity with the supplying company. Many websites attempt to put these fears to rest by incorporating sections that speak to the security arrangements made by the company in question. Endorsements by valued third-party organizations also help improve buyer confidence.

The Internet readily lends itself to customer care activities. A variety of approaches are taken here, including developing website content that will help buyers install and use the product, providing information on new and complementary products, and listing answers to frequently asked questions. Many companies publish a newsletter that is electronically distributed to interested persons, while others enable return visitors to gain rapid access to relevant material, rather than going through another log-in process. Another vehicle for staying in touch with customers is through online questionnaires, which request feedback on the company and its offerings.

Exporter Type and Decisions

Exporters make important decisions virtually on a daily basis. At various points, however, they must find answers to questions of a more strategic nature, such as export start-up, market selection, entry and servicing methods, and strategy adjustment. Figure 8.1 illustrates the sequence of decisions, and also identifies three types of companies: the first-time exporter, the expanding exporter, and the continuing exporter.

The critical question facing the first-time exporter is whether to grow through expanding domestic or foreign market operations. Most companies prefer the former, since it tends to be less costly and risky, and often brings quicker returns. However many companies are unable to meet their profit targets within their domestic marketplace. This is particularly true for companies producing specialized products and services. The decision to enter export markets is a significant choice for most companies, best made after considerable research and reflection.

Once exporting has been chosen, first-time exporters move on to deal with the subsequent questions, that is, questions 2 to 5 in Figure 8.1. Choosing to export to a foreign market is critical, since it determines the arena in which the company will compete for business. Once a market has been chosen, attention then turns to how this market should be entered. Will the company deal with foreign buyers directly or deal with foreign-based partners? This decision will have a major bearing on the way a company's products and services will be offered in the market in question. Given their plan to enter one or more new

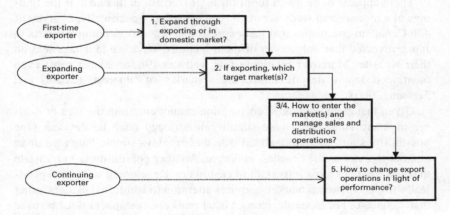

Source: Adapted from Seringhaus and Rosson (1990).

Figure 8.1   Exporter types and critical questions

export markets, expanding exporters must also answer questions 2, 3 and 4 in Figure 8.1. Their situation is aided by the fact that they have some export experience to draw upon. Continuing exporters are not required to deal with such fundamental questions. Unless there is a major problem of performance to be dealt with, they are more concerned with fine-tuning existing operations.

As can be seen, the three types of exporters face different questions, and thus have contrasting requirements. Table 8.1 presents some ideas about ways in which Internet technology might help exporters resolve their problems, and manage their operations. The main benefits Internet technologies bestow on exporters are the abilities to (1) conduct high-quality and timely research, (2) communicate effectively with prospective partners, customers and other interested parties, and (3) test ideas before committing themselves to full-scale operations.

Localization Efforts

Dealing with foreign languages has always been an issue for companies involved in foreign trade. As SMEs diversify their market base and employ Internet technologies, decisions must be made about the language(s) used on their websites. This is a matter of growing importance, since (a) a majority of online users were non-English speakers by 1998; (b) the USA accounted for a declining share of Internet commerce (forecast to be 55 per cent in 2002); and (c) web surfers are three times more likely to buy when the offering is made in their native language (Gibbs, 1999).

There appears to be much room for improvement in this area, if the findings of a more recent study are at all representative. Specifically, a survey of 426 Canadian companies that had expressed an interest in doing business in Japan revealed that only seven of them included Japanese language text on their website. Moreover relatively few websites (98, or 23 per cent) even mentioned Japan, despite this being a market of 'interest' (Coates and Tiessen, 2000).

Given that even the largest corporation cannot entertain the idea of dealing in many languages, some simplifying strategy must be devised. One possibility is an 'internationalized' site that employs simple language in an attempt to cater to the broadest audience. Another possibility is to translate the areas that are most important to customers. Developing websites specifically for international markets requires attention to additional matters, other than language. For example, icons, visual puns and metaphors must be used with care, and day/month/year ordering, as well as the use of commas in references to numbers, should match local practice (Nielsen, 2000).

Table 8.1 Export decisions and the role of the Internet

Exporter type	Critical question	Required decision	Potential Internet role
First-time	1. Should exporting be initated?	growth potential versus domestic market, problems to be overcome to tap export potential, likely cost/benefit of export involvement	size up key markets, buyers, competitors, distributors, check industry and government sources
Expanding	2. Which market(s) should be entered next?	determine market potential and barriers to entry, choose from feasible market alternatives,	compare market statistics, examine trade leads, test market via website, participate in virtual trade missions and fairs,
	3. What entry and servicing method is best?	viability of market entry options, selection of foreign partner	contact key buyers, distributors
Continuing	4. How can performance be maintained or improved?	need to adjust/change existing operations for the market in question, decide what new initiatives are required	track market dynamics, fine-tune processes, scout opportunities for improvement

Source: Adapted from Seringhaus and Rosson (1990).

Global E-business Developments

Historically most companies have moved into export markets following home market success. This often involved a steady roll-out, starting with markets that offered the greatest opportunity, which required the least amount of change or satisfied some other criterion. Internationalization along these lines was far from universal, but characterized the process for most companies. A question that arises in the literature is: does this model still make sense?

For three reasons, Sawhney and Mandal (2000)[3] argue that this model does not make sense. First, because competition is increasingly on an international basis, companies do not have the luxury of taking time to expand from a strong home base. Second, the Internet makes company strategies more transparent and thus susceptible to copying or matching. Third, research shows that early entrants tend to gain the largest market share. Delaying expansion is therefore potentially costly. These developments are not entirely new, but the Internet appears to accentuate global and competitive trends. In this new environment, the challenge for SMEs is to find a way of capitalizing on the opportunities while, at the same time, steering clear of associated problems. This poses several questions to SMEs that feel compelled to compete in this environment:

- What types of e-commerce businesses will go global first?
- What foreign markets or regions should you aim at first?
- With whom should you partner in building your global businesses?
- How should you structure your international organization?
- How well is your business model suited for globalization?

The ability of companies to globalize in part depends on the nature of their business. It is easier to move digital information (bits) than it is to carry out transactions (money) or to move physical products or services (atoms). Information simply requires a good telecommunications infrastructure, whereas transactions and products/services require payment and distribution infrastructure, respectively. US portals and infomediaries (such as Yahoo!) have expanded internationally both quickly and successfully, because they do not rely on the presence of a payment or distribution system. In contrast, business models involving commerce (E*Trade) and fulfillment (Amazon) have proved harder to operate in foreign settings, since infrastructure levels vary so much. Given shipping and payment difficulties, B2C e-commerce is regarded as the hardest model to globalize. It is, therefore, argued that the first movers into foreign markets will be portals and infomediaries, followed by infrastructure providers (SAP, Cisco), B2B market-makers (e-steel) and, finally, B2C e-commerce.

Regarding market/region selection, a prior strategic consideration is whether to try to dominate a region or to opt for the establishment of many global beachheads. Sawhney and Mandal (2000) comment on the appropriateness of each strategy. Following the choice of either a dominant or a beachhead strategy is the market/region selection. Key factors include market attractiveness, offering fit, capability fit and competitive intensity.

Partnering is another important consideration. Increasingly even the largest companies find that their resources will not permit them to run totally independent operations. SMEs, in particular, must consider partnering arrangements in foreign markets. An array of possibilities exists, including local Internet start-ups (as partners or acquisition targets), local venture capitalists, local incubators, large companies and local entrepreneurs (ibid.).

Finally, as a company develops substantial and widespread operations, it would be appropriate to consider what form its organization should take. The degree to which operations need to be localized should be a guiding principle, and a suitable architecture should be established, rather than developing a patchwork of solutions. Three layers are recommended. The global core should provide vision, leadership and strategy. The middle layer should provide a set of shared services, which include procurement, human resource management, marketing services and partner management. These are provided to all regional marketing units. The local market units constitute the outer layer and offer rich local expertise on customers, regulations, partnerships and supply-chain management. Such a structure enables a business to think globally but act locally, and to enjoy the benefits of standardized services. Although these ideas are not uniformly applicable to all SMEs, they offer promising insights for companies that are planning to go global or are already in the midst of Internet-enabled foreign market expansion.

SURVEY OF SUCCESSFUL CANADIAN EXPORTERS

Profiles of Canadian SMEs that have successfully employed a wide range of Internet technologies in exporting are presented below. A list of candidate companies was compiled from several sources: Industry Canada, Foreign Affairs and International Trade Canada offices in Ottawa and across the country, company case studies on the Electronic Commerce Task Force website,[4] media stories and personal knowledge. Following examination of company websites, the long list of candidates was reduced to about 20, ensuring an adequate representation by region, sector, B2B versus B2C, technological/innovative diversity and established (bricks and mortar) versus Internet start-up businesses. Ten companies were invited to participate in the study, and interviews were conducted with each of them. Table 8.2 lists the companies and a summary of the interviews, presented below, provides additional insights.

Table 8.2 Characteristics of the featured companies

Company	Province	Product/service	B2C or B2B	Established or Internet start-up
ABoriginArt Galleries	Ontario	aboriginal art	B2C (some B2B)	Internet
Blast Radius	British Columbia	website development	B2B	Internet
Draganfly Innovations Inc.	Saskatchewan	indoor flying objects	B2C	Internet
Innovative Brewing Technologies	Prince Edward Island	microbrewery/ brewpub manuals	B2B	established
Just White Shirts & Black Socks	Ontario	men's clothing	B2C (some B2B)	established
Michel Pratte Sports	Quebec	sports clothing and equipment	B2C	established
Sabian Ltd	New Brunswick	musical cymbals	B2C	established
Shana Corporation	Alberta	electronic forms	B2B	established
Taybridge Communications	New Brunswick	electronic design and online services	B2B	Internet
Unique Patterns Design Ltd	Nova Scotia	custom dressmaking patterns	B2C (adding B2B)	established

ABoriginArt Galleries

Believing that the Internet provided a perfect space to retail the work of Inuit, First Nations and northwest coast artists, Simon Griffiths and Peter Hickman founded ABoriginArt Galleries (AG) in late 1997. The experience and know-how of the co-owners complemented each other nicely; Simon was familiar with aboriginal art and galleries, while Peter's background was in information technology and the Internet.

It took a year for the business to develop to the point where the website could go 'live'. Plans had to be developed, resources and inventory put together, and the website designed and made operational. The design of the website was outsourced to a company managed by a friend. The friend was prepared to work at a discount in order to obtain valuable experience. A decision was made to have the site hosted by a large and reputable Internet service provider (ISP) as a large storage space was required and AG wanted the site to be fast and the connection dependable. The company ensured that it was listed in the first 20 names when certain key word combinations were submitted to search engines. ABoriginArt – the company name – helps in alphabetical listings.

AG has customers in most provinces in Canada, almost all US states including Alaska, and has done business around the world. The site is in English, with main pages in French and German. AG conducts its business on a personal basis: once an order is received, a phone call is made. Hickman explains, 'Art is a very personal thing and we find that customers want to talk about the prints and sculptures.' At the outset, it was not clear whether there would be a threshold price beyond which Internet sales would prove difficult. This has not materialized: although most sales are in the $500–800 range, AG regularly sells items priced at $5000, or more.

The company handles credit checks via its own terminal. Some customers prefer the security of providing credit card details by phone. ' We price our products in US and Canadian dollars,' notes Griffiths, but payments are accepted in various currencies. Given that there is often confusion about posted and actual exchange rates, the company has resisted incorporating a currency converter function on its website. For interested customers, however, it would provide an estimate of an item's price in a local currency. Once the sales transaction is approved, the item is packed and shipped. AG uses Canada Post exclusively, shipping by ground or air, depending on the destination and timeliness required. The company no longer uses courier companies because of breakage and other problems.

The AG website is updated and refreshed regularly. Customers have to be encouraged to return, and therefore the site features new pieces and sale items on a weekly basis. The site also offers discounts for repeat customers, as well as special services for corporate clients that may wish to purchase an item for recognition purposes. At present, AG's supply chain is not integrated with those of its suppliers. However some product sourcing is done through artists' and wholesalers' websites.

Griffiths and Hickman both hold down full-time jobs, in addition to running AG in their 'spare time'. Over time, and with expansion, they will hand over the business to their employees. For the time being, however, there is plenty of work to be done to ensure AG's continued success, which results from its unique art holdings, global presence and superior personal service.

Product/service	Aboriginal art
Location	Toronto, Ontario
Age	two years
Annual sales	$400 000–500 000
Employees	Four
Export sales (%)	90
Major market	USA
E-commerce focus	how we do business

→ www.canadian-art.com

Blast Radius

Having established Blast Radius (BR) in a one-bedroom apartment in Vancouver, in November 1996, the founders realized very quickly that to succeed in the website development business they needed to think on a large scale. With few major companies in Vancouver, local opportunities were quite limited and, therefore, within months of starting up, a decision was made to open an office in New York to further business prospects. More recently, the development of the company's business and client base led it to establish an office in Los Angeles. Another office is planned to open in Toronto. The remote offices handle client interaction and management. All technical work is done in Vancouver, where larger premises now accommodate an expanding workforce. Some technical work is also to be conducted in the new Toronto office.

What sets BR apart from many of its competitors is its approach to customer service. Substantial strategic development and planning is done with client firms to ensure the resulting website will attract the attention and sustain the interest of target customers. Most of BR's clients focus on the 12 to 34-year-old demographic, a segment the company knows well.

BR has found that its best developers and designers want to work with the top brands and interesting projects, which in turn want the best developers. This circular process helps perpetuate the firm's growth. Securing the right client becomes essential in this environment. In fact, BR works with only 20 per cent of those that approach it. The company prefers to develop long-term relationships with clients, rather than engaging in one-time web development projects. Clients with global brands are preferred, and business is accepted from very few start-up companies. Consequently the list of BR clients reads like a 'Who's Who' in consumer goods marketing, including Nike, Casio, Universal Studios, Atlantic Records and Lego.

Maintaining a physical presence in its active markets helps BR develop and deepen relationships with clients. Despite the hype of virtual offices and telecommuting, the company finds that a physical presence is crucial in gaining the trust and support of its partners.

Close to 90 per cent of BR's business has been international, mostly from the USA, with some recent projects coming from Europe. Given the small Canadian market, the firm had to be competitive internationally from the beginning. The company has developed a site for special products aimed at Asians living in North America. This website was written in Chinese, and provided BR with useful experience, should it decide to expand its geographic interests in Asia.

Brent Dykes, BR's marketing manager, realizes that a web presence is essential for SMEs that want to conduct business internationally, provided they have a plan and are ready to deal with issues such as product fulfillment. While they have conducted work outside of North America, they view English as the language of web commerce, and have no plans to change this at the present time. The company is, however, preparing to embrace other languages, as it begins to play a more important role in e-commerce (particularly in Europe).

The company's website serves as a showcase, presenting their designers' work to prospective clients and would-be employees. It is important to present an image consistent with the company's beliefs and capabilities. BR has invested close to $100 000 in the current site, and it is a prime vehicle for promotional purposes.

Product/service	Website development
Location	Vancouver, British Columbia
Age	four years
Annual sales	$10–15 million
Employees	140
Export sales (%)	85–90
Major markets	USA, Europe
E-commerce focus	showcase

→ www.blastradius.com

Draganfly Innovations Inc.

Hobby shops and model kits always fascinated Zenon Dragan. However living in Saskatchewan severely limited the time he could spend outdoors flying toys. As a result, he set about designing a flying saucer for indoors that could be used year-round.

Zenon Dragan founded his company, Draganfly Innovations Inc. (DI) in 1996, and initially tried selling the saucers at a local shopping mall. However sales were very slow to materialize and he barely broke even. A friend introduced him to the Internet and he immediately saw the potential it presented for selling unique and niche market items. Prior to going live with the website, he sent out a press release featuring a colored photo of the flying saucer, along with a product write-up. This caused word to spread, and the press release was paid off in the first hour of the site's operation. DI's first website was very simple and only cost $400 to develop; it got him started and proved that the Internet could work for his business. Although people in Saskatoon were not interested in buying DI's product, it was clear that a market existed in many other parts of the world, and the Internet made it easy to gain access to these markets. In fact, exports to Israel are greater than sales in Canada. In the first year, DI shipped over 30 000 saucers and generated revenues of over $1 million.

The site was upgraded as sales continued to increase, and new marketing methods were tried. Given the novelty of the company's products, many magazines have been very cooperative in featuring Dragan's press releases. This publicity provides exposure that would otherwise be impossible for such a small company. Advertising space in magazines like *GQ*, *Playboy* and *Popular Mechanics* would normally cost thousands of dollars. The company estimates it generates over a million dollars' worth of free publicity every year, and credits this as one of its major success factors. While DI made some mistakes early on, such as spamming news groups with advertising messages, the company continues to use publicity as a key marketing device. Many foreign publications have also carried DI's products, which resulted in increased traffic to its website. English is the sole language used on the site, and it currently have no need to add other languages.

The price of DI's flying toys range from $27 to $30 000, and all products are listed in US dollars. With competition intensifying, developing and launching innovative products is DI's greatest challenge. The company aims to introduce a new product every six months. It has experienced a first-mover advantage and obtained valuable insights, which enables DI to continue to lead the field.

The current site is about two years old, and has started to push its technical limits. Internet technology has advanced, and so there are many new features

Dragan would like to add. The back-end is not yet integrated with the site, one area that will be emphasized in the next round of site improvements. These updates will be expensive, costing approximately $15 000. A local developer carries out most of the work, since it does not make sense to undertake the design and development functions in-house.

Product/service	Indoor flying objects and toys
Location	Saskatoon, Saskatchewan
Age	four years
Annual sales	$1–1.5 million
Employees	four
Export sales (%)	99
Major markets	USA, UK, Spain, Germany
E-commerce focus	promotion, online sales

→ www.rctoys.com

Innovative Brewing Technologies

Innovative Brewing Technologies (IBT) is an entrepreneurial unit within DME Brewing Services of Charlottetown, Prince Edward Island. Founded in 1990, DME's business involves providing turnkey microbrewery or brewpub services. Microbreweries produce craft beer, whereas brewpubs feature the brewing operation in a restaurant setting. DME designs, produces and installs facilities for clients around the world. Much of its early work took place on the West Coast of the USA but, over time, the microbrewery trend has grown in Canada and other countries. Currently DME sales total $6–10 million, and the company has about 70 employees. In the course of working for DME, it became apparent to Kelly Dunne that there was no easy way for interested parties to learn about microbrewery operations. With support from the president, four DME employees established IBT in 1998, to produce and sell educational manuals. The four employees worked after hours to launch the company but, today, perform both functions during the normal workday. IBT operations complement those of DME. In fact, the manuals help expand demand for DME.

Both DME and IBT have websites, but they serve different functions. DME's site (www.dmebrewing.com) was implemented in 1996, and is at present an electronic brochure. It describes the company and its capabilities, and provides examples of projects undertaken in the past. The site was designed in-house at minimal cost, and has been revised four times. The fifth update, which was substantial, costing about \$30 000, was introduced in October 2000. It enabled clients to order parts online, and to contact the company's representatives in Australia, Brazil and Japan. IBT's website is only a year old, and in English only. The company worked with Island Tel, as well as a local web developer. IBT acted as an e-commerce guinea pig for the telephone company and, as a result, received a very good rate. Both sites have been maintained internally, which means a low expense.

The IBT website offers customers several payment methods, including credit card, through a secure site hosted in Toronto. Shipments may be made either by ground mail or by courier. The latter sometimes charges more than the value of the manuals (prices range from US \$9.99 to \$39.00). As a result, the company plans to place inventory with its representatives, which would allow them to respond locally and inexpensively.

Dunne emphasizes the importance of launching the website. This was carried out after careful planning for IBT, with all the appropriate steps taken, including mail-outs, META tags (reference tags that help search engines locate websites), and search engine listings. When the DME site was launched in 1996, the company did not take these steps directly. Fortunately a link was made to the 'Real Beer Page' in San Francisco, which connected DME to search engines. This produced numerous inquiries for the US\$2000 annual cost. However DME was one of only two or three companies in North America providing the microbrewery service at the time. Today, with the growing demand for microbreweries and brewpubs, the number of suppliers has doubled. IBT and DME recognize that they have to work harder and smarter in a more competitive arena.

Although selling to geographically distant and culturally different markets creates many challenges, IBT vice-president Kelly Dunne and her colleagues are determined to master the necessary skills. E-commerce is an important strategic thrust for the two companies now.

Product/service	Microbrewery/brewpub manuals
Location	Charlottetown, Prince Edward Island, Canada
Age	two years
Annual sales	\$30 000
Employees	four
Export sales (%)	95
Major market	USA
E-commerce focus	promotion, online sales

→   www.innovativebrew.com

Just White Shirts & Black Socks

Founded in 1994 by three business executives who were paying inflated prices for quality dress shirts, Just White Shirts & Black Socks (JWS) has seemingly defied the odds, achieving rapid success in a congested market-place. In the early days, JWS offered a very restricted line of shirts and socks. Although customers liked the product, they soon asked for greater choice of fabric, color and style, as well as accessories such as ties and belts. More recently, the trend toward the 'business casual' form of dress resulted in requests for shirts and slacks that maintained JWS quality standards, but fit the new work environment. JWS's success has led to market diversification too. The company has used its experience in the Canadian market to seek export sales in key markets.

JWS started life as a mail-order company, but saw the potential the Internet presented, and established its first website in 1996. The English language site has gone through five versions on two platforms in a few years. JWS felt Internet sales might approach 20 per cent of total sales, and the savings from handling transactions online would probably offset the cost of developing and maintaining a web presence. These ideas held true until 1999, when Internet sales mushroomed to 40 per cent of total sales. Vice-president of marketing, Michael Sachter, is impressed with the contribution that online sales are now making to JWS, but points out that the company is 'distribution channel agnostic'. In other words, JWS relates to the customer as he/she prefers.

JWS has been active in the USA for three years, and established a joint-venture relationship with an Australian company for providing local market-ing and fulfillment in 1999. It also welcomes business from customers in other countries. The JWS website streams visitors to separate Canadian, US, Australian and other sections, with pricing in their respective currencies.

JWS runs most operations from Toronto. It sources materials on a world-wide basis, and fully controls manufacturing in Pakistan. Shipments are made from JWS warehouses in Toronto and New York, except those for Australia and Asia, which are handled from Australia. Buyers choose either courier or a cheaper shipment method, with varying carriers depending on the destination.

Now that the website has proved to be scalable, the next priority for JWS is to fully integrate the site with the back-end supply chain systems. JWS uses two companies for website development: one focuses on design and the other handles technical matters. Sachter states that start-up costs fall in the range of $5000, for a 'basement' project, to $100 000 to $2 million, for a fully inte-grated site. JWS costs fell in the middle of this range. Annual maintenance costs are extra.

According to Sachter, some SMEs make fundamental errors in Internet marketing. First, companies usually emphasize site development over site marketing, devoting insufficient funds to drive traffic to the site. Second, few companies realize that measuring and testing practices, developed for and used in direct marketing, can help with Internet marketing. Third, there is not a lot of attention given to peer relationships, which Sachter uses to find out what is, and is not, working.

New initiatives reveal the plans and determination of JWS. The company has established a corporate sales division, hoping to transfer the lessons of its success with individuals into sales of clothing (with logos) to organizations. Other priorities involve encouraging repeat business, and providing rewards for repeat purchase and business referrals.

Product/service	Men's apparel
Location	Toronto, Ontario
Age	six years
Annual sales	$3–4 million
Employees	17
Export sales (%)	not available
Major market	Canada
E-commerce focus	another customer touch point

→ www.justwhiteshirts.com

Michel Pratte Sports

Michel Pratte Sports (MPS), established in 1987, has expanded beyond the storefront operation to service the North American market. Recognizing that its retail location in Ste. Adèle, Quebec, restricted the opportunities for growth, the company produced a mail order catalogue, in 1989, which has been sent to over 30 000 customers annually, throughout North America. Approximately 80 per cent of sales originated from the USA, where MPS has built a solid reputation among serious outdoor adventurers. Ski clothing and equipment is the bread and butter of MPS's business, but mountain bikes and hiking gear are growing in importance.

In 1995, a Montreal-based web developer approached the company to explore MPS's interest in developing a presence on the Internet. With the mail order infrastructure already in place, this seemed to be a natural move that would not involve much dislocation. The first website was relatively simple, and offered a limited selection of merchandise. Unfortunately technical difficulties caused many problems. Specifically the payment function took a long time to process, causing some visitors to give up without purchasing.

Despite small sales volumes, the company still saw the business potential the Internet could provide. The website was revamped in 1998 with the goal of increasing sales. At an approximate cost of $75 000, this update allowed for listing more products and adding new features to the site. For instance, links to ski organizations, camps and skiing conditions at locations around the world were added. Although this additional content is expensive to update it gives visitors a reason to bookmark the site and return at a later time, increasing the likelihood of a future purchase. The website has two versions, French and English, reflecting the company's home-base in Quebec, and acknowledging its American customers, which represent the majority of its clients. While there are occasional sales from outside North America, they have not been very significant. The company historically used Canada Post for shipments to its mail order customers, and has retained this method for orders originating from Internet marketing.

Despite the fact that visits and sales have greatly increased with its present website, MPS is currently restructuring its operations. The plan is to run everything from a central database, with retailing, catalogue and web operations all merged together. Such integration will permit inventory to be tracked and displayed in real time; efficiency will be greatly enhanced, while all the three sales channels are jointly managed. Response times will also improve, and MPS expects to be able to compete more effectively against its competitors. The new website features prices in Canadian dollars for domestic customers as well as in US dollars. Altogether the changes will make it possible for the company to maximize its marketing efforts across the entire operation. In summary, the redeveloped site will provide greater functionality and enhance customer service.

It seems as though MPS has quickly embraced the Internet, but owner Normand Lachaine worries that his company is not moving as rapidly as its American rivals. MPS provides great customer service, and a unique selection of products; however competitors are just a click away. Being on guard is essential for survival, let alone growth and profitability.

Product/service	Sports clothing & equipment
Location	Ste. Adèle, Quebec
Age	13 years
Annual sales	$3 million
Employees	15
Export sales (%)	90
Major market	USA
E-commerce focus	promotion, online sales

→ www.mprattesport.com

Sabian Ltd

Founded in 1982 in Meductic, New Brunswick, Sabian Ltd has achieved a leadership position in the musical cymbals world. Readers of *Modern Drummer* magazine recently voted Sabian the most innovative and customer service-oriented cymbal company in the world. The company traces its origins back to Turkey, where the art of hand-hammered cymbals was perfected centuries ago. The combination of traditional technology and modern business practices has proved unstoppable. With sales approaching $25 million, and with about 100 employees, Sabian will soon break free from the SME category.

Sabian cymbals are used by leading artists in all musical genres, including rock star Phil Collins, jazz giant Jack DeJohnette, the New York Philharmonic Orchestra and the Phantom Regiment Drum and Bugle Corps. The company sells its numerous musical cymbals, gongs and other percussion instruments through 90 distributors, in more than 100 countries. Branches in Los Angeles, Marshfield, Massachusetts, Glasgow and Monte Carlo support the company's diverse marketing efforts.

The prime objective of Sabian's website is to provide support for the marketing and sales operations of its distributors. In addition, since the critical demographic segment for the company is 13- to 17-year-old males, an Internet presence is essential for communication purposes. The website is large, containing a full product catalogue, and uses sounds and video to good effect.

The site contains information on cymbals, artists and dealer locations. The latest company news is presented via an interactive newsletter. 'The Zone' is a dedicated area, permitting members to hear the sounds created by each cymbal, take a factory tour or chat with other members. A new area has been added to the website: a virtual store, which offers a variety of branded clothing, accessories and multimedia items. Sabian does not sell cymbals directly to customers. These are handled through the established distributor and dealer marketing channels. Given the international nature of Sabian operations, some sections of the website are available in French, German, Portuguese and Spanish.

The only transactions that occur on Sabian's website are for purchases from the virtual store. Prices are set in US dollars, and a company in Texas provides credit card verification services. Buyers can choose from a variety of shipping services, depending on their price and time preferences. Shipping to the USA has often caused problems for Sabian. Clothing items, in particular, are sensitive to tariffs, and customs procedures are often unpredictable.

Sabian put up its first website in 1996, and its third version became operational in September 2000. The website is tightly integrated with print and other communication activities and, for that reason, has been designed by the company's advertising agency. Mardi Thornton, marketing operations manager at Sabian, regards expert website help as crucial, stating, 'a web site has to be cutting-edge, quick, interesting and fresh, or else visitors will just click on by. Although our web site has been well received, the new version will be full-screen, flatter and easier to navigate.' A Mandarin Chinese language catalogue will also be included in the next round. None of this comes cheaply. Start-up costs for Sabian were in the $150 000 region, and maintaining the site costs $50 000–$70 000 annually.

Product/service	Musical cymbals
Location	Meductic, New Brunswick
Age	18 years
Annual sales	$25 million
Employees	100
Export sales (%)	90 plus
Major markets	USA and Canada (60%)
E-commerce focus	support local distributors

→ www.sabian.com

Shana Corporation

Founded in 1985, Shana has long been a pioneer in the form management systems field. Its business has evolved with technology advances over time. Recently Shana embraced the Internet as a way to better serve existing clients, and also to seek out new prospects. Given that forms make up about 85 per cent of all business documents, this is an industry that can offer firms solutions to their paper problems.

Shana was the first company to offer a form management solution for users of the Macintosh platform in the mid-1980s, and introduced its first cross-platform system in 1996. This was an industry first. The Informed Series incorporates the 'Informed Designer', which allows firms to create their unique designs, and the 'Informed Filler', which provides functionality by completing and storing the forms.

However it was the introduction of the 'Informed Deployment Server' four years ago that really changed the company's focus. This product sits on a corporate Intranet and ensures that all employees use exactly the same version of a form (10 000–20 000 different forms are not uncommon in a large organization). By concentrating on one application, Shana has been able to focus its limited resources on providing top-quality solutions to the largest global corporations.

Shana's English language website does not include a transaction capability. Customers such as Boeing are not interested in simply buying the product on the Internet. Rather they and other companies wish to hire Shana, not just as a provider of the product, but also for its consulting and integration expertise. The website does, however, provide significant sales support. Firms can download demos from the site, and test the software during the sales process. Moreover, through interactive communications applications, such as 'NetMeeting', remote presentations can be arranged, saving both the potential customers and client time and travel expenses. With close to 90 per cent of its sales originating from outside Canada, this feature of the site provides customers with significant savings.

Shana has currently licensed its technology in over 65 countries. The Internet also acts as a convenient and effective customer service tool. Telephone support can be very expensive, especially in today's 24-hour work-day globalized environment. By placing much of the technical literature online with a search engine, clients can often find what they need, eliminating phone expenses. Shana not only saves money, it also provides the client with enhanced services, since they never have to wait for answers. According to Nigel Brechi, Shana's marketing manager, 'we couldn't do business without the Net'.

Partnerships with leading players, such as Entrust Technologies, allow Shana to offer the most advanced encryption and public key infrastructure-enabled solutions to clients. Solutions such as digital signatures mean that many forms may never need to be submitted on paper. As the infrastructure improves, this is bound to add additional value for clients. All of this is possible because of the tremendous advances in Internet technologies and infrastructure developments, mainly on the client side. Shana plans to continue incorporating these advances into its products as it grows and evolves to meet the continuing needs of its clients.

Product/service	Electronic forms
Location	Edmonton, Alberta
Age	15 years
Annual sales	$2 million
Employees	35
Export sales (%)	90
Major markets	USA, Australia
E-commerce focus	Promotion, customer and sales support

→ www.shana.com

Taybridge Communications

David Lewis started his company in 1992 and managed it on a part-time basis while working for information technology and computer-based training companies in British Columbia and New Brunswick. In 1998, all the business signals were positive and, as a result, David decided to take the plunge, starting to work full-time for his company, and running its business from his home in Taymouth, 30 minutes outside Fredericton, New Brunswick.

Taybridge Communications provides a variety of services to organizations in both the private and public sectors. The work that Lewis undertakes ranges from website development and technical writing to customer support via e-mail and the Internet. Customers are located as close as Fredericton, and as far away as San Diego, California. Distance does not present any problems for Taybridge, since it operates almost exclusively in an electronic environment, moving design and other files back and forth via the Internet.

One of the most useful aspects of the company's website is that it presents a portfolio of David's work. Many websites include lists of clients, but Taybridge goes much further, presenting more than a dozen examples of the work it has undertaken. In the past, the Taybridge website featured prices for typical projects, as well as hourly rates for other work. Lewis found this to be problematic; few projects proved to fit the label 'typical' and, by posting rates, prices were locked-in. The website no longer lists prices or rates. However a feature that generates a steady response is the 'request a quote' button. Prospects complete an online survey regarding their needs and budget constraints, and are promised a quote within one business day – often arriving sooner.

Lewis indicates that prices for a basic website start at about $5000, with a full, customized e-commerce site reaching $60 000 or more. His advice is that SMEs considering setting up a fully transaction-enabled website might proceed simply. It does not make much sense for smaller companies to create their own back-end systems (for credit and fulfillment, for example), Lewis says, when these tasks can be effectively outsourced to another company's web server. Taybridge's website design prices include one-year maintenance. Otherwise SMEs should expect to pay, on average, $100 per month for simple text changes. Page changes are more complicated, and are usually priced on an hourly rate. Lewis favors a cautious approach towards foreign language websites. These are clearly important as foreign business grows; at the same time, the development and maintenance costs can easily rocket as languages are added.

When he has time, Lewis ponders how the Taybridge website might be enhanced. New features have to pass the test of improving the company's revenue-generating ability. At present, no great modifications are planned; the site seems to work well. Lewis designed and hosts ARCNET, a site that enables aboriginal businesses in Canada to network and promote themselves in the global marketplace. This work reflects David's Mohawk heritage. He is currently exploring opportunities in other English-speaking markets. David says, 'I do not think in terms of national boundaries any more, but of time zones'.

Product/service	Electronic design and online services
Location	Taymouth, New Brunswick
Age	two years (full-time)
Annual sales	$100 000–150 000
Employees	one (subcontracting on larger projects)
Export sales (%)	95
Major market	USA
E-commerce focus	providing online information services

→ www.taybridge.com

Unique Patterns Design Ltd

Tanya Shaw Weeks has taken Unique Patterns Design (UPD) a long way from the custom dressmaking business she founded in 1994. The genesis of the business was Weeks's view that many women were not well served by the dressmaking pattern industry. Existing companies provided patterns that were geared to standard sizes and shapes and, as a consequence, many women found substantial work was required to customize the patterns. UPD was set up to offer a better and automated system for the large number of women who enjoyed making their own clothing.

With the help of a local university, UPD developed software for the customization of patterns. The resulting process is simple: (1) the customer provides the necessary measurements; (2) these are entered into the system to produce a custom pattern; and (3) the pattern is printed on high quality paper, which is then shipped to the customer. As Weeks states, 'No more guessing or trying to make things fit.'

Initially, customers followed a three-step process: (a) choosing patterns from a catalogue sent to them, (b) mailing in their measurements, and (c) receiving the resulting custom pattern by mail. As interest increased in the Internet, UPD saw the potential to reach a wider audience and enhance customer service at the same time. Putting the catalogue online would help UPD easily gain access to new markets, rather than producing, promoting and mailing their catalogues, which can often be expensive. In 1995, the concept was tested, and proved to be a great success. Although most business is still based on catalogue sales, the Internet trade currently represents about 20 per cent of total sales and is growing rapidly. The company has more than 7000 registered members.

The Internet allows UPD to constantly update its content and quickly respond to changing consumer needs and trends. The site is updated weekly, giving users a reason to return. The company's English-only website is continually evolving as more features are added. The current site cost about $100 000 for design, content and development. Most of the technical development work is done in-house.

It is technically possible for customers to download the images in order to print the patterns. However UPD is concerned that the calibration of customers' printers might affect the size of the pattern. For this reason, patterns are still delivered through traditional channels. Shipping patterns to foreign customers is not only expensive, but can also take a long time. Given that 90 per cent of sales are outside Canada, UPD decided to establish a remote office in Seattle to service the American and Asian customers. This office is connected to the Dartmouth head office using Internet technologies. Orders are processed in Dartmouth, Nova Scotia, with patterns printed and shipped from Seattle. This arrangement reduces both cost and time for many customers. As sales grow in other areas, additional remote sites may become necessary.

A recent development for UPD was the establishment of a sister company, Virtually Yours Inc. This company markets software to e-tailers that enables customers to 'try on' clothing online. After providing body measurements, a customer can select items from a retailer's inventory and decide whether the fit (sizing and color) is satisfactory. This is a new and evolving industry, which has undergone considerable technological change. Software licensing arrangements with e-tailers will permit UPD to leverage its existing technology for maximum advantage. There is no doubt that further innovation will occur in the future.

Product/service	Custom dressmaking patterns
Location	Dartmouth, Nova Scotia
Age	six years
Annual sales	less than $1 million
Employees	15
Export sales (%)	90
Major market	USA
E-commerce focus	promotion, sales

➜ www.uniquepatterns.com

LEARNING FROM SUCCESS

We now draw on lessons from the ten companies featured above. A number of common themes are presented first, followed by suggested 'best practices'.

Common Themes

- *Technical or technological infrastructure*   Companies have not experienced any major technical difficulties in becoming Internet-enabled. It appears that the technical supply infrastructure is good in all parts of Canada. Although some companies were forced to enter into relationships with distant partners in the early days of Internet marketing, local providers are more than able now to meet current company needs. Various providers are active on the web-designing front, including specialized web developers, advertising agencies and mainstream information technology companies.
- *The cost and complexity factor*   An encouraging finding is that an Internet site can be constructed to fit any budget. For start-up companies that have little money to devote to Internet marketing, a simple site can be designed and made operational for $5 000, and can be maintained in-house inexpensively. Of course, companies that need to operate larger and more complex sites may have to spend a very significant amount of money. Two points emerge from this. First, simple sites often meet customer needs quite adequately; second, cost has not prevented many companies from moving into the world of e-commerce.
- *The language factor*   English is the predominant language of e-commerce for the featured companies. Seven companies provide services in English only, one in English and French, and two offer services in three or more languages. Only the main pages were translated, as opposed to the entire site. These language strategies may be adequate for companies currently focusing on the US market. However, as other regions of the world become more important to e-commerce, an English-only approach may be counterproductive.
- *Currency denomination and price levels*   Prices are usually listed in US dollars. Four companies' prices are exclusively in US dollars, two in Canadian and US dollars, and one in three currencies. Three companies do not list prices on their websites. Pricing in US dollars seems to be acceptable for Canadian and other non-US customers for the time being. A related point concerns price levels in Internet marketing. As might be expected, the ten featured companies sell business and consumer products and services at varying price levels. An important finding, for companies selling relatively expensive

items, is that individual customers appear willing to purchase them via the Internet.

- *Physical shipments*   A reassuring finding is that the companies have not experienced any major problems in shipping their products. This runs counter to stories in the media that identify fulfillment as a real challenge, especially in the B2C sector, where problems are reported when moving products over the so-called 'last mile'. To some extent, the lack of a shipping problem probably reflects the dominant role played by the US market, and the relative ease of shipping to customers there (versus elsewhere). It appears that the combination of postal and courier services provides a sufficient number of options for most shippers and customers.
- There has been little or no *integration of back-end systems with websites* up to this point. However several companies are planning to move in this direction in the near future.
- *Terms of use*   None of the featured sites includes 'terms of use' or 'privacy' policies. Although the absence of these policies has not created any overt problems to date, some sales may have been lost, since individual customers question security and privacy matters. As e-commerce matures, policies of these kinds – and, perhaps, others – are likely to be seen as mandatory rather than optional. The prospect of liability claims suggests that the inclusion of such policies would be a prudent, if not a necessary, step.
- *Selection of export markets*   Few of the Internet start-up companies seem to have done much in the way of market selection or planning. Rather these companies have looked to the USA (and to a lesser extent, Canada) for business. Beyond those two markets, business is 'accepted' from customers in other locations. This may be a sustainable approach in the near future, but could require a different strategy as markets outside North America gain prominence. Brick and mortar companies mostly use their websites to support existing operations, implying they have not had to choose or plan for new markets.

Best Practices

- *Superior service*   Internet marketing depends on advanced technology. However technology, on its own, does not create business. Superior service is the key to winning and keeping customers. Successful exporters match their marketing methods to the preferences of customers and delight them with superior service.
- *Frequent updates*   Although technology is not the final arbiter of success, it is important. It is also moving very quickly. Therefore periodic upgrades are made in order to offer greater functionality to

customers and/or partners. Content is updated and changes are made on a regular basis, in order to produce a website that is informative, current and dynamic.

- *Website functionality*   The featured companies have moved beyond the electronic brochure level of Internet marketing. Seven of the ten websites offer a transaction capability, while four sites support sales and distributors or customers. (In the case of Sabian, distributor support is the primary function, but accessory sales are also made.) Further, the purpose of each site is clear; its function is to inform, sell and/or support.
- *The website's feel and look*   The look and feel of websites correspond to the target customer groups. For a graphic example of this principle in action, contrast the sites of Sabian Ltd. (www.sabian.com) and Shana Corporation (www.shana.com). The former focuses on young percussionists, whereas the latter is directed to corporate systems professionals.
- *Ease of use*   The websites of the featured companies were straightforward in terms of navigation. For transaction-based sites, the pathway to completing a purchase presented no problems. Other sites, which provide information or support, were similarly easy and logical to navigate. Three sites were restricted to members only.
- *Added flexibilities*   Successful exporters provide a range of contact, payment and shipping options. The resulting flexibility means that customers with differing capacities and preferences can be easily accommodated. In some cases, the preference relates to security ('I'd rather not provide my credit card information via the Internet'), whereas others relate to service level ('Delivery in a week is satisfactory').
- *The final 'best practice' is more general*:   the featured companies all responded enthusiastically to the opportunity to talk about their business. They are clearly proactive, enthusiastic and quick to respond. These characteristics are important in any business setting; but, perhaps, more so in exporting. Other companies were contacted, but did not respond, declined or could not be tied down to an interview.

We now present some concluding comments, focusing on the implications of the research for managers and government officials.

IMPLICATIONS

The first point to be made is that the successful use of the Internet by the ten featured companies does not reveal any fundamentally new exporting models.

For the most part, the SMEs have used the Internet as a new or additional method for reaching and serving customers. In this respect, it facilitates rather than creates business. Put another way, the Internet represents an evolutionary rather than revolutionary way of conducting business. That said, the Internet is a powerful medium. The experiences of the ten featured companies demonstrate that the Internet offers numerous relevant advantages.

First, the Internet makes it possible for companies to break free from their relatively small domestic (Canadian in the above cases) market, and compete in an environment with reduced geographical barriers. The Internet is a perfect vehicle for niche marketing, which is the strategy that most SME exporters practice, whether serving B2B or B2C sectors. The Internet also permits companies to practice one-to-one marketing. It is a powerful way to search for, connect with and retain single customers.

Second, the Internet can play a significant role. For example, all ten companies profiled generate more than 80 per cent of their revenues outside Canada and, in some cases, the Internet accounts for all of this business. In other cases, the proportion of sales accounted for by the Internet is growing, often sharply. Where transactions are not handled electronically, company websites are increasingly being used for purposes such as demonstrating the product, showcasing past work and providing customer support.

Third, it appears that the Internet operations of the featured companies are viable. Many are profitable and others are close to breaking even. Many of the companies have invested relatively modest amounts to take advantage of the Internet, while others have spent on a larger scale. Whether the approach has been cautious or more aggressive, the profitable (or almost profitable) operations of the exporters are significant, in the light of huge losses reported by many so-called 'dot.com' firms.

A further point is particularly relevant for Canadian companies but may have application to others that serve the US market. Current pricing practices enhance export profitability. Specifically the featured companies mostly incur their expenses in Canadian dollars but, since most of their business is done in the USA, the companies price items with those buyers in mind. This is helped by the fact that most US buyers are unaware that the product originates in Canada. When they are, many probably do not appreciate the difference between the two currencies. As a result, a good premium is currently being enjoyed thanks to the wide currency differentials. It could be argued that this is a general feature of Canadian exporting at present. However it appears to be accentuated in Internet exporting, given the dominance of US Internet buyers and the use of US dollar pricing at this time.

The experience of the featured companies is that the Internet offers real benefits for SMEs that have foreign business aspirations. Internet-enabled exporting is a significant activity for the above ten companies and it is yielding positive financial results. Other companies should look at the Internet as a vehicle for entry and/or expansion into today's (relatively) borderless international markets.

This leads to the question of government support for e-commerce in general and Internet exporting in particular. The Canadian federal government has invested substantially in infrastructure and policy development to make Canada an e-commerce leader. Programs have also been developed to encourage the adoption of the Internet on the part of SMEs. The experiences of the ten featured companies show that these investments are wise. At the same time, it should be reiterated that the Internet is no panacea for economic development. As Samiee (1998) reminds us, it is committed companies with a competitive edge that are the winners in domestic or world markets. Internet technology seldom provides the edge in question; however, it certainly can be a strong enabling factor.

NOTES

1. Industry Canada (1999) reports higher levels of usage by SMEs.
2. This section draws extensively on Bygdeson (1999). Many of the principles apply in a domestic as well as an export market context.
3. This section draws extensively on Sawhney and Mandal (2000).
4. This may be found at http://strategis.ic.gc.ca/virtual_hosts/e-com/english/44.html.

REFERENCES

Bygdeson, Jonas (1999), 'Using the Internet as a tool of international business', Swedish Trade Council, February (retrieved from: www.e-global.es/suecia.doc).
Canadian Federation of Independent Business (1999), 'Virtually a reality: results of the 1999 CFIB survey on Internet use among small- and medium–sized firms, Toronto, August (retrieved from: www.cfib.ca).
Coates, Kenneth and James H. Tiessen (2000), *Canadian Firms, Electronic Commerce and the Japanese Market*, Ottawa: The Japanese–Canadian Trade Council.
Forrester Research (2000), 'Global ecommerce approaches hypergrowth' (retrieved from: www.forrester.com/ER/Marketing/1,1503,212,FF.html).
Gibbs, Hope Katz (1999), 'Global website planner: taking global local', *Global Business Online*, 12 December (retrieved from: www.exporttoday.com/archive/dec99/article2.html).
Hamill, Jim and Karl Gregory (1997), 'Internet marketing in the internationalization of UK SMEs, *Journal of Marketing Management*, **13**, 9–28.
Hanson, Ward (2000), *Principles of Internet Marketing*, Cincinnati: South-Western College Publishing.
Industry Canada (1999). 'Canadian Internet commerce statistics: summary sheet', SES Canada research, web entrepreneurship survey, Ottawa, Spring, (retrieved from: http://e-com.ic.gc.ca/using/en/e-comstats.pdf).

International Data Corporation (1999), 'The Internet and its impact on small business functions: first quarter 1999', IDC, Toronto, July.

KPMG (1999a), 'Electronic commerce research report 1999', London.

KPMG (1999b), 'Electronic commerce: a survey of small and medium sized enterprises', KPMG and Demon Internet, London.

Ng, Hooi-Im, Ying Jie Pan and T.D. Wilson (1998), 'Business use of the world wide web: a report on further investigations', *International Journal of Information Management*, **18** (5), 291–314.

Nielsen, Jakob (2000), *Designing Web Usability*, Indianapolis: New Riders Publishing.

OECD (1998), 'Small and medium-sized enterprises and electronic commerce', Paris, background report for the Ottawa Conference, September.

Pastore, Michael (2000), 'Small business provides opportunities for service providers' (retrieved from: http://cyberatlas.internet.com/markets/smallbiz/article/0,1323, 10098_712211,00.html).

PriceWaterhouseCoopers (1999), 'SME electronic commerce study (TEL05/97T)', final report for Asia Pacific Economic Cooperation, 24 September.

Samiee, Saeed (1998), 'Exporting and the Internet: a conceptual perspective', *International Marketing Review*, **15** (5), 413–26.

Sawhney, Mohanbir and Sumant Mandal (2000), 'Go Global', *Business 2.0*, May, 178–215.

Seringhaus, F.H. Rolf and Philip J. Rosson (1990), *Government Export Promotion: A Global Perspective*, London: Routledge.

Small Business Administration (1999), 'E-commerce: small businesses venture online', Office of Advocacy, Washington, July.

The Economist (1999), 'A survey of business and the Internet', 26 June, 5–6.

von Goeler, Kate (1998), 'Internet commerce by degrees: small business early adopters', 8 November (retrieved from: www.instat.com).

Yankee Group (1998), 'Yankee Group finds small and medium business market missing the Internet commerce opportunity', 17 November (retrieved from: www.yankeegroup.com).

9. Economic efficiency in traditional and dot.com firms: a theoretical approach

Khaled Soufani and Terence Tse

INTRODUCTION

Dot.com-centered activities in the newly emerging global economy expose businesses worldwide to a significantly larger number of customers and markets where the buying and selling of information, products and services are increasingly exercised via computer networks. This global situation exposes enterprises of all sizes operating in different business activities, industries and sectors to strategic challenges that require them to consider the potential threats and opportunities that face them with some degree of urgency. One of the important opportunities that can be considered by many firms, especially smaller enterprises, is their ability to become more competitive in order to expand in both domestic and international markets through increased economic efficiency. Economic efficiency relates to choosing the least-cost combination of inputs and also producing the maximum feasible output from the existing resources (Sawyer, 1985). Economic efficiency in any market critically depends on the amount and the nature of information about products, costs, competition and customer taste that are available to both buyers and sellers (Whinston *et al.*, 1997). When the three economic agents that are engaged in major economic activities in any market (consumers, firms and the government) are not endowed with proper information, the market may be inefficient or even fail to function. Market failure does not mean that nothing good has happened, but it means that the best attainable results have not been achieved (Raynauld *et al.*, 1994). International businesses have never before been equipped with tools that facilitate the acquisition of fast, precise and general information at the least possible cost as is possible today through the Internet and the World Wide Web.

The primary objective of this chapter is to develop a theoretical framework that portrays the conceptual role of information on the World Wide Web in enhancing the economic efficiency of dot.com-centered activities. Another objective is to develop an efficiency-chain model that addresses factors and variables that pertain to the role of information in enhancing efficiency. The model theoretically evaluates the effects on each stage in the efficiency chain when more information is derived from, or permeated through, the Internet. This can set the stage for developing a robust analysis to evaluate the effects of Internet information on the economic efficiency of firms that use dot.com operations both theoretically and empirically.

ECONOMIC EFFICIENCY

Efficiency relates to the use and the allocation of resources. In the use of resources, economic efficiency requires that any given output is produced at a minimum cost, which in turn implies that both waste and technological inefficiency are avoided and that appropriate input prices are used to find the cost-minimizing production process (Bannock *et al.*, 1984). Optimal allocation of resources and economic efficiency are achieved when it is no longer feasible to change the existing resource mix to make someone (for example, a supplier, manufacturer, wholesaler, retailer or consumer) better off without making someone else worse off.

Economic efficiency in any market critically depends on the amount and nature of information about the input and output factors and processes, including those of raw materials, competition, customer taste, costs and prices. Information enables producers and consumers to maximize the difference between what they are willing to sell (buy) a good or service for and what they actually sell (buy) it for, which relates to the economic concept of producer surplus and consumer surplus. It is argued that economic efficiency is achieved at the theoretical point of intersection between supply and demand in a competitive market: Pareto optimality (Varian, 1999). Although this is practically difficult to achieve, attaining any improvement towards that state is certainly desirable. Economists have recognized that information could play an important role in achieving a more efficient state of affairs (Mishan, 1981; Pindyck and Rubinfeld, 1999; Perloff, 1998).

The development of the World Wide Web (WWW) has made it possible to establish, and to increase, the role of dot.com activities in the international economy, which in turn has increased the flow of information available to and from all economic agents, including consumers, producers or firms, and the government. The transformation of information technology through the Internet has contributed largely to a transition from the traditional ('bricks and mortar' system to the New Economy. The New Economy carries many of the factors that contribute to the enhancement of economic efficiency, as more information is widely available and easily accessible to producers and consumers. Therefore the development of a theoretical model containing the elements necessary for the improvement of an efficiency chain will be useful for evaluating the benefits and the economics of electronic commerce and dot.com-centered activities.

DEFINITION OF DOT.COM

Given that the impact of the World Wide Web varies from industry to industry and that the primary aim of this chapter is to generate a general model, we define dot.com in a fairly broad sense. 'Dot.coms' refers to those companies, a chain of companies, a market or an activity that involve some elements of the Internet or the WWW. On the other hand, 'traditional' relates to the non-usage of the Internet for business activities.

This study develops an efficiency-chain model that addresses the factors and variables that pertain to the role of information in enhancing efficiency. The model theoretically evaluates the effects on each stage in the efficiency chain when more information is derived from, or permeated through, the Internet.

THE ECONOMIC EFFICIENCY MODEL

Traditional economic theory does not provide a specific definition of the role of dot.com activities in enhancing economic efficiency, which is mainly due to the fact that the importance of economic activity and business operations on the Internet has become more evident over the past few years. There appears to be a gap in the academic literature that focuses on establishing a link between traditional economic theory and the role of the Internet. This gap in the literature is a strong element in the justification for this study.

We are unaware of any existing formalized model in economics literature that depicts a traditional economic efficiency chain. Therefore, for the purposes of comparison, we present what constitutes such a chain in Figure 9.1. The model assumes the simplest form of a chain, starting from raw material suppliers and extending to consumers (end-users). We will start with the final stage or the end-users in the chain. In the traditional economy, consumers experience a cumbersome selection process. This is because information can only reach a limited audience, which in turns entails significant search costs (Evans and Wurster, 1997). For instance, a consumer in search of a product has to choose a street, then a shop, then a department, then a shelf, and then a product; the process (and cost) is likely to be repeated if he or she intends to look further.

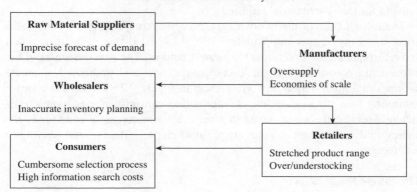

Traditional Economic Efficiency Chain

Note: In such chains the non-usage of the Internet in achieving economic efficiency means not benefiting from the enhancement led by information.

Figure 9.1   The traditional progression of a supply chain

As for a retailer interested in catering to customers of various types, it may have to carry a wide range of products to prepare for all potential customers' eclectic tastes and preferences. This might lead to either an overstocking or an understocking of goods as a result of the lack of adequate a priori information concerning the customers' needs and wants. Evans and Wurster's (1999) observation that 'inventory is merely the physical correlate of deficient information' sums up this situation very well.

On the basis of the above logic, retailers would order a suboptimal combination of various goods from wholesalers. These retailers' pattern of ordering would probably lead the wholesalers to suffer from similar suboptimal inventory planning. Manufacturers, as a result, would experience difficulties in forecasting demand with precision. Consequently the entire system would carry excess inventory to cover for lack of adequate information. Fisher *et al.* (2000) found that the markdowns of department stores in the USA grew from 8 per cent of store sales in 1971 to 33 per cent in 1995 and concluded that this was the result of manufacturers' oversupply.

Perhaps one of the best-known approaches to attaining economic efficiency is to engage in scale economies. Even so it may not be the most profitable approach. This is because it only increases value gradually and in a linear fashion. Small effort produces small results; large effort gives large results (Kelly, 1998). As we argue below, information availability in the New Economy can result in reduction of economic waste (for example, excess inventory) and yield increasing returns, making economies of scale obsolete. At the raw material suppliers' level, it is expected that there will be a problem in forecasting the demand for the raw material required.

The introduction of the Internet may have had a major impact on the traditional economy. Evans and Wurster (1997) suggested that it has dismantled and reformulated the traditional business structures. The new dynamics of the information economics has made companies, new and traditional, evaluate their optimal input/output mix. We present in Figure 9.2 a theoretical concept exhibiting how the availability of information can influence economic efficiency. Specifically we postulate that there are three types of economic efficiency enhancements: single stage and ripple effects, and customer satisfaction.

The Single Stage Effects

By 'single-stage enhancement', we refer to the fact that the Internet improves the information availability and subsequently the organization of *each stage* in the chain. At the consumers' level, it is generally agreed that incomplete information prevents them from making optimal decisions. Evans and Wurster (1997) believe that the Internet has mitigated the limitations of informational reach. The economic efficiency gained by consumers by maximization of consumer surplus is becoming increasingly significant as search costs are drastically reduced. More importantly, previously unattainable information can now be obtained and as a result the decision-making process of suppliers and consumers becomes both a less expensive and a more efficient exercise than before.

As for retailers, the ability to track customers' preferences and spending patterns can be extremely valuable. This is particularly valid for pure dot.com companies. Rather than maintaining a broad and general marketing program and placing a general advertisement in the newspaper, these online sellers can tailor-make their marketing programs to promote specific products that fit the specific customer's needs, taste and spending patterns. The ability to do so can be translated into economic efficiency enhancements as marketing can become less expensive and possibly more effective. A clearer picture of the customers' preferences can also lead to better inventory, displaying and shelving planning and management. Economic efficiency is therefore further enhanced.

The attainment of better information by the wholesalers allows them to forecast demand conditions with greater accuracy. This higher accuracy in demand projection enables tighter inventory control thanks to the newly gained ability of wholesalers to improve their procurement and inventory management policy. This is possible as, first and foremost, information helps to identify the purchasing pattern, thereby ensuring that supply matches

New Economic Efficiency Chain: Single Stage Enhancement

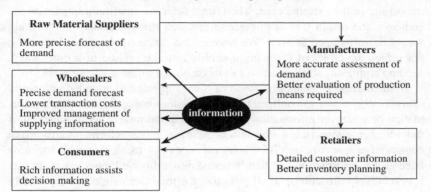

Raw Material Suppliers

More precise forecast of demand

Wholesalers

Precise demand forecast
Lower transaction costs
Improved management of supplying information

Consumers

Rich information assists decision making

information

Manufacturers

More accurate assessment of demand
Better evaluation of production means required

Retailers

Detailed customer information
Better inventory planning

Note: Each stage enhances its economic efficiency using the information that is relevant to it; such information, pertaining to only one stage, is not shared by another (thus the stages are not connected).

Figure 9.2 The economic impact of information in a single stage

demand, which in turn maximizes economic efficiency. Second, it could lower transaction costs by reducing inventory and streamlining administration costs, as argued above. An example of administration costs is dispatching sales representatives to gather intelligence concerning specific groups of customers in terms of either geography or characteristics. With the advance of e-commerce, all customer information, down to the smallest detail, can be obtained, stored and analyzed at a much lower cost and with greater ease.

With regard to the manufacturers, greater availability of information yields a more accurate assessment of demand, which in turn could circumvent the aforementioned oversupplying problem. Information could also help them to align the quantity and quality of raw materials better with the production needs. Consequently manufacturers have better information for assessing the tangible production assets they have to purchase.

It should now be clearer that economic efficiency is gained when each stage of the chain receives more information. For the next type of economic efficiency enhancement, we examine the effect of information on economic efficiency when the stages are connected together by information flow (Figure 9.3).

The Ripple Effect

The ripple effect is our second type of economic efficiency enhancement, which relates to the case when the impact of any additional information available to any stage in the chain would permeate all levels, perhaps up to the origin: in the extreme case, when there is an informational impact on the end-user, the origin (for example, the required raw materials) of the chain would be influenced as well. We have called this a ripple effect because it resembles the effect of throwing a pebble into the middle of a quiet pond, sending ripples in all directions. Let us elaborate on how it may work.

In the traditional economy, consumers are subjected to bounded rationality (Simon, 1957): they are obliged to make decisions based on incomplete information or whatever information they possess at the time. The introduction of the Internet allows these consumers to have more information to make comparative assessments. This, however, does not mean that they can now have all the information and that bounded rationality no longer exists. In fact it is relatively difficult, if at all possible, for the information to be perfectly symmetric to both consumers and suppliers. Nevertheless we believe that, even though information asymmetry always prevails, the slightest (positive or negative) change in information availability can have an impact on consumers' purchasing behavior and desires. Any game theory example can illustrate such a modification in purchasing attitude.

In our economic efficiency model, we postulate that, when consumers have

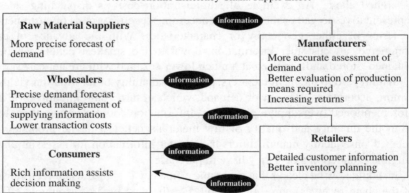

New Economic Efficiency Chain: Ripple Effect

Note: The ripple effect results when stages are connected by information (thus the linkage between stages), creating a network. It takes place when the impact of a piece of information fed into one of the stages permeates the whole network. It can be argued that new information injected into the knowledge realm of consumers will be beneficial to all the stages in the chain. In addition to those from stage-specific information, each stage benefits from the information flowing through the network. For example, the manufacturers can earn increasing returns, as opposed to the linear returns from economies of scale.

Figure 9.3   The ripple effect

better quality information, not only can they enjoy the benefits of rich information, but also better quality information will be passed on throughout the chain. For instance, when a particular consumer has more information to make a more accurate assessment of his or her purchasing decisions than before, the retailer which sells him or her the goods will also be able to obtain a more accurate picture of his or her preferences and purchasing patterns. For restocking the inventory, for example, the retailer now has a more precise idea of the demand for the goods. As the information follows up along the chain, the wholesaler can compile more precise data concerning the demand and demography in each of its retailing regions. Even the manufacturer further up is now in a better position to determine what and how much must be produced to satisfy the potential demand. In this example, the information 'quality ripple' is sent through from the consumer's end, causing a positive influence on each stage.

The use of the Internet and the WWW creates conditions which enable small and medium-sized enterprises to expand their options in looking for something online. As the web-based commerce becomes easier and cheaper, it will reach various customer bases and markets and the ease and affordability will be factors conducive to enhancing efficiency. There also appears to be another enhancement of economic efficiency. With the improvement of the quality and the transfer speed of information, the speed of the supply chain is accelerated. Such speed is especially vital to products that have short life cycles. The holy grail of retailing – being able to offer the right product at the right place at the right time for the right price – has remained frustratingly elusive (Fisher *et al.*, 2000). We expect that, with the improvement of economic efficiency in the New Economy, the retailing world will be one step closer to achieving this.

When information is shared among all stages of the chain, we can expect the usefulness of the information available to the network (within the chain) to increase proportionally to the square of the number of users (stages). This is a function known as Metcalf's law. In fact the value of information increases as the number of members who use it increases (Downes and Mui, 1998). For instance, instead of simply earning linear returns from economies of scale, the manufacturers can enjoy increasing returns in a network with value increasing exponentially as 'small efforts reinforce one another so that results can quickly snowball into an avalanche' (Kelly, 1998).

To sum up, it appears that information available on the web can enhance economic efficiency at a single-stage level as well as between and among the different stages. We can therefore draw on the two types of economic efficiency enhancement discussed above. The benefits of the increase in the availability of information are equal to the sum of all enhancements attained at the stage level *plus* the values created between the different stages *plus* the

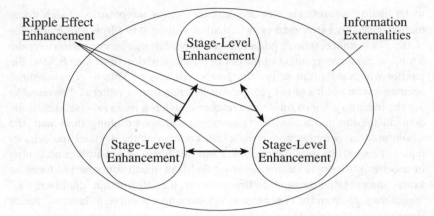

Figure 9.4   The combined effects of the stage-level and ripple effect
enhancements

information externalities resulting from the new opportunities and the incre-
ment of information value accruing to repetitive uses. This conclusion is
depicted in Figure 9.4. Given the above explanation, it would be fair to expect
that a network with three members might be much more powerful than three
networks with one member each. It is therefore useful to explore this hypothesis empirically.

Customer Satisfaction

There is an additional dimension to economic efficiency. As mentioned before,
economic efficiency results from the choice of the most cost-effective
input–output mix, but, in the traditional economy, suppliers predominantly
determine this mix. Consumers lacking information can only act partially, if
not passively. With the emergence of the dot.com activities, consumers have
become more powerful and selective, largely owing to the effect of interactiv-
ity and the growth of human intelligence. Consumers become more active and
are able to search for the desired goods at any time of the day, month or year
without needing to make any physical trips to a commercial location. Sellers
must now consider consumers' actual desires in order to adjust for the right
input–output mix. Furthermore, as information is becoming much more accessible, the Internet allows consumers to digress from focusing solely on the
product. What is provided on the website is much more than the product itself.
People also see the context of the product (Hampden-Turner, 1998). All this
leads businesses to pay more attention to customer satisfaction than ever
before. This has led economic resources to be diverted and reallocated in order

to create customer satisfaction and relationships, which were previously less of a concern.

The value of customer relations is, after all, the proprietary information that suppliers have about their customers and that their customers have about the company of their choice and their products (Evans and Wurster, 1997). As the information barrier breaks down, we can expect customer relations, or customer value, to become the fundamental operating principle of many businesses. In fact this principle is becoming paramount, not only to dot.com firms, but also to the traditional ones (Vandermerwe, 1999). It is also expected that, with the increasing symmetry of information, companies will no longer be able to profit from limiting the spread of information. As the information flow increases, companies are less able to hide their costs and pass on inefficiencies to customers (Downes and Mui, 1998). Evans and Wurster (1997) suggest, for example, that automobile dealers' profit margins depend on exploiting information asymmetry, which in turn confirms the arguments made by Akerlof (1970) regarding the used cars market and problems associated with asymmetric information. We therefore hypothesize that economic efficiency found in dot.com firms could be different from that of traditional firms as the composition of input differs: more resources in dot.com firms have to be spent on developing customers' satisfaction, rather than wasted on the exploitation of information deficiency. Whereas most physical resources are used in the majority of inputs in traditional firms, intangible information constitutes a substantial portion of input in the dot.com companies. While the former input is generally exhaustible, the latter not only can be reused, but is also attainable at very low, if not zero, cost. Therefore we expect that the unique nature of information will create a unique input–output mix and thus widen the differences between the economic efficiency of the two types of firms.

CONCLUSION

This chapter presents a theoretical approach to the way in which information can contribute to enhancing economic efficiency. One of the most important elements brought in by the Internet was the previously unseen (or even unimaginable) number of channels for disseminating information. Through linked communication and the creation of networks, we conceptualize the significant impact that information alone can have on the economic efficiency chain faced by businesses and their customers. Given the findings and the proposals of this study, we hope that this chapter will serve to stimulate robust future research and analysis to evaluate the global implications of this issue. In addition, the model can be utilized as guidance for managers in their attempt to restructure their organizations for higher efficiency and competitiveness to meet the challenges of the borderless global economy, which will inevitably be based on some form of dot.com activities.

REFERENCES

Akerlof, George A. (1970), 'The market for "lemons": quality uncertainty and the market mechanism', *Quarterly Journal of Economics*, **84**, 488–500.

Bannock, Graham, R.E. Baxter and Ray Rees (1984), *The Dictionary of Economics*, 3rd edition, Harmondsworth: Penguin.

Downes, Larry and Chunka Mui (1998), *Unleashing the Killer App: Digital Strategies for Market Dominance*, Boston, MA: Harvard Business School Press.

Evans, Philip and Thomas S. Wurster (1997), 'Strategy and the new economics of information', *Harvard Business Review*, September–October, 7–82.

Evans, Philip and Thomas S. Wurster (1999), *Blown to Bits: How the New Economics of Information Transform Strategy*, Boston, MA: Harvard Business School Press.

Fisher, M., A. Raman and A.S. McClelland (2000), 'Rocket science retailing is almost here, are you ready?', *Harvard Business Review*, July–August, 115–24.

Hampden-Turner, C. (1998), 'Living in a world of paradox: from chaos to self-organization in the knowledge economy', *Siemens Business Service's 21st Century Symposium Workshop*, 4.

Kelly, Kevin (1998), *New Rules for the New Economy: 10 Radical Strategies for the Connected World*, New York: Penguin Books.

Mishan, Edward J. (1981), *Economic Efficiency and Social Welfare: Selected Essays on Fundamental Aspects of the Economic Theory of Social Welfare*, London: George Allen and Unwin.

Perloff, Jeffrey M. (1998), *Microeconomics*, Reading, MA: Addison-Wesley Longman.

Pindyck, Robert S. and Daniel L. Rubinfeld (1999), *Microeconomics*, Scarborough: Prentice-Hall Canada.

Raynauld, Jacques, Yvan Stringer and Peter C.G. Townley (1994), *Markets and Prices: A Policy Perspective*, Scarborough: Prentice-Hall Canada.

Sawyer, Malcom C. (1985), *The Economics of Industries and Firms*, London: Croom Helm.

Simon, Herbert (1957), *Models of Man: Social and Rational; Mathematical Essays on Rational Human Behavior in Society Setting*, New York: Wiley.

Vandermerwe, Sandra (1999), *Customer Capitalism: The New Business Model of Increasing Returns in New Market Spaces*, London: Nicholas Brealey Publishing.

Varian, Hal (1999), *Intermediate Microeconomics: A Modern Approach*, New York and London: W.W. Norton.

Whinston, Andrew B., Dale Stahl and Choi Soon-Yong (1997), *The Economics of Electronic Commerce*, Indianapolis: Macmillan Technical Publishing.

10. The knowledge network of e-commerce and internationalization of entrepreneurship

Hamid Etemad and Yender Lee

INTRODUCTION

The number of books, articles, reports and other on-line publications, studying numerous problems in e-commerce in different fields rival the rate of publication in any well-established and active field.[1] Each of these fields is examining a relevant e-commerce problem from their own disciplinary and then multidisciplinary perspectives. These developments point collectively to two clear facts: that an interdisciplinary field is emerging and that e-commerce will be developing much faster than its constituent disciplinary fields as it will be drawing upon their established base as well as respective growth rates. Although e-commerce has been very inclusive in its early stages of development, both in terms of content (that is, many disciplines, from computer sciences to technology and trade) and geographical reach (that is, spanning boundaries and time zones), it is practically impossible for practitioners and scholars to keep up with these developments. These rapid developments, especially their wide coverage, call for a systemic tracing of worldwide collections on the subject. This chapter is an attempt to use the theory of knowledge networks (Etemad and Lee, 2003a) in order to reveal the early scholarly foundations documented by and spread in many books and journals.

In contrast to this rapid development in e-commerce by the early champions of this emerging field, the broader field of entrepreneurship to which e-commerce entrepreneurs belong (and from which e-commerce has departed), experienced a long formation period. While the beginning of entrepreneurship can be traced to the incremental work of a few principal founders, including Cantillon (1755), Jean Baptiste Say (1803, 1815), Ely and Hess (1893) and Schumpeter (1911, 1942, 1947) over the long formation period of some 250 years, (Etemad, 2003b; Etemad and Lee, 2003a), the early works in e-commerce are less than three decades old. In fact the first cited scholarly works appeared in the early 1990s. For example, the first two cited scholarly articles in *MIS Quarterly* and in the *Journal of Management Information*, written by J.Y. Bakos, appeared in 1991 (see notes of Table 10.1 for full reference and Table 10.2a for citation details). The first two books in the field, *Frontiers of Electronic Commerce*, by Kalakota and Whinston, and *Digital Electronic Commerce*, by Tapscott (see notes of Table 10.1 for full reference and Table 10.2b for the citation), appeared in 1996 (see Tables 10.2b and 10.4 for details) less than ten years ago. (For tables see end of chapter.) The first of dedicated scholarly journals in the field began publishing only in the early 1990s (see Tables 10.3 and 10.4 for details). In spite of its embryonic state, e-commerce followed the developmental structure and evolutionary path (Culnan and Swanson, 1986) of one of its constituent fields, management information systems (MIS), and has begun to exhibit signs of becoming a field of its own (Culnan, 1987). Given this rapid rate of development, amassing a body of literature in a short time, and the importance of this literature to international entrepreneurship and also in attracting other scholars for further development of this emerging field, this chapter will attempt (a) to provide a preliminary perspective on the rapid development of the field, (b) to identify the diverse array of constituent fields (from which e-commerce draws, and upon which it builds its further development), and (c) to generate a selected list of high-impact e-commerce-related references. These references should manifest characteristics of knowledge networks and could serve as a scholarly basis for the future research and development in internationalization of entrepreneurship as a field both of scholarly enquiry and of practice.

As an emerging interdisciplinary field, e-commerce draws and builds upon its constituent elements to form integrated platforms for its further development. The working hypothesis of this chapter is that e-commerce, even in its current embryonic state, relies heavily, and builds upon, many other well-developed fields for its further development. We refer to these fields as the constituent fields of e-commerce, which include, for example, Accounting, Auditing, Business Law, Computer and Information Science, Consumer Behaviors and Consumer Psychology, Economics, Finance, Information Systems and Technologies (IS/IT), International Business, Marketing, Operations Management and Supply Chain Management (SCM) among others. This early dependence of e-commerce on its constituent fields appears to have stimulated its rapid development. The evolutionary paths of most sciences gravitate towards more specialization within each field. The implication of this tendency is that specialists in each field would need to know of similar specialized developments elsewhere. The Internet's inner connectivity may have served it well, and may have also served as a catalyst in the interdisciplinary development of e-commerce by extension. Conversely this specialization and the heightened need for access to the knowledge of the other fields may have served the development both of e-commerce and of its associated knowledge base (that is, the knowledge network of e-commerce)[2] very well. On the one hand, no other field has drawn upon so many diverse fields to deliver potential benefits to such a large number of human endeavors as e-commerce has already done in its short life span. On the other hand, no other field has required communication and coordination within and across so many fields as e-commerce. E-commerce's need for such beneficial relations seems to have served the development of both e-commerce and its constituent fields symbiotically (Etemad *et al.*, 2001) and synergistically at the same time (Etemad, 2003a, 2003b). However interdisciplinary fields experience lower rates of development elsewhere (Etemad, 1999; Etemad and Lee, 2003a, 2003b).

The above argument suggests that the rapid development of e-commerce can be attributed in part to its wide reach and multidisciplinary nature, which allows it to draw heavily from, and capitalize on, each of its constituent fields' development, including international business (which has a broad reach, wide scope and multidisciplinary nature). It is also in part due to the embryonic state of the field, which allows it to rely on pertinent materials of the other established fields. The former characteristics may have also reinforced e-commerce's need to remain a cross-disciplinary field of enquiry. Owing to the nature of the field, e-commerce now has a high potential for further coordination and integration as well as cross-fertilization of its constituent fields, which in turn help e-commerce's further development. These developments would undoubtedly be beneficial to e-commerce as a field of application and practice as well as scholarly inquiry.

The rapid technological development in IT (a constituent field of e-commerce) as well as the global nature of information technology (that is, its potential to reach hundreds of millions of people in remote locations at low cost through a variety of platforms and possibilities) may have further heightened e-commerce's development in the last two decades. The possibility of interactive access through the Internet to an enormous volume of global resources may have been another contributing factor, which has fueled and continues to stimulate the rapid growth of the supporting infrastructures. For ease of reference, we will call this infrastructure the hardware-based part of the World Wide Web (WWW), supporting e-commerce application and research with the assistance of specialized software-based techniques and technologies on the WWW. This interconnected infrastructure links enormous volumes of information residing on the various servers on the Web, making access to remote knowledge resources straightforward. Each of these servers can then be viewed as a reservoir of information and knowledge in the vast interconnected network, which we call the knowledge network (KN) of e-commerce. This knowledge network provides many potential benefits to individuals, as customers, entrepreneurs and users, as well as to organizations and to society as a whole. It also exposes them to an array of innovations and their inherent disruptive effects that did not exist before. Naturally the benefits attract more users, who in turn support the further expansion and development of e-commerce's knowledge network world wide (see the next section). Similarly the hazards also serve as challenges to the scholarly community in terms of research problems in need of solutions.

In short, e-commerce continues to expand its reach world wide and is assumed to have become one of the fundamental instruments of international trade and commerce. In fact, more of the relatively smaller enterprises are resorting to e-commerce to reach international customers in global markets than their larger counterparts. At the same time, the relatively larger enterprises are also using e-commerce networks to optimize the management of their supply chains, which have already reached all corners of the world.

The structure of this chapter is as follows. Following this introduction, the next section discusses the potential impact of e-commerce. A brief discussion of the theory of knowledge networks is presented in the third section. This theoretical framework guides the research and the results presented in the chapter. Similarly, bibliometric epistemology is adopted as the main research method. This methodology is used to develop a preliminary perspective on the knowledge network of e-commerce. In view of the space available, only the highlights of this knowledge network, including a brief list of frequently cited authors, documents (books, chapters and reports) and often used media sources with the highest impact are presented here. Conclusions and implications are discussed at the end.

THE POTENTIAL IMPACTS OF E-COMMERCE

The impact of e-commerce has been profound and pervasive. It has affected individuals, organizations and society as a whole. Three groups of individuals are affected by the rapid developments of the Internet and e-commerce: individual users of e-commerce resources, consumers and entrepreneurs. We concentrate first on individual customers and entrepreneurs, who are affected by e-commerce and can in turn have an impact upon the further development of the field with their respective actions. Secondly, we assess the impact of e-commerce on organizations and society as a whole.

Impact on Individuals as Customers

Consumers and customers[3] are the primary beneficiaries of e-commerce. The benefits are tangible for individual consumers and corporate customers and can be attributed to three broad factors:

1. *the stimulating role* of removing a host of barriers and restrictions, which furthers involvement in e-commerce;
2. *the facilitating role* of application and deployment of innovative Web-based techniques and technologies, which reduce transaction costs and enable enterprises to perform effectively at all e-commerce levels;
3. *the enabling role* of the infrastructure, which empowers players (for example, individuals and organizations) to conduct their affairs effectively in many innovative ways almost unimaginable in the past.

As a direct result, typical players can minimize their total transaction costs (that is, both time and financial components) and maximize their convenience by shopping or conducting other transactions asynchronously, 24 hours a day, all year round, from almost anywhere in the world, irrespective of restrictions associated with location and local business hours. The popular press refers to this as 'the death of time and distance and the global reach of the Internet' (Strauss and Frost, 2001, p. 4).[4]

Additionally e-commerce takes advantage of well-recognized and distinct features of the World Wide Web: access to e-commerce-oriented websites provides much richer information and wider selection choices to potential customers. As these attributes add value, buyers can hardly ignore or forgo the benefits associated with either the expanded choice or the convenience factor. E-commerce can allow a typical customer to interact with any number of enterprises, vendors and service providers on-line, supplying the expanded choice of products (or services) with as much intensity as they desire until they are satisfied.[5] There is no pressure, requirement or obligation to transact with such on-line entities unless the user feels content and perfectly satisfied, which is not necessarily the case in conventional transactions. The inner connectivity of the Web also enables potential customers to visit a much larger number of information nodes and thereby exhibit behaviors quite unlike their off-line and traditional practices. Consider a plausible scenario with a typical customer who visits a number of websites directly or indirectly (for example, through portal, electronic brokers, information intermediaries or purchasing agents). The customer can proceed to compare their offerings, enter or exit each site with a couple of clicks of the mouse, and make the selection that would offer him the maximum satisfaction based on the proposed value. He may simultaneously seek advice from rating agents on-line or seek guidance from information intermediaries (called infomediaries in the e-commerce terminology) in arriving at his final decision.

When the customer starts his prospecting with a search engine, it is very likely that e-commerce enterprises with URLs (universal resource locators) listed on the first page of the search results are visited first. Although this process is not too far from consulting consumer reports for the consumer ratings of land-based stores before visiting them, infomediaries appear to have a stronger, and even an undue, influence on the decision-making process of potentially new customers. While off-line rating agents are supported mainly by buyers, on-line rating agents are financed mainly by suppliers. The noteworthy point is that the incremental time cost of examining the much expanded consideration set, as compared to visiting additional stores, is in practice very little both to the provider and to the prospector. The popular press refers to this as being a click away from any site, regardless of time and distance (Strauss and Frost, 2001, pp. 6–7).[6]

Impact on Consumer Expectations

The low access cost is partly due to the 'public good' nature of information (or marketing knowledge in this case) residing on the Web and partly due to the Internet functioning as a knowledge network for e-commerce by providing easy access to the desired (or necessary) information on command. The ease of access to pertinent information and the possibility of comparing responses almost instantaneously (especially with the help of purchasing intermediaries, which rate and exhibit their results[7]) create greater competition among the suppliers and provide consumers with greater bargaining power. The higher information transparency also provides for the maximization of consumer surplus (or value) based on consumers' perceived value. Further confirmation by the supplier's rating, in relation to the prevailing value off-line at the time, either finalizes or aborts (in the case of disconfirmation) their initial preferences. It may also cause an upward revision in consumer expectation over time, if not right away. This tendency combined with inherent characteristics of the Internet (acting as a knowledge network of e-commerce, making access to information readily available), may further contribute to the upward movement of consumer expectations continually over time. In a conventional transaction, the maximization of value is generally due to the increased quality or reduced total cost to the buyer, but rarely a combination of the two. However e-commerce seems to be capable of improving on both the quality and the cost side of the value proposition. The lowering of total costs, whether real or perceived, for example, can come from a reduced financial or temporal component of costs. The increased convenience combined with the perceived higher quality (which may or may not correspond to reality) gives rise to increased competition for delivering increased value in real terms.

Impact on Competition and Suppliers

Ironically, as suppliers compete to remain in a typical customer's consideration set, in the hope of providing objective satisfaction by delivering much higher value, more choice, higher volume and more transparent information and higher quality of goods and services than before, they contribute to two mechanisms. The first is the escalation of consumer expectations: for much higher levels of information, transparency, choice, quality and value, which will further fuel competition. The second is the escalation of competition. Suppliers contribute to the momentum of higher competition, if not actually forcing it upon the participating suppliers.

Although such momentum adds to the customer's perceived advantage and may deliver actual benefit to them, it also leads to the ultimate shake-out in the on-line service providers due to escalating competition. Those who cannot continuously provide higher value (for example, in terms of higher quality combined with lower real or perceived prices) to compete under such sustained and increasing pressure will have to exit the market eventually. The consequent thinning in the suppliers' ranks is bound to slow down both the expectation and competition escalation mechanisms and eventually stabilize both pressures, at least temporarily, before more innovative on-line entrepreneurs fuel the expectation and competition mechanisms once more.

Implications

The above suggests that e-commerce enterprises should try to increase the ease and convenience of on-line transactions as well as reduce their actual financial or temporal costs. E-commerce innovative techniques and technologies can help achieve the latter easily by, for example, shortening almost all required time cycles. Shorter cycles could be accomplished through faster, more effective and easier interfaces between the buyers and suppliers, faster production and expedited delivery. The end result is higher value in terms of higher customer satisfaction due to a combination of added choice, higher responsiveness, information transparency, buyer empowerment and true improvements in the delivered quality of most goods and services, especially for 'digitized products and services' (for example, digital books, music and software).

The public policy implications are equally profound. Countries that cannot provide fast and efficient access to information for their own on-line entrepreneurs will be effectively creating barriers to e-commerce transactions within their jurisdiction. They will also be preventing their e-commerce entrepreneurs from competing effectively as rapid and efficient access to websites and on-line information are critical to successful competition in cyberspace.

Impact on Entrepreneurs and Intrapreneurs

E-commerce offers a rich set of opportunities to both entrepreneurs and intrapreneurs, ranging from simple automation of order processing to

complete presence and participation in international markets. Dana *et al.*
(2004) maintain that mere 'internetization' of knowledge leads to increased
participation in international commerce almost independent of the enterprise's
size, age and experience, as entrepreneurs take advantage of the emerging on-
line opportunities and contribute to added market efficiencies. This resonates
well with Schumpeter's destructive construction (1934), whereby newer and
more innovative enterprises add to the overall efficiencies and force the older
and less efficient firms to exit.

Although conventional internationalization has been reportedly correlated
with both size and age (Poutziouris *et al.*, 2003) as well as with the experientially gained knowledge set of the enterprise (Johansson and Vahlne, 1977,
1990, 1992), on-line enterprises may not follow the tradition. This is mainly
due to the contributions of the e-commerce knowledge network to on-line
enterprises. In fact, the Scandinavian School of Internationalization is
anchored by the concept of gaining knowledge experientially (Johanson and
Wiedersheim-Paul, 1975) in psychologically close (Stöttinger and
Schlegelmilch, 1998) countries before moving to establish further international presence elsewhere.

In contrast, the knowledge network of e-commerce is already capable of
bridging the explicit knowledge gap by connecting foreign enterprises with the
interested local enterprise to cover the tacit, locally embedded and experiential (Polanyi, 1969; Nonaka and Takeuchi, 1996) knowledge gaps. Therefore
e-commerce-centered entrepreneurs (or intrapreneurs) can champion corporate presence in cyberspace and thereby override the barriers of time, distance
(both physical and psychological), culture and experience by offering a rich
set of choices corresponding to the diversity of international markets. The
Internet can provide a neutral, yet efficient and effective, electronic environment, through which information (and then physical) access can be provided.
The possibility of providing a much expanded choice alone, each corresponding to a set of culturally centered preferences at no additional cost, overcomes
the conventional barriers of corporate size, age and experience as factors
inhibiting international consumers and contributing to their conventional resistance.[8] This is at the root of customer relations management (CRM) applied
internationally (Etemad, 2003a, 2003b). The delivery of value higher than
customers' expectations, based on well-tailored offerings centered on the local
consumers' needs (or expectations) may lead directly to increased satisfaction,
loyalty and repeat purchases.

Implications
The above is tantamount to providing entrepreneurs (or intrapreneurs) of
smaller, younger and less-endowed enterprises with the opportunity of gaining
access to global markets, which are practically difficult, if not impossible, to

reach conventionally in the real world. In other words, the knowledge network of e-commerce coupled with international entrepreneurship through alliances (Yoshino and Rangan, 1995) can provide a matchless set of expanded opportunities for potential cyberspace enterprise. Therefore the access to e-commerce techniques and technologies (that is, the software-based part of e-commerce) and the information infrastructure (that is, the information backbone or the hardware-based part of e-commerce) can be viewed as *enablers to aspiring international entrepreneurs*. Naturally their absence will disadvantage a potential local enterprise in global competition.

Impact on Organizations

E-commerce affects nearly all aspects of organizations and can benefit them in many profound ways. Most of these impacts are initially market-driven, but affect internal functions and cross corporate boundaries as well. However the consequent intercorporate interactions radiate inward with time and encompass most corporate actions in the partner organizations.

The demand side

On the demand side, e-commerce holds the potential of expanding an organization's competitive space from local to national and eventually international markets, with comparatively low capital outlays. As a result, an enterprise can quickly and interactively reach more customers by reaching numerous local distribution channels, increasing economies of scale, diversifying its customer base and market segments and managing its supply chain, marketing and distribution on a timely basis (for example, on a just-in-time basis), if not more efficiently and effectively, all with the help of e-commerce-centered techniques and technologies at a much lower cost and with fewer delays than their conventional counterparts.

The supply side

On the supply side of the enterprise value chain, e-commerce has the potential to enhance both the primary and the supporting functions in a typical value chain and thereby create additional value for suppliers and partners. In contrast to CRM, managing partners' relations in delivering more value to all partners is called 'partner relations management' (PRM). On the primary side, PRM can facilitate the management of procurement functions through on-line, in-time and continuous (when necessary) management of information flows pertaining to communication, documentation, order processing (for example, acknowledgment and verification of orders and shipments), financing and collection with suppliers and business partners worldwide on a temporally optimal basis. Such management of the supply chain's critical flows, for example, minimizes the volume of goods-in-process and inventory. It also makes the supply chain much more responsive to both consumers and the changes in the market place.

In addition to the above fine-tuning of procurement, production, logistics, marketing and distribution functions, e-commerce can further enhance the performance of support functions along the value chain. For example, e-commerce-related and Web-based technologies can expedite the storing, processing and retrieving of pertinent information associated with order placement and processing and their corresponding financial flows, which used to be mostly paper-based and manually processed, with long delays. In fact generic e-commerce support technologies include enterprise resource programs (ERP), PRM and even customer relations management (CRM), which are all automated, interactive and functional without much intervention by the much slower personnel. Computers can be enabled to 'talk to each other' in real time and manage the system optimally without undue delays. These technologies support e-commerce-related processes and technologies and allow them to reduce the costs of the overheads, finished and in-process goods as well as inventories by creating 'pull-type supply chains': that is, once demanded, the product is designed, produced and delivered quickly (Etemad, 2003a).

Implications
E-commerce can therefore help the organization to decrease the cost of creating, processing and distributing goods and services, on the one hand, and increase customer satisfaction by responding to particular needs in shorter process cycles, on the other hand. Combined, these factors add to a firm's value proposition, increasing its competitiveness and augmenting its flexibility in rapidly changing markets as well as reducing the costs of bringing well-suited, if not tailor-made, products and services to the market place.

Impact on Society

Society as a whole also benefits from e-commerce through three principal mechanisms, as follows.

Improvements in interactions across the enterprise boundaries
As stated above, e-commerce-centered techniques and technologies improve the efficiency of the market/exchange mechanism on both the demand and the supply side by reducing systemic waste as well as increasing the responsiveness of the system, resulting in a better allocation of resources across the organization.

Fine-tuning of internal processes
The introduction of Web-based and well-tuned routines for managing CRM and PRM processes requires a corresponding fine-tuning in both the enterprise resource planning (ERP) and the organizational structures to accommodate them, which facilitates a potentially better exchange and timely allocation of resources within the organization.

Overall societal efficiency
The required efficiencies across supply chain and production lines, in response to market and competitive demands and inter-firm arrangements, as discussed earlier, require a much better allocation of resources both internally and across corporate boundaries. On the human resource side of the equation, for example, e-commerce enables more individuals to work at home through Internet connectivity, which in turn provides for economies associated with 'working smartly and effectively' and even doing more with less as waste is reduced (that is, less time, to do more, and even more effective, work with the help of augmenting technologies readily available on-line, especially for e-commerce-related processes). On the socioeconomic side, virtual work communities may also reduce waste in terms of travel time, transportation, energy and even traffic jams, which all combine to lead to more efficient and effective production across numerous supply chains. In other words, e-commerce can lower the cost of e-commerce-augmented goods and services and allow them to be supplied at substantively lower prices, which in turns allows for market expansion nationally and internationally as less affluent customers can afford to participate in international markets and purchase an expanded basket of products or services and thereby raise their living standards. In summary, e-commerce can lower the cost of living while raising the standard of living thanks to increased productivity without much additional cost to the individual or to the productive system as a whole, as waste and redundancy are systematically minimized.

Implications
Both the enterprise and society need to adopt e-commerce-oriented strategies and deploy e-commerce techniques and technologies for their inherent efficiencies, without which they cannot compete with others as effectively and efficiently.

THE THEORY OF KNOWLEDGE NETWORKS OF E-COMMERCE AND THE RESEARCH QUESTIONS

Description of Knowledge Networks

Knowledge is simply the output of the learning (or knowing) process, just as plans are the output of the planning process. In Western culture, science and knowledge are often used interchangeably or combined to form scientific knowledge (Gibbons *et al.*, 1994). Chandy and Williams (1994) suggest that every discipline can be seen as a particular knowledge system that is a component of a more general system. For example, Administrative Sciences are a part of Social Sciences. The concept of network has been used in engineering for designing and managing complex systems for a long time. Similar to complex systems, each local component of the network is a part (or subpart) of the larger network and is designed to perform a particular task effectively within its mandate. Since the early 1980s, the concept of a knowledge network has been accepted as one of the principal metaphors for portraying the essential characteristics of interrelated and complex knowledge and information systems which underlie a socioeconomic system, such as e-commerce. Implicit in the concept of network is that certain resources are concentrated in certain locations (nodes, which are scattered around the network) but are accessible through the network thanks to the interlinkages among the nodes holding those knowledge resources. Consequently, a knowledge network can be viewed as the invisible structure of knowledge and intellectual capital of a field residing within a set of interconnected nodes, in which each node contains a family of related knowledge resources consisting of concepts, ideas (or inventions), frameworks (or models), and technologies (and techniques or routines) – CIFTE – for solving problems. The knowledge network of a field can therefore be portrayed as a framework for identifying both the CIFTE residing in the various nodes, and the cross-cutting ties among them, whether richer, stronger or weaker.

Similarly a general system of knowledge generation (or some diffusion process among the producers and users of the CIFTE over time) in any discipline can be viewed as an ever-evolving landscape of interlinked concentrations of important knowledge resources and technologies essential to supporting the field and residing in the innerconnected nodes accessible by others, as if they themselves were the repository of the essential knowledge (or technology).[9] Certain key nodes serve as pillars and are critical to the initial formation and understanding of the evolutionary path of a given discipline, particularly in its emerging stages. The interconnection of servers throughout the World Wide Web, with their store of e-commerce-related information data banks and techniques or technologies, can easily characterize the Internet as the e-commerce knowledge network.

Epistemological Bibliometrics

The understanding of these characteristics and the developmental processes inherent in a knowledge system are usually referred to as the epistemology and are specific to that discipline. While epistemology is formally defined as the study of the nature of knowledge, the objective of an epistemological inquiry is the understanding, and even the justification, of the knowledge through analysis of its origin and nature, identity of intellectual architects and understanding of its development, including its associated developmental path(s) over time. Traditionally, and especially in Europe, the scope of epistemology is restricted to scientific knowledge. We take the liberty of extending these boundaries in order to understand the various characteristics of e-commerce inclusively.

Portraying the E-commerce Knowledge Network through Bibliometric Epistemology

Bibliometrics refers to efforts designed to quantify what constitutes knowledge within a given knowledge network through proxy measures applied to the communication, in written and published forms, among knowledge workers in a field (Laudon and Laudon, 1993, p. 488). Among a variety of methods developed in the last three decades, citation analysis is the earliest and the most widely used, as well as the most important method of bibliometrics. As Merton (1979) pointed out, citation indexing has been a standard of scientific bibliography, but its sociological and historical research potentials have not been fully exploited.

Following Latour (1987), we use bibliometric epistemology to characterize the knowledge network of e-commerce in terms of its intellectual designers (the 'who'), their respective contributions (the 'what') and the time and place in which they were published (the 'when and 'where'). According to Latour (1987), these are four of the six principal attributes of knowledge which help to portray a knowledge network. The landscape of a mature knowledge network contains a large number of citations, from a sufficiently large number of sources, written by many authors (or the intellectual architects) in the field and published in various publication media of the field (for example, journal articles, book volumes, reports and so on) and elsewhere. Naturally the landscape in a young or emerging field may not be as rich, or as easily recognizable, especially in the earlier stages where the citations may be scattered across a vast territory shared with other fields from which the emerging field is departing or on which it is building. Although the latter is the case of e-commerce, this embryonic field has developed an impressive collection of techniques and technologies and accumulated a large amount information and knowledge, as discussed earlier.

On the explicit side of information and knowledge (Polanyi, 1969), a large number of publications have appeared in various media in different continents ever since the early 1990s, when e-commerce was introduced. An increasing number of individuals, organizations and societies aspire to embrace e-commerce and enter the 'information age'. Following the brief discussion of knowledge networks presented above, e-commerce publications can be grouped in four general streams: (a) development of new theories, algorithms or e-commerce models, for e-commerce applications (that is, e-commerce CIFTE), although some of them are descriptive and structural in nature; (b) the application of e-commerce CIFTE, including models, theories, techniques and technologies in various sectors and fields; (c) application of other fields' CIFTE to e-commerce; and (d) a mixed extension and the combinations of the above. These categories help us to identify the most likely media in which to find the information. For example, one would expect to find the first category in e-commerce-oriented media while the second category would most likely be found in the other fields' communication media (such as books and journals). Given the large number of e-commerce-related applications, as highlighted earlier, two factors complicate a typical bibliometric research: a large number of documents, including papers, books and technical reports, both online and off-line, would have to be found; and the scope of the search would have to include a large number of media belonging to a wide and diverse set of fields. This is a tall order for a typical scholarly research. A typical searcher can easily feel overwhelmed by the scope of the topic and the diversity of media over which the search must be conducted.

A complicating factor is that the research questions may become equally diverse and even path-dependent. A typical research question in the first stream would then be whether a particular component of the e-commerce CIFTE has made a significant contribution to building theory or theory essentials fundamental to the further development of e-commerce as an emerging field. In the second stream, a set of related research questions regarding the application of e-commerce CIFTE to other fields (or application of other fields' CIFTE to e-commerce) could be raised. This would include, for example: in which sectors have such e-commerce CIFTE (for example, models, techniques and technologies) been applied successfully? which sectors have experienced difficulty or have lagged behind the others? what are the underlying reasons for respective successes and failures? and which field's CIFTE has had a lasting impact on e-commerce?

In the third and the fourth streams, one could ask: which publications have contributed either to theory development or to successful applications in e-commerce and/or other fields? The extent of the importance of a given publication in one stream and its relation to articles in the others would certainly depend on the researcher's orientation. The selected path for conducting the research may also have an impact on the results.

We suggest that the concept of knowledge networks and bibliometric epistemology are critical to answering the family of research questions, of which some are noted above. We redefine a knowledge network simply as a collection, or a combination, of knowledge resources in an invisible network of interconnected knowledge resources capable of portraying the developmental pattern and diffusion processes in e-commerce-centered knowledge systems. In this simple portrayal, each part of the knowledge network serves a specific purpose in the study of the e-commerce research. As stated earlier, this chapter utilizes the bibliometric epistemology methodology to uncover and then portray, if not characterize, the various manifestations of the knowledge networks that underlie e-commerce. According to Latour (1987), it will have to contain the influential e-commerce materials (in books and journal articles), authors and their corresponding publication media, including journals.[10]

RESEARCH METHODOLOGY

The current chapter reports the preliminary results of a multi-phase research study, with each phase requiring a different approach for examining a different aspect of e-commerce as an emerging field of scholarly research inquiry and commercial development. As discussed above, the embryonic state of the field posed special difficulties and challenges. The following sections expand on the above and highlight the methodologies used in two phases.[11]

Phase I: Identification of Data Bases and Design of Search Processes

As a relatively new field, e-commerce lacked its own dedicated publication media in its early life to allow us to conduct a focused search. Furthermore, as a multidisciplinary field, e-commerce formed its initial developments on platforms based on its constituent disciplines. Most of these disciplines are well-established fields and have their own communication and publication media. In the absence of well-established media in e-commerce, the early authors in this emerging field were forced to publish their work in publication organs of other fields. Furthermore most of these early writers came from their own disciplines and they published in the communication media of those disciplines (for example, Bakos's pioneering article on e-commerce, as noted earlier, appeared in *MIS Quarterly*). These complexities posed challenges to this research,[12] which turned out to be neither obvious nor trivial. The use of conventional bibliometric methods would not have worked as we were forced, for example, to search for sources before searching for e-commerce material scattered in those sources. We could not follow the most logical approach, that is, examining all potential constituent fields as potential platforms for e-commerce applications. This was far beyond the scope of the given project, ridden with boundary ambiguities and not straightforward. These complexities forced us to use the most conservative approach. We examined both the Social Science Citation Index (SSCI) and Science Citation Index (SCI) in the search for data bases as potential sources containing e-commerce-oriented materials to construct our initial source data bases. The SSCI and SCI contain citations from over 4000 refereed journals. Unfortunately, and unlike other prior studies, the data for this research could not be simply drawn from a sample of journals chosen by the researchers. Instead the entire data base of SSCI and SCI had to be searched as potentially relevant fields for conducting the analysis. Therefore the results reported in this study are not limited to any specific field or area. In spite of these difficulties, the results confirm the true interdisciplinary nature of this emerging field, as they include a relatively large number of disciplines.

Once the potential data bases containing e-commerce-related materials were identified, the appropriate search procedures were sought. Three conventional search strategies have been used in the past. The first one would be analogous to selecting all e-commerce articles published in 'only one' of the most accepted (or most popular) journals in a given field. The *Quarterly Journal of Electronic Commerce* is arguably the most influential journal publishing e-commerce papers, but it did not exist in the early 1990s. The advantages of this type of search strategy are the 'guaranteed quality' of its published papers, the clarity of what are the acceptable methods and topics in the field (as defined by the editorial policies of the journal) and the possibility of using refined search boundaries without any loss of substance. However the use of this strategy would expose the study to the risk of missing many of the other e-commerce-related papers published elsewhere, especially in the early days of the field. Therefore this approach alone would not be sufficient.

A second strategy would be analogous to collecting all e-commerce-related articles published in a number of major (or most accepted) journals between certain dates: for example, the top five to eight journals between 1990 and 2000. Following this strategy, one would be required to identify prestigious journals such as *Academy of Management Review* (AMR), *Academy of Management Journal* (AMJ), *Administrative Science Quarterly* (ASQ), *Management Science* and *MIS Quarterly*. Once again, because of the multidisciplinary nature of e-commerce, this approach is bound to miss many other e-commerce publications as e-commerce papers have appeared in a large variety of journals across many disciplines and continents.

A third strategy, used for disciplinary research in the past, is to adopt the 'keyword intersection' approach by using keywords associated with key concepts in the field or with a particular topic to define boundaries and delimit the search for identifying the associated content. This method can be restricted to the publications of a field or applied regardless of the publication media and location. This method can be used in conjunction with, or as a complement to, the other methods. A clear advantage of this approach, especially when applied without restrictions, is that it first forces the researchers to establish an objective list of key words and concepts to delimit the subject under study, e-commerce in this case. Naturally this list must be revised from time to time by future research studies and complemented by other methods, including the two strategies mentioned above, as the field (or the topic) evolves with time. We selected this method and the following four steps to highlight a set of specific procedures and algorithms to collect the citation data for this study.

Step 1: the selection of keywords and key concepts to define the scope of the search
Given the rapid growth of this emerging field, we tried to be as comprehensive as possible in order not to overlook less obvious publications.

Step 2: the use of Boolean combinations of specific keywords in the search field
We used a variation of keywords to search several fields, including the title, the abstract and/or keyword fields in SSCI and SCI data bases for two decades (1981 to 2000). The resulting search identified all documents (for example, books and journal articles) with the specified keywords appearing in their title, abstract and/or keyword fields. This data set constitutes what we refer to as our *Initial Source Files*. The full citation records of these articles were then downloaded year by year from SSCI and SCI data bases and stored in editable formats to form our *Initial Working Files*.

Step 3: the transformation of initial working files
These Initial Working Files (one for each year for a total of 20 years) were then edited, line-by-line and record-by-record, by an editing software in order to prepare the raw data, resulting from Step 2, for a systematic data analysis in a common data base management system such as dBase III plus.

Step 4: final compilation in a single data source
After the above editing, the annual working files were combined to form a single source data file in which each line represents a micro-unit of the citation, containing a citation of a specific document on an e-commerce topic. This step resulted in the formation of a data base that we have called the *Citation Data Base*.

The summary results of the above search and the sampling methods for forming both our Source and Citation Data Bases are presented in Table 10.1 (see end of chapter).

Phase II: Data Mapping and Analysis

In this phase, we analyzed the data obtained and prepared in Phase I. Owing to space limitations only the most significant part of the research findings is presented in this chapter. For example, we found a relatively large number of cited articles for this young field. Some 79 books and journal articles were identified as frequently-cited documents. To save space, only an abridged version of this list is shown in Table 10.2. We set the minimum cut-off point for inclusion and reporting in this chapter at five citations for papers and four citations for books, as the extent of significance and the contribution of documents with lower citation figures are not clear at present.[13] Table 10.2a presents the results of this search and sampling for much-cited journal articles; while Table 10.2b shows the results for frequently-cited books (both in abridged form).

Following Latour (1987), the remaining results pertain to quantitative proxy measures used to portray (or characterize) the formation stages of the e-commerce knowledge network.[14] Leading scholars (that is, the 'who' of the knowledge network) and their respective contributions (that is, the 'what' of the knowledge network) and dates (that is, the 'when' of the knowledge network), as well as the initial supporting domains from which their e-commerce work was drawn (that is, the 'constituent fields' of the knowledge network) are presented in Tables 10.3 and 10.4. Nested throughout Tables 10.2 to 10.4 are the publication media (that is, the 'where' of the knowledge network), which have published the e-commerce-centered resources under examination.

RESEARCH CONTRIBUTIONS, IMPLICATIONS AND CONCLUSION

The contributions of this research to the emerging field of e-commerce are highlighted below in four parts.

The Interlinkages amongst Concepts in the E-commerce Context

As indicated earlier, e-commerce draws upon a wide range and rich diversity of topics, functions and institutions which require the researchers of this field to adopt an interdisciplinary[15] perspective to research and examine issues from a variety of vantage points. This makes research in the field more challenging and rewarding as well as slower to develop or publish than other fields. The possibility of 'publishing' e-commerce advances on the Internet may, however, mitigate the expected publishing difficulties. Such publication, regardless of the media, could be much more rewarding for its potential impact on individuals, institutions and society, as discussed earlier. The impact could also be greater and more profound than that of publications in an off-line medium in disciplinary fields for the easy accessibility of the Internet and the interlinkages of e-commerce with other fields. As noted earlier, the concept of a knowledge network is in part predicated on the possibility of drawing upon the resources scattered across the network and yet accessible through the network for solving more complex problems beyond a member's scope and capabilities. In other words, the network can be viewed as a repository of knowledge, from which to draw the necessary resources to respond to challenges, or resolve difficult problems facing some members of the network, and to deposit them asynchronously onto the network for the benefit of all concerned when they require them. The knowledge network of e-commerce has come close to functioning as such a network and the implications of publishing in such knowledge networks are worthy of consideration by scholars and practitioners alike.

The Implicit Alliance of the Stakeholders, including Researchers and Practitioners

Although alliances are implicit in the theoretical concept of a knowledge network, the current Internet-based practices exhibit much commonality with a typical knowledge network and, therefore, e-commerce knowledge networks can be viewed as a theoretical model of Internet-based e-commerce. In fact the implicit understandings and alliances among active e-commerce actors have contributed to the smooth functioning of information components of e-commerce on the Internet. The Internet appears to be supporting e-commerce practice while resembling a knowledge network beyond e-commerce. Scholars' and practitioners' contributions may actually further advance not only the state of e-commerce research, theory and practice, but also that of knowledge networks in general.

The Contribution of this Chapter to the Emerging Field

The methodology developed and the results presented in this chapter can readily empower aspiring scholars (new and old) and practitioners alike. This research can serve to facilitate and therefore save much time and effort in identifying the influential published works, authors and journals. Ignoring the potentials of this methodology to prepare for new developments and following conventional methods exposes scholars, especially new and aspiring researchers, to the high risks of duplication and irrelevance and society and its institutions to less optimal allocation of resources and forgone opportunities. In the final analysis, the requisite interconnectivity for efficient conduct of e-commerce may ensure a more optimal allocation of efforts and resources than otherwise.

Implications for Research and Public Policy Formulation

As implications of e-commerce for individual consumers and customers (in the case of business to business transactions), entrepreneurs, organizations (including small enterprises) and society as a whole were presented following the pertinent discussion of e-commerce impact in Part I, there is no need to replicate them here. However suffice it to conclude that the weight of the accumulating evidence, of which this research uncovered only the scholarly aspects, is in favor not only of e-commerce staying and flourishing as a field of research and application but also of its becoming a potent force for change with which to reckon. Individuals, entrepreneurs, enterprises and societal organizations can only ignore it at the risk of their own ineffectiveness, if not at their peril, in the unforgiving international competition.

NOTES

1. This chapter draws on two earlier works: a much earlier and shorter version prepared for presentation in the Third Biennial Conference on International Entrepreneurship in September 2002 in Montreal and a paper prepared for presentation at the 2003 Annual meeting of the Administrative Association of Canada in Halifax, Nova Scotia using the same data base.
2. Very few families of innovative technologies have relied on and encompassed as many fields. As a result, e-commerce has had a profound impact on mankind in a short time period.
3. We adopt the standard marketing terminology here. In businesses where a series of intermediaries are involved, the ultimate buyers are consumers, while all others are customers. This definition resonates with the adopted e-commerce terminology of B2C (consumer-centered) and B2B (business-centered) transactions.
4. Although this is of limited utility to many typical locally oriented buyers and suppliers for the time being, the potential benefits of bridging time and distance increase as more businesses go on-line and more buyers and suppliers adopt international scope in their business conduct as time progresses.
5. This is due mainly to the information-intensive nature of e-commerce in general and websites in particular. A customer can therefore satisfy his information needs according to his own pace and desires.
6. In fact the expansion of considerations set comes at no cost to the customer as search engines provide a list of potential suppliers from which the customer can choose. However this allows the customer to favor certain sites over others, which is equivalent to implicit competition in the real world where perceived inferiority rules against service providers, regardless of objective measures.
7. There are many rating agents on the Internet, including bizrate.com, asksimmon.com and so on. In addition most infomediary agents also exhibit website listings based on their own ranking criteria, which may or may not be objective.
8. One can easily argue that such strategies fall within the realm of customer relations management (CRM). E-commerce techniques and technologies overcome the national–international boundary conditions and internationalize CRM at almost no additional cost.
9. For an expanded exposition of the theory of knowledge networks, see Etemad and Lee (2003b).
10. A truly reflective portrayal of the e-commerce knowledge networks must naturally be based on a sufficiently large data base and appropriate search techniques.

11. The objective of the final phase of this research, not reported in this chapter, is to expand upon the analysis of this chapter in order to identify the future research directions of high impact.
12. Although most e-commerce-related developments went far beyond what was drawn from the constituent disciplines, with the addition of at least integrating and coordinating materials with others for its application, and use of its own as well as further developments, they had to be published in the constituent fields' media. This phenomenon made the field of search for e-commerce material wide open. The identification of boundary conditions was very difficult.
13. These citation limits were used for sampling from the pool of initial source data bases.
14. In this phase, we will construct the proposed e-commerce knowledge network in which nodes represent important or influential e-commerce work and linkages represent the interrelations among them. Once the e-commerce knowledge networks are developed, we will further develop models to integrate and extrapolate the information provided by the knowledge networks. The objective of developing quantitative models is to utilize the knowledge network results to perform high-level analysis. Finally we may compare our research approach with other data analysis approaches such as meta-analysis and regression analysis, using a common statistical package (SPSS or EQS).
15. This discussion applies to other multidisciplinary fields as well. For example, as an emerging multidisciplinary field, international entrepreneurship faces the same difficulties and challenges. Scholars of this emerging field are well served if they search other constituent fields for particular concepts and constructs before developing them.

REFERENCES

Cantillon, Richard (1755), *Essai sur la Nature du Commerce en Général*, London and Paris: R. Gyles; translated (1931), by Henry Higgs, London: Macmillan and Co.

Chandy, P.R. and T.G.F. Williams (1994), 'The impact of journals and authors on international business research: a citation analysis of JIBS articles', *Journal of International Business Studies*, **25**(4), 715–28.

Culnan, M.J. (1987), 'Mapping the intellectual structure of MIS, 1980–1985: a cocitation analysis', *MIS Quarterly*, September, 341–52.

Culnan, M.J. and E.B. Swanson (1986), 'Research in management information systems, 1980–1984: points of work and reference', *MIS Quarterly*, September, 289–301.

Dana, L.P., H. Etemad and I. Wilkinson (2004), 'Internetization: a new term for the new economy', *Journal of International Entrepreneurship*, **2** (4).

Ely, Richard T. and Ralph H. Hess (1893), *Outline of Economics*, New York: Macmillan.

Etemad, H. (1999), 'The emerging knowledge network of international entrepreneurship', *Global Focus*, **11** (3), 55–62.

Etemad, H. (2003a), 'Managing relations: the essence of entrepreneurship', in H. Etemad and R. Wright (eds), *Globalization and Entrepreneurship: Policy and Strategy Perspectives*, Cheltenham, UK, and Northampton, MA: Edward Elgar, pp. 223–42.

Etemad, H. (2003b), 'Marshalling relations: the enduring essence of international entrepreneurship', in L.P. Dana (ed.), *Handbook of International Entrepreneurship*, Cheltenham, UK, and Northampton, MA: Edward Elgar.

Etemad, H. and Y. Lee (2003a), 'The knowledge network of international entrepreneurship: theory and evidence', *Small Business Economics*, **20** (1), 5–23.

Etemad, H. and Y. Lee (2003b), 'The emerging interdisciplinary field of e-commerce: highly-cited documents, authors and journals', paper presented at the 2003 Annual Conference of the Administrative Sciences Association of Canada, Halifax, Nova Scotia, 12–14 June.

Etemad, H. and R. Wright (2003), 'Internationalization of SMEs: towards a new paradigm', *Small Business Economics*, **20** (1), 1–4.

Etemad, Hamid, Richard Wright and L.P. Dana (2001), 'Symbiotic international business networks: collaboration between small and large firms', *Thunderbird International Business Review*, **43** (4) August, 481–500.

Gibbons, M., C. Limorges, H. Norswothy, S. Schwartzman, P. Scott and M. Trow, (1994), *The New Production of Knowledge: the Dynamics of Science and Research in Contemporary Societies*, London: Sage, p. 161.

Johanson, J. and J.E. Vahlne (1977), 'The internationalization process of the firm – four Swedish case studies', *Journal of Management Studies*, **12** (3), 305–22.

Johanson, Jan and Jan-Erik Vahlne (1990), 'The mechanism of internationalization', *International Marketing Review*, **7**(4), 11–24.

Johanson, Jan and Jan-Erik Vahlne (1992), 'Management of foreign market entry', *Scandinavian International Business Review*, **1**(3), 9–27.

Johanson, Jan and Finn Wiedersheim-Paul (1975), 'The internationalization of the firm: four Swedish cases', *Journal of International Management Studies*, **12** (3), October, 36–64.

Latour, B. (1987), *Science in Action: How to Follow Scientists and Engineers through Society*, Cambridge, MA: Harvard University Press, p. 265.

Laudon, K.C. and J.P. Laudon (1993), *Business Information System: A Problem Solving Approach*, Fort Worth, TX: Dryden.

Merton, R. (1979), 'Preface', in E. Garfield, *Citation Indexing: Its Theory and Application in Science, Technology and Humanities*, New York: John Wiley.

Nonaka, I. and H. Takeuchi (1996), *The Knowledge Creating Company: How Japanese Companies Create the Dynamics of Innovation*, New York: Oxford University Press.

Podolny, J.M., T.E. Stuart and M.T. Hannan (1996), 'Networks, knowledge and niches: competition in worldwide semiconductor industry, 1984–1991', *American Journal of Sociology*, **101**, 1224–60.

Polanyi, M. (1969), 'The Logic of Tacit Inference', *Knowing and Being*, London: Routledge and Kegan Paul.

Poutziouris, P., K. Soufani and N. Michaelas (2003), 'On the determinants of exporting – UK evidence', reprinted in H. Etemad and R. Wright (eds), *Globalization and Entrepreneurship*, Cheltenham, UK, and Northampton, MA: Edward Elgar, pp. 15–38.

Say, Jean Baptiste (1803), *Traité d'économie politique ou simple exposition de la manière dont se forment, se distribuent, et se consomment les richesses*; revised (1819); translated (1830) by C.R. Prinsep, *A Treatise on Political Economy: Or Familiar Conversations On the Manner in Which Wealth is Produced, Distributed and Consumed by Society*, Philadelphia: John Grigg and Elliot.

Say, Jean Baptiste (1815), *Catéchisme d'économie politique*, translated by John Richter (1821), *Catechism of Political Economy*, London: Sherwood.

Schumpeter, Joseph Allois (1911), *Theorie der wirtschaftlichen Entwicklung*, Munich and Leipzig: Dunker and Humblot; translated by R. Opie (1934), *The Theory of Economic Development*, Cambridge, MA: Harvard University Press.

Schumpeter, Joseph Allois (1942), *Capitalism, Socialism and Democracy*, New York: Harper and Row.

Schumpeter, Joseph Allois (1947), 'The creative response in economic history', *Journal of Economic History*, **7**, November, 149–59.

Stöttinger, B. and B. Schlegelmilch (1998), 'Explaining export development through psychic distance: enlightening or elusive?', *International Marketing Review*, **15** (5), 357–72.

Strauss, J. and R. Frost (2001), *E-Marketing*, Upper Saddle River, NJ: Prentice Hall.

Whitley, R. (1984a), 'The fragmented state of management studies: reasons and consequences', *Journal of Management Studies*, **21**(3), 331–48.

Whitley, R (1984b), 'The scientific status of management studies as a practically-oriented social science', *Journal of Management Studies*, **21**(4), 369–90.

Yoshino, M. and U.S. Rangan (1995), *Strategic Alliances: An Entrepreneurial Approach to Globalization*, Boston, MA: Harvard Business School Press.

Table 10.1 *Sampling of source documents using e-commerce as the keyword in different search fields*

Method	Search Fields		Sampling Year							Subtotal
			1981–94	1995	1996	1997	1998	1999	2000	
Ecomm in title (t)	G1	Title (t)	9	8	41	27	44	64	106	299
Ecomm in keywords (k)	G2	Keyword (k)	0	0	1	2	11	16	38	68
Ecomm in abstract (a)	G3	Abstract (a)	5	7	13	29	45	82	135	316
Ecomm in any field	G4	Basic (any fields)	0	0	1	3	2	3	6	15
Subtotal	G5	Basic (t+k+a)	14	15	56	61	102	165	285	698
The Associated Citation										
Ecomm in title (t)	G1	Title (t)	3	20	167	179	374	1 111	1 964	3 818
Ecomm in keywords (k)	G2	Keyword (k)	0	0	50	54	435	411	1 281	2 231
Ecomm in abstract (a)	G3	Abstract (a)	115	20	341	454	1 212	1 719	2 871	6 732
Ecomm in all fields	G4	Basic (any fields	0	0	3	26	129	79	155	392
Subtotal	G5	Basic (t+k+a)	118	40	561	713	2 150	3 320	6 271	13 173

212

Average Citations per Document

Ecomm in title (t)	G1	Title (t)*	0.3	2.5	4.1	6.6	8.5	17.4	18.5	12.8
Ecomm in keywords (k)	G2	Keyword (k)			50.0	27.0	39.5	25.7	33.7	32.8
Ecomm in abstract (a)	G3	Abstract (a)	23.0	2.9	26.2	15.7	26.9	21.0	21.3	21.3
Ecomm in all fields	G4	Basic (any) fields			3.0	8.7	64.5	26.3	25.8	26.1
Subtotal	G5	Basic (t+k+a)	8.4	2.7	10.0	11.7	21.1	20.1	22.0	18.9

Notes:
1. Different sample groupings represent different degrees of relatedness, from the lowest (G1) to the highest (G4) and they refer to the search for the designated keyword encompassing progressively more fields than previously.
G4 = G3 + G2 + G1; and G3 = G2 + G1.
2. The first article (with keyword in title) collected from SSCI; J. Meyer (1992), 'The challenge of electronic e-commerce', *ABA Journal*, **78**(Mar), 85–95. The second article is J. Kao (1993), 'The Worldwide Web of Chinese business', *HBR*, **71**(2), 24–33; the third is M.J. Cronin (1993), 'Internet business resources', *Database*, **16**(6), 47. However, these three articles did not contain any references. Since there are a lot of magazine articles (e.g., *Fortune*) without cited references, G1 (with e-comm in titles) has generally fewer average cited references than general academic articles.

213

Table 10.2   Highly cited documents in e-commerce

Fq	Type	Year	2a Full Citation Index for Journals
26	J	1987	MALONE-TW-1987-COMMUN-ACM-V30-P484
21	J	1996	HOFFMAN-DL-1996-J-MARKETING-V60-P50
17	J	1991	BAKOS-JY-1991-MIS-QUART-V15-P295
17	J	1995	BENJAMIN-R-1995-SLOAN-MANAGE-REV-V36-P62
14	J	1995	RAYPORT-JF-1995-HARVARD-BUS-REV-V73-P75
14	J	1997	ALBA-J-1997-J-MARKETING-V61-P38
12	J	1985	PORTER-ME-1985-HARVARD-BUS-REV-JUL-P149
12	J	1996	QUELCH-JA-1996-SLOAN-MANAGE-REV-V37-P60
12	J	1997	BAKOS-JY-1997-MANAGE-SCI-V43-P1676
10	J	1996	ARMSTRONG-A-1996-HARVARD-BUS-MAY-P134
9	J	1987	MCAFEE-RP-1987-J-ECON-LIT-V25-P699
9	J	1994	RAYPORT-JF-1994-HARVARD-BUS-REV-V72-P141
8	J	1989	DAVIS-FD-1989-MANAGE-SCI-V35-P982
8	J	1989	DAVIS-FD-1989-MIS-QUART-V13-P319
8	J	1995	IACOVOU-CL-1995-MIS-QUART-V19-P465
8	J	1996	BHIMANI-A-1996-COMMUN-ACM-V39-P29
7	J	1961	VICKREY-W-1961-J-FINANC-V16-P8
7	J	1989	EISENHARDT-KM-1989-ACAD-MGT-REV-V14-P532
7	J	1992	DELONE-WH-1992-INFOR-SYSTEMS-V3-P60
7	J	1994	PREMKUMAR-G-1994-J-MGT-INFO-V11-P157
7	J	1995	BATY-JB-1995-J-MANAGEMENT-INFORMA-V11-P9
7	J	1996	BERTHON-P-1996-J-ADVERTISING-RES-V36-P43
7	J	1996	JOHNSON-DR-1996-STANFORD-LAW-R-V48-P1367
7	J	1997	BURKE-RR-1997-J-ACAD-MARKET-SCI-V25-P352
7	J	1997	PETERSON-RA-1997-J-ACD-MARKET-SCI-V25-P329
6	J	1997	JARVENPAA-SL-1996-INT-J-ELECT-COMM-V1-P59/97
6	J	1983	IVES-B-1983-COMMUN-ACM-V26-P785
6	J	1985	RAYMOND-L-1985-MIS-QUART-V9-P37
6	J	1988	DELONE-WH-1988-MIS-Q-V12-P51
6	J	1991	BAKOS-JY-1991-J-MANAGEMENT-INFORMA-V8-P31
6	J	1991	GURBAXANI-V-1991-COMMUN-ACM-V34-P59
6	J	1995	HANDY-C-1995-HARVARD-BUSINESS-MAY-P40
6	J	1998	BAKOS-Y-1998-COMMUN-ACM-V41-P35
5	J	1929	HOTELLING-H-1929-ECON-J-V39-P41
5	J	1982	MILGROM-PR-1982-ECONOMETRICA-V50-P1089
5	J	1983	BAILEY-JE-1983-MANAGE-SCI-V29-P530
5	J	1987	BENBASAT-I-1987-MIS-QUART-V11-P369
5	J	1988	JOHNSTON-HR-1988-MIS-Q-V12-P153
5	J	1990	HUBER-GP-1990-ACAD-MANAGE-REV-V15-P47
5	J	1992	TREVINO-LK-1992-COMMUN-RES-V19-P539
5	J	1993	GROVER-V-1993-DECISION-SCI-V24-P603
5	J	1994	BLOOM-PN-1994-J-MARKETING-V58-P98
5	J	1994	RIGGINS-FJ-1994-J-MGT-INFORMA-V11-P37
5	J	1995	GULATI-R-1995-ACAD-MANAGE-J-V38-P85

Fq	Type	Year	2a Full Citation Index for Journals
5	J	1995	MAYER-RC-1995-ACAD-MANAGE-REV-V20-P709
5	J	1995	MUKHOPADHYAY-T-1995-MIS-QUART-V19-P137
5	J	1996	APPLEGATE-LM-1996-J-ORG-COMPUTG-ELEC-V6-P1
5	J	1996	COCKBURN-C-1996-INT-J-INFORM-MGT-V16-P83
5	J	1996	KUMAR-K-1996-MIS-QUART-V20-P279
5	J	1996	SPAR-D-1996-HARVARD-BUS-REV-V74-P125
5	J	1997	FOX-WF-1997-NATL-TAX-J-V50-P573
5	J	1997	HARTWELL-L-1997-MOL-BIOL-CELL-V8-P1
5	J	1998	SPILLER-P-1998-INT-J-ELECT-COMM-V2-P29

			2b Full Citation Index for Books
21	B	1996	KALAKOTA-R-1996-FRONTIERS-ELECT-COMM
18	B	1983	ROGERS-EM-1983-DIFFUSION-INNOVATION/1995
13	B	1975	WILLIAMSON-OE-1975-MARKETS-HIERARCHIES
10	B	1980	PORTER-ME-1980-COMPETITIVE-STRATEGY
10	B	1985	PORTER-ME-1985-COMPETITIVE-ADVANTAG
10	B	1996	TAPSCOTT-D-1996-DIGITAL-EC
9	B	1985	WILLIAMSON-OE-1985-EC-I-CAPITALISM
8	B	1997	HAGEL-J-1997-NET-GAIN-EXPANDING-M
7	B	1995	HAIR-JF-1995-MULTIVARIATE-DATA-AN
7	B	1997	KALAKOTA-R-1997-ELECT-COMMERCE-MANAG
7	B	1997	CHOI-SY-1997-EC-ELECT-COMMERCE
6	B	1967	THOMPSON-JD-1967-ORG-ACTION
6	B	1978	NUNNALLY-JC-1978-PSYCHOMETRIC-THEORY
6	B	1988	ZUBOFF-S-1988-AGE-SMART-MACHINE
6	B	1992	DAVIDOW-WH-1992-VIRTUAL-CORPORATION
6	B	1993	HAMMER-M-1993-REENGINEERING-CORPOR
6	B	1994	CRONIN-MJ-1994-DOING-BUSINESS-INTER
5	B	1977	GALBRAITH-JR-1977-ORG-DESIGN
5	B	1992	QUINN-JB-1992-INTELLIGENT-ENTERPRI
5	B	1995	NONAKA-I-1995-KNOWLEDGE-CREATING-C
4	B	1975	FISHBEIN-M-1975-BELIEF-ATTITUDE-INTE
4	B	1990	SENGE-PM-1990-5TH-DISCIPLINE-ART-PRA
4	B	1996	STERN-LW-1996-MARKETING-CHANNELS
4	B	1997	STEWART-TA-1997-INTELLECTUAL-CAPITAL
4	B	1998	SWIRE-PP-1998-NONE-YOUR-BUSINESS-W
4	B	1998	US-DEP-COMM-1998-EM-DIG-EC

Notes:
1. In the second column, J denotes journal article and B denotes books.
2. There are 53 highly cited journal articles (J) with citation frequencies > = 5 and 26 highly cited books (B) with citation frequencies > = 4.
3. These highly cited journal articles and books are listed in descending order of their respective cited frequencies.

Table 10.3 *Highly cited scholars in the e-commerce field and their respective contributions*

Total citations	Author	Contribution	Representative Publication (frequency/type/year/full citation index)			
48	Bakos-JY	6	17	J	1991	BAKOS-JY-1991-MIS-QUART-V15-P295
33	Malone-TW	3	26	J	1987	MALONE-TW-1987-COMMUN-ACM-V30-P484
32	Porter-ME	3	12	J	1985	PORTER-ME-1985-HARVARD-BUS-REV-JUL-P149
26	Williamson-OE	3	13	B	1975	WILLIAMSON-OE-1975-MARKETS-HIERARCHIES
25	Hoffman-DL	2	21	J	1996	HOFFMAN-DL-1996-J-MARKETING-V60-P50
23	Rayport-JF	2	14	J	1995	RAYPORT-JF-1995-HARVARD-BUS-REV-V73-P75
21	Kalakota-R	2	21	B	1996	KALAKOTA-R-1996-FRONTIERS-ELECT-COMM
21	Benjamin-R	2	17	B	1995	BENJAMIN-R-1995-SLOAN-MANAGE-REV-V36-P62
18	Rogers-EM	1	18	J	1983	ROGERS-EM-1983-DIFFUSION-INNOVATION/1995
14	Alba-J	1	14	J	1997	ALBA-J-1997-J-MARKETING-V61-P38
13	Delone-WH	2	7	J	1992	DELONE-WH-1992-INFOR-SYSTEMS-V3-P60
12	Davis-FD	*	8	J	1989	DAVIS-FD-1989-MANAGE-SCI-V35-P982
12	Quelch-JA	2	12	J	1996	QUELCH-JA-1996-SLOAN-MANAGE-REV-V37-P60
11	Clemons-EK	3	4	J	1993	CLEMONS-EK-1993-J-MANAGEMENT-INFO-V10-P9
11	Hagel-J	2	8	B	1997	HAGEL-J-1997-NET-GAIN-EXPANDING-M
11	Premkumar-G	2	7	J	1994	PREMKUMAR-G-1994-J-MGT-INFO-V11-P157
10	Hammer-M	2	6	B	1993	HAMMER-M-1993-REENGINEERING-CORPOR
10	Ives-B	2	6	J	1983	IVES-B-1983-COMMUN-ACM-V26-P785
10	Armstrong-A	1	10	J	1996	ARMSTRONG-A-1996-HARVARD-BUS-MAY-P134
10	Tapscott-D	1	10	B	1996	TAPSCOTT-D-1996-DIGITAL-EC
9	Teece-DJ	3	3	B	1987	TEECE-DJ-1987-COMPETITIVE-CHALLENG-P185
9	Riggins-FJ	2	5	J	1994	RIGGINS-FJ-1994-J-MGT-INFORMA-V11-P37
9	McAfee-RP	1	9	J	1987	MCAFEE-RP-1987-J-ECON-LIT-V25-P699
8	Benbasat-I	2	5	J	1987	BENBASAT-I-1987-MIS-QUART-V11-P369
8	Milgrom-PR	2	5	J	1982	MILGROM-PR-1982-ECONOMETRICA-V50-P1089

8	Bhimani-A	1	8	J	1996	BHIMANI-A-1996-COMMUN-ACM-V39-P29
8	Iacovou-CL	1	8	J	1995	IACOVOU-CL-1995-MIS-QUART-V19-P465
7	Coase-RH	2	4	J	1937	COASE-RH-1937-ECONOMICA-V4-P386
7	Daft-RL	2	4	J	1986	DAFT-RL-1986-MANAGE-SCI-V32-P554
7	Markus-ML	2	4	J	1987	MARKUS-ML-1987-COMMUN-RES-V14-P491
7	Baty-JB	1	7	J	1995	BATY-JB-1995-J-MANAGEMENT-INFORMA-V11-P9
7	Berthon-P	1	7	J	1996	BERTHON-P-1996-J-ADVERTISING-RES-V36-P43
7	Burke-RR	1	7	J	1997	BURKE-RR-1997-J-ACAD-MARKET-SCI-V25-P352
7	Choi-SY	1	7	B	1997	CHOI-SY-1997-EC-ELECT-COMMERCE
7	Eisenhardt-KM	1	7	J	1989	EISENHARDT-KM-1989-ACAD-MGT-REV-V14-P532
7	Hair-JF	1	7	B	1995	HAIR-JF-1995-MULTIVARIATE-DATA-AN
7	Johnson-DR	1	7	J	1996	JOHNSON-DR-1996-STANFORD-LAW-R-V48-P1367
7	Petterson-RA	1	7	J	1997	PETERSON-RA-1997-J-ACD-MARKET-SCI-V25-P329
7	Vickrey-W	1	7	J	1961	VICKREY-W-1961-J-FINANC-V16-P8

Notes:

1. There are 39 highly cited scholars, each with a minimum subtotal citation of 7.
2. Subtotal citation denotes the total number of the author's contributions cited by any of the significant documents (which has at least 3 citations in the e-commerce area). For example, Bakos-JY had contributed 6 documents with subtotal 48 citations to our citation sample (of 13 173 citations).

Table 10.4 Highly cited documents in the e-commerce area and their research outlet

Area	Fq	Title	Type	Year	Full Citation Index	Total
Ads	7	JadvRes	J	1996	BERTHON-P-1996-J-ADVERTISING-RES-V36-P43	7
Bio	5	MolBio	J	1997	HARTWELL-L-1997-MOL-BIOL-CELL-V8-P1	5
Bus	12	HarBusRev	J	1985	PORTER-ME-1985-HARVARD-BUS-REV-JUL-P149	
Bus	10	HarBusRev	J	1995	RAYPORT-JF-1995-HARVARD-BUS-REV-V73-P75	
Bus	6	HarBusRev	J	1995	HANDY-C-1995-HARVARD-BUSINESS-MAY-P40	
Bus	5	HarBusRev	J	1996	ARMSTRONG-A-1996-HARVARD-BUS-MAY-P134	
Bus	5	HarBusRev	J	1996	ARMSTRONG-A-1996-HARVARD-BUS-REV-V74-P134	
Bus	5	HarBusRev	J	1996	SPAR-D-1996-HARVARD-BUS-REV-V74-P125	
Bus	18	Book	B	1983	ROGERS-EM-1983-DIFFUSION-INNOVATION/1995	
Bus	8	Book	B	1997	HAGEL-J-1997-NET-GAIN-EXPANDING-M	
Bus	6	Book	B	1992	DAVIDOW-WH-1992-VIRTUAL-CORPORATION	
Bus	6	Book	B	1993	HAMMER-M-1993-REENGINEERING-CORPOR	
Bus	5	Book	B	1995	NONAKA-I-1995-KNOWLEDGE-CREATING-C	
Bus	5	Book	B	1992	QUINN-JB-1992-INTELLIGENT-ENTERPRI	91
Comm	26	CommACM	J	1987	MALONE-TW-1987-COMMUN-ACM-V30-P484	
Comm	8	CommACM	J	1996	BHIMANI-A-1996-COMMUN-ACM-V39-P29	
Comm	6	CommACM	J	1998	BAKOS-Y-1998-COMMUN-ACM-V41-P35	
Comm	6	CommACM	J	1991	GURBAXANI-V-1991-COMMUN-ACM-V34-P59	
Comm	6	CommACM	J	1983	IVES-B-1983-COMMUN-ACM-V26-P785	
Comm	5	CommACM	J	1992	TREVINO-LK-1992-COMMUN-RES-V19-P539	
Comm	6	Book	B	1988	ZUBOFF-S-1988-AGE-SMART-MACHINE	37
Ecomm	6	IJEcom	J	1997	JARVENPAA-SL-1997-INT-J-ELECT-COMM-V1-P59	
Ecomm	5	IJEcomm	J	1998	SPILLER-P-1998-INT-J-ELECT-COMM-V2-P29	
Ecomm	21	Book	B	1996	KALAKOTA-R-1996-FRONTIERS-ELECT-COMM	

Category	Count	Journal	Type	Year		Citation
Ecomm	7	Book	B	1997	46	CHOI-SY-1997-EC-ELECT-COMMERCE
Ecomm	7	Book	B	1997		KALAKOTA-R-1997-ELECT-COMMERCE-MANAG
Econ	5	EconJ	J	1929		HOTELLING-H-1929-ECON-J-V39-P41
Econ	5	Econmet	J	1982		MILGROM-PR-1982-ECONOMETRICA-V50-P1089
Econ	9	JeconLit	J	1987		MCAFEE-RP-1987-J-ECON-LIT-V25-P699
Econ	13	Book	B	1975		WILLIAMSON-OE-1975-MARKETS-HIERARCHIES
Econ	10	Book	B	1996		TAPSCOTT-D-1996-DIGITAL-EC
Econ	9	Book	B	1985	38	WILLIAMSON-OE-1985-EC-I-CAPITALISM
Finance	7	Jfinanc	J	1961	7	VICKREY-W-1961-J-FINANC-V16-P8
Internet	6	Book	B	1994	6	CRONIN-MJ-1994-DOING-BUSINESS-INTER
Law	7	StandfordLawR	J	1996	7	JOHNSON-DR-1996-STANFORD-LAW-R-V48-P1367
Method	7	Book	B	1995		HAIR-JF-1995-MULTIVARIATE-DATA-AN
Method	6	Book	B	1978	13	NUNNALLY-JC-1978-PSYCHOMETRIC-THEORY
Mgmt	5	AMJ	J	1995		GULATI-R-1995-ACAD-MANAGE-J-V38-P85
Mgmt	7	AMR	J	1989		EISENHARDT-KM-1989-ACAD-MGT-REV-V14-P532
Mgmt	5	AMR	J	1990		HUBER-GP-1990-ACAD-MANAGE-REV-V15-P47
Mgmt	5	AMR	J	1995		MAYER-RC-1995-ACAD-MANAGE-REV-V20-P709
Mgmt	12	MgtSci	J	1997		BAKOS-JY-1997-MANAGE-SCI-V43-P1676
Mgmt	8	MgtSci	J	1989		DAVIS-FD-1989-MANAGE-SCI-V35-P982
Mgmt	5	MgtSci	J	1983		BAILEY-JE-1983-MANAGE-SCI-V29-P530
Mgmt	12	SloanMR	J	1996	59	QUELCH-JA-1996-SLOAN-MANAGE-REV-V37-P60
MIS	5	DeciSci	J	1993		GROVER-V-1993-DECISION-SCI-V24-P603
MIS	5	IJInfoMgt	J	1996		COCKBURN-C-1996-INT-J-INFORM-MGT-V16-P83
MIS	7	InfoSys	J	1992		DELONE-WH-1992-INFOR-SYSTEMS-V3-P60
MIS	7	JmgtInfo	J	1995		BATY-JB-1995-J-MANAGEMENT-INFORMA-V11-P9
MIS	7	JmgtInfo	J	1994		PREMKUMAR-G-1994-J-MGT-INFO-V11-P157
MIS	6	JmgtInfo	J	1991		BAKOS-JY-1991-J-MANAGEMENT-INFORMA-V8-P31
MIS	5	JmgtInfo	J	1994		RIGGINS-FJ-1994-J-MGT-INFORMA-V11-P37
MIS	17	MISQ	J	1991		BAKOS-JY-1991-MIS-QUART-V15-P295

Table 10.4 continued

Area	Fq	Title	Type	Year	Full Citation Index	Total
MIS	9	MISQ	J	1994	RAYPORT-JF-1994-HARVARD-BUS-REV-V72-P141	
MIS	8	MISQ	J	1989	DAVIS-FD-1989-MIS-QUART-V13-P319	
MIS	8	MISQ	J	1995	IACOVOU-CL-1995-MIS-QUART-V19-P465	
MIS	6	MISQ	J	1988	DELONE-WH-1988-MIS-Q-V12-P51	
MIS	6	MISQ	J	1985	RAYMOND-L-1985-MIS-QUART-V9-P37	
MIS	5	MISQ	J	1987	BENBASAT-I-1987-MIS-QUART-V11-P369	
MIS	5	MISQ	J	1988	JOHNSTON-HR-1988-MIS-Q-V12-P153	
MIS	5	MISQ	J	1996	KUMAR-K-1996-MIS-QUART-V20-P279	
MIS	5	MISQ	J	1995	MUKHOPADHYAY-T-1995-MIS-QUART-V19-P137	116
Mktg	7	JAMktSci	J	1997	BURKE-RR-1997-J-ACAD-MARKET-SCI-V25-P352	
Mktg	7	JAMktSci	J	1997	PETERSON-RA-1997-J-ACD-MARKET-SCI-V25-P329	
Mktg	21	JMktg	J	1996	HOFFMAN-DL-1996-J-MARKETING-V60-P50	
Mktg	14	JMktg	J	1997	ALBA-J-1997-J-MARKETING-V61-P38	
Mktg	5	JMktg	J	1994	BLOOM-PN-1994-J-MARKETING-V58-P98	54
OB	5	JorgCompE	J	1996	APPLEGATE-LM-1996-J-ORG-COMPUTG-ELEC-V6-P1	
OB	6	Book	B	1967	THOMPSON-JD-1967-ORG-ACTION	
OB	5	Book	B	1977	GALBRAITH-JR-1977-ORG-DESIGN	
Stra	10	Book	B	1980	PORTER-ME-1980-COMPETITIVE-STRATEGY	
Stra	10	Book	B	1985	PORTER-ME-1985-COMPETITIVE-ADVANTAG	36
Tax	5	NatTaxJ	J	1997	FOX-WF-1997-NATL-TAX-J-V50-P573	5

Note: The area supporting e-commerce studies is mainly the Information Science domain, with some support from Management, and Organization Studies. Other areas include MIS, Business, Marketing, Economics, and Communication.

11. The internationalization efforts of growth-oriented entrepreneurs: lessons from Britain

Harry Matlay and Jay Mitra

INTRODUCTION

In the second half of the 20th century, the flow of goods, services, information, capital and labor across national and regional frontiers increased considerably, giving rise to the notion that economic activity is becoming increasingly globalized. Much of the impetus for the globalization process of economic activity was initially provided by large firms through their cross-border expansionary strategies (Taylor, 1995). During the 1980s and 1990s, there was a notable acceleration in the globalization process, which increasingly involved not only large, transnational corporations, but also small and medium-sized organizations (Storper, 1997). The OECD (1997) report shows that internationalized SMEs account for about 25–35 per cent of the world's manufactured exports, with the contribution of exports to GDP representing 12 per cent of Asian economies and 4–6 per cent for OECD countries. These statistics suggest a radical shift in the internationalization status of SMEs from the 1970s and 1980s. In the UK, for example, while SMEs contributed up to 25 per cent of GDP, they accounted for only 10 per cent of manufactured exports (Willis, 1981). Perceptions are sometimes as important as reality, and the negative perception of size (as in 'smallness' being a barrier to internationalization) countered possibilities of growth of SMEs in the international market. In recent years, globalization has increasingly affected the strategies of small, growth-oriented organizations (Karagozoglu and Lindell, 1998). For a growing number of entrepreneurs, the challenges posed by the 'Global Village' offered opportunities and threats, which they were no longer prepared (or able) to ignore (Fitzgerald, 1997).

Depressed demand following the oil crisis of the 1970s, international competition and technological and structural change have all contributed to the emergence of different international players in the market. Large firms have restructured and 'downsized', and new technology-based developments have spawned robust small firms (often described as 'born global') capable of 'taking on' the international market from birth. These developments have also influenced both the decision and policy makers to examine the role of SMEs in the international market place.

In Britain, the process of globalization was further compounded by the Single European Market initiative at the European Union level (Preston, 1997; Moini, 1992; Nothdurft, 1992). As a result, British industry, in recent years, has undergone a major restructuring, as organizations of all sizes and economic activity streamlined, refocused and sought to form alliances or joint ventures with firms operating in international markets (Taylor, 1995). The globalization process in Britain is increasingly recognized as a major driving force behind the reshaping of the socioeconomic and political structure of the country (Bruland, 1989; Casson, 1991). Growth-oriented firms, operating in the small business sector, are playing a significant role in the restructuring response to the globalization process evident in modern Britain (Matlay, 1999; Howells and Wood, 1993; Robertson, 1992; Dunning, 1992). The growing importance of small businesses in relation to globalization, and the unique opportunities and threats they face, call for a careful and systematic research of the topic.

The evidence supporting the belief that both small and large firms are participants in the global free market belies the notion that globalization is a universal phenomenon. Different dynamics prevail in the small and large firms, in terms of markets, strategies, functions, technologies and human resources, which represent the diversity in the economy. Just as the global free market is not made of a single regime, the 'democratic capitalism' universal (Matlay, 1999), that is, the positioning of small firms in the global market place, does not mean that SMEs pursue strategies and tactics similar to those adopted by large firms. The economic modernization of the large firm can be quite different from that of the smaller business; and the 'locus of control' in the owner/manager often distinguishes methods used by SMEs from those taken up by large firms.

This chapter sets out to explore the main factors that affect the globalization tendencies of British entrepreneurs. It aims to promote a deeper and better understanding of the motives, barriers and strategies of a growing number of entrepreneurs that are increasingly affected by globalization.

SMALL BUSINESSES IN A GLOBAL CONTEXT

The globalization of economic activity is a complex and far-reaching process that encompasses a wide variety of cross-border enterprise operations.

International investment, trade, strategic alliances, joint marketing campaigns, and cross-border manufacturing of goods and the rendering of services can be considered part of the globalization process affecting the economies of most developed and developing nations (Oberhansli, 1997). The theory underlying the internationalization of small organizations argues that entrepreneurial firms thrive and grow in competitive new markets by exploiting their inherent advantages and also by reducing their business risks and costs significantly (Matlay, 1997, 1998). Underlying international small business activities, and partly driving them, are advances in new technology, the continuing liberalization of markets and the increased mobility of production factors (Archibugi and Michie, 1997; Cox, 1997). For a growing number of domestic small firms, the globalization process creates fundamentally new opportunities, as well as renewing threats to their survival (OECD, 1996; Karagozoglu and Lindell, 1998).

To date, only a limited number of empirically rigorous research studies have been published on the topic of globalization in smaller firms. This is not surprising in view of the considerable conceptual and contextual difficulties encountered in the study of small businesses in general and comparative, cross-border research in particular (Matlay, 1999). Furthermore the notion of 'globalization' is a relatively fuzzy concept. Typically the economic activity of most firms, in a given research population, could be expressed in degrees of globalization, rather than in absolute terms of whether or not they are globalized. Similarly globalization can seldom be measured directly, as it usually reflects a composite of several interrelated dimensions. As a concept, globalization is generally perceived to include a variety of inward and outward aspects of economic activity (OECD, 1997, p. 21) including the following:

- the knowledge and flexibility that allows movement across national borders,
- the ability to take advantage of opportunities anywhere in the world,
- the capacity to move capital and source/distribute products/services in other countries,
- a commitment to transnational management of factors of production,
- the capability to market and/or adapt a portfolio of products/services to specific markets successfully, and
- the ability to be simultaneously active in a number of independent businesses and/or be members of strategic alliances in other countries.

There is also a degree of conceptual confusion between the 'internationalization' and 'globalization' activities of small firms (Matlay, 1999). Most research appears to use these two concepts interchangeably, focusing on the export activities of small firms that actively seek to complement their domestic turnover by identifying compatible overseas markets (Stewart, 1997; Hamill and Gregory, 1997; Mahone, 1995). There is a little or no distinction made between the 'process of increasing involvement in international operations' (Welch and Luostarinen, 1988) and operations in the home market or in the international market due to global influences. Such influences may, for example, include and incorporate the intangible dimension of information and knowledge flows, including financial flows, intermediate service flows, formal international cooperation on joint ventures, strategic alliances or collaborative research, global knowledge flows in scientific communities and across the media, and transfers of tacit knowledge through greater personal mobility and exchanges in industry, politics, science and culture (Hamill and Gregory, 1997).

The export response that appears to motivate and underline the internationalization of some small firms is relatively narrow when compared to the much more complex and involved activities that usually result from the globalization efforts of fast-growing SMEs (Coviello and Munro, 1997; Morgan, 1997; Lindell and Karagozoglu, 1997; Crick and Chaudhry, 1995). Nevertheless an increasing number of small business strategists view the ability to engage in global activities as a significant ingredient in the survival and growth of small firms in general (D'Souza and McDougall, 1989; O'Farrell *et al.*, 1996) and new ventures in particular (Bloodgood *et al.*, 1996; Oviatt and McDougall, 1994; McDougall and Oviatt, 1996). It is when clarity is obtained to enable distinctive argument that the researcher can begin to unravel the different paths that small and large firms follow in their international operations in a global market.

Theoretical insights, such as those in Cyert and March's (1963) behavioral theory of the firm, which have been used to develop sequential internationalization models (Johanson and Vahlne, 1977, 1990, Wiedersheim-Paul *et al.*, 1978), elaborate on different stages of international involvement. However it is not clear whether sequential internationalization states anything different for small firms or offers much relevance to the 'born globals' or high technology start-ups. Networking theory, which tends to examine the maturation of alliances and relationships (Styles and Ambler, 1994) and describes markets as systems of relationships, does not help to distinguish small and large firm behavior. The resource-based view (Bell *et al.*, 1998) offers better insight, in that it concentrates on the diverse mix of resources and competencies of different types of firms. Others (Reid, 1983; Coviello and Munro, 1997) have given credence to multiple influences, conditions and decision-making styles, which go some way in helping to locate different types of firms in varying international markets.

Some small business owner–managers perceive the globalization process in terms of new opportunities for outward expansion and growth. For others, globalization poses considerable competitive threats. It is important to note that, regardless of an owner–manager's perception of the globalization process, most small businesses in Britain appear to face challenges pertaining to their limited human and financial resources, informal planning, control and administrative procedures/systems, and restricted access to relevant import/export information and support (Matlay, 1997, 1998). However internationally sustainable competitive advantage appears increasingly to depend upon a firm's unique assets (Lindell and Karagozoglu, 1997; Barney, 1991; Hamel and Prahalad, 1990). In this respect, small firms generally exhibit greater flexibility, speed and advantage-seeking behavior than their larger counterparts (Fiegenbaum and Karnani, 1991; Hitt *et al.*, 1991). As Fitzgerald (1997) argues, the entrepreneurial drive of some owner–managers motivates them to search constantly for new opportunities, and to challenge aggressively the market position of their competitors. On balance, however, it appears that the early globalization successes achieved by some entrepreneurs are usually checked or even sabotaged by their own managerial limitations, and also, in particular, by their reluctance to employ and delegate control to experienced managers (Karagozoglu and Lindell, 1998; Lindell and Karagozoglu, 1997).

RESEARCH SAMPLE AND METHODOLOGICAL CONSIDERATIONS

Scase (1996) notes with concern that, despite a growing interest in small businesses, the state of knowledge associated with this sector of the British economy remains relatively inconsistent. He suggests a number of reasons for this. First, there are considerable definitional problems regarding size, sector and type of economic activity in firms operating in the small business sector. Second, in view of the scope and diversity of the sector, error margins in the classification and conceptualization of research samples become significant. Third, the nature and range of small firms are bound to vary considerably across enterprise/sectoral characteristics, rendering untenable most attempts to generalize from small-scale empirical results. Fourth, problems of access and data collection add further to the methodological difficulties inherent in the study of small business topics. In contrast, it appears that not only is the study of large organizations more prolific, but the generalization of results is considered both desirable and academically valid (Marginson *et al.*, 1993). As a result, research 'evidence is so fragmentary and the theories so empirically specific that there are severe limitations to the development of cumulative small business theory' (Scase, 1996, p. 580).

This self-funded research study, undertaken over the 1996–98 period, was designed to combine three different analytical approaches. It incorporated an exploratory telephone survey of 6000 organizations randomly selected from the Yellow Pages Business Database of Great Britain. The telephone survey aimed to collect quantitative data on the globalization process of firms operating in the small business sector of the British economy. It achieved a respectable response rate of 87 per cent. A subsample of 600 owner–managers was chosen from the wider quantitative sample, and interviewed once a year for the duration of the research study. These semi-structured, face-to-face interviews generated a wealth of qualitative data relating to the globalization attempts, successes and failures of the responding owner–managers. On average, face-to-face interviews lasted about three hours. Over the same period, 60 'matched' case studies were conducted, in order to detail the main strategies, and approaches that owner–managers adopted in relation to their globalization needs and strategies. These three distinct methods were combined to triangulate and corroborate the results that emerged from the wider research study.

SIZE DISTRIBUTION OF THE RESEARCH SAMPLE

The size distribution of the quantitative sample was tabulated and analysed in conformity with the European Commission's standardized business definition (EC, 1996). The randomly selected quantitative sample of 6000 businesses (Table 11.1), showed a considerable degree of consistency with the overall composition of the Yellow Pages Business Database of Great Britain for 1996.

The telephone survey sample comprised 2211 firms (36.85 per cent) from manufacturing, and 3789 (63.15 per cent) from the service sector. This reflected the decline in the traditional manufacturing structure in Britain and the commensurate expansion of the service sector. The vast majority of firms in the research sample (5383) were micro-businesses, employing fewer than ten individuals. Of these, 1963 (36.47 per cent) were manufacturing and 3420 (63.53 per cent) were service-oriented businesses. The research sample also included 457 small businesses, with a payroll of 11 to 49 employees. Of these,

Table 11.1   Size distribution of the 1996–98 research sample

Size band	Size definition	Number of employees	Number of firms	Manufacturing (N=2211)	Services (N=3789)
A	Micro-business	1–9	5 383	1 963	3 420
B	Small business	10–49	457	194	263
C	Medium-sized	50–250	129	42	87
D	Large business	251+	31	12	19

194 firms (42.45 per cent) operated in manufacturing and 263 (57.55 per cent) in the service sector. Service organizations were also predominant amongst medium-sized and large businesses in the sample; 87 and 19, respectively, operated in this sector, compared to 42 and 12 in manufacturing. The size distribution and composition of the research sample appears to reflect closely the overall structure and firm distribution of the modern British economy.

DECISION-MAKING PROCESSES IN SMALL BUSINESSES

The locus of organizational control and decision-making processes in the 6000 respondent businesses was analyzed across four size bands (Table 11.2). In small firms in general, and in micro-businesses in particular, organizational control was likely to rest with one individual, who usually made most, if not all, of the important decisions. Although there were considerable size-related differences amongst the businesses in the sample, the locus and nature of decision-making processes showed marked similarities across both manufacturing and service firms. In micro- and small businesses, the locus of organizational control rested entirely with the owner–manager. The locus of financial and human resource decision-making processes was also concentrated mainly in the hands of the owner–manager(s). In micro-businesses, the owner–manager was identified as the gatekeeper of all decisions relating to financial and human resources. Only a fraction (11.32 per cent) of small business owner–managers chose to delegate financial and human resource decision-making processes to other managers, and in all cases they still retained 'the final say' in such matters. Financial and human resource plans and budgets were only encountered in a fraction of micro- (3.18 per cent) and small businesses (4.82 per cent).

Table 11.2   The locus of decision-making processes in small firms

Band code	Number of employees	Size definition	Locus of financial and human resource decisions		
			Owner–manager (%)	Other managers (%)	Other personnel (%)
A	1–10	Micro-business	100.00	0.00	0.00
B	11–49	Small business	88.68	11.32	0.00
C	50–250	Medium-sized	14.95	85.05	0.00
D	251+	Large business	0.00	100.00	0.00

In medium-sized organizations, the locus of control was typically devolved to the management team and/or board of directors level. The owner–manager's involvement in the financial and human resource functions had been reduced significantly (14.95 per cent), while that of other managers increased proportionally (85.05 per cent). Importantly all managers claimed to use relevant plans and budgets as part of their strategy. The locus of organizational control in large businesses rested with the board of directors and its chairperson. A variety of operational functions were devolved to designated management teams or to the individual managers. Both the finance and the human resource development functions had their own department and appointed manager in charge. Detailed financial and human resource development plans and budgets were drawn up routinely as part of the wider business strategy and organizational control. No other category of personnel appears to have been involved in the financial or human resource decision-making processes in these firms.

GLOBALIZATION TENDENCIES OF SMALL FIRMS IN BRITAIN

The 6000 responding owner–managers in the telephone survey reported three types of positions with regard to globalization: 'nil', 'direct' and 'indirect' globalization activities (Table 11.3). Direct globalization activities involved the production of goods and the rendering of services to markets situated beyond the borders of Britain. Indirect globalization involved goods and services which were destined for foreign consumption, but which were initially directed at businesses located within Britain. These goods and services, however, formed an integral part of the global sales portfolio of the recipient domestic businesses. Although the indirect export activities of small businesses do not fall within 'traditional' definitions of globalization, they are reported in this chapter as an integral part of the data provided by the respondents.

Direct globalization tendencies of respondent firms in the research sample appear to increase in proportion with their size. Only 2.38 per cent and 3.50 per cent of owner–managers of micro- and small businesses, respectively, reported incidences of direct globalization. The proportion of medium-sized and large businesses involved in globalization processes increased to 14.73 per cent and 48.39 per cent, respectively. Similar trends were observed in indirect globalization tendencies, with the exception of large businesses, which did not appear to be involved in this type of activity. In the case of micro- and small businesses, 11.42 per cent and 12.25 per cent of respondents reported activities that fell into this category. Just over a quarter (28.68 per cent) of medium-sized businesses also reported indirect globalization activities. Only a very small proportion of

Table 11.3 Globalization tendencies of small firms in Britain

Band code	Number of employees	Size definition	Globalization tendencies of small firms		
			Nil globalization (%)	Direct globalization (%)	Indirect globalization (%)
A	1–10	Micro-business	86.20	2.38	11.42
B	11–49	Small business	84.25	3.50	12.25
C	50–250	Medium-sized business	56.59	14.73	28.68
D	251+	Large business	51.61	48.39	0.00

Table 11.4   Sectoral spread of globalized small firms in Britain

Band code	Number of employees	Size definition	Globalization tendencies of small firms	
			Manufacturing sector (%)	Service sector (%)
A	1–10	Micro-business	84.37	15.63
B	11–49	Small business	81.25	18.75
C	50–250	Medium-sized businesses	84.21	15.79
D	251+	Large business	73.33	26.67

products and services originating from indirect globalization activities of micro- and small-sized businesses were directed at medium-sized organizations. The largest proportion of this output was aimed at large businesses that exhibited sizeable global portfolios.

An analysis of the data that related to the sectoral spread of directly globalized businesses (Table 11.4), has established a clear bias towards manufacturing firms, even though the overall research sample was numerically dominated by enterprises in the service sector. In total, 84.37 per cent of globalized micro-firms and 81.25 per cent of small businesses operated in the manufacturing sector. Similarly 84.21 per cent of globalized medium-sized businesses and 73.33 per cent of large organizations were also producing manufactured goods. It appears that, even though service-oriented establishments are numerically dominant in the British economy, these businesses find it more difficult to globalize their activities than manufacturing firms.

SMALL BUSINESS OWNER–MANAGERS' MOTIVES TO GLOBALIZE

When asked about the reasons behind their globalization drive (Table 11.5), 61.98 per cent of owner–managers in the manufacturing sector and 82.61 per cent in services claimed they saw greater strategic opportunities in foreign markets. Linked to this motive, 38.02 per cent of manufacturing owner–managers perceived that they were operating in a stagnating/declining domestic market. Furthermore 26.45 per cent of them believed that the type of products they manufactured had currently reached saturation levels in the domestic market. In their view, they had little choice but to seek broader opportunities for their product portfolio in foreign markets. The second most important reason to globalize, as given by manufacturing owner–managers (52.07 per cent), involved inquiries from foreign agents or firms marketing

Table 11.5   Small business owner–managers' motives to globalize

Small business owner–managers' motives to globalize	Respondents operating in manufacturing (%)	Respondents operating in services (%)
Greater strategic opportunities in foreign markets	61.98	82.61
Inquiries from foreign agents/firms	52.07	47.83
Stagnating/declining domestic market	38.02	78.26
Product/service saturation of domestic market	26.45	21.74
The globalization drive of known competitors	14.05	17.39
Personal/professional contacts abroad	5.79	4.35
Competitive pressures from large firms	4.96	4.35
Other motives	13.22	13.04

similar products. Interestingly most of these inquiries originated in non-EC countries. The respondents suspected that at least half of this type of inquiry related to perceived barriers to entry into other EC countries. In the case of owner–managers operating in the service sector, the second most important motive to globalize involved a stagnating or declining domestic market. Inquiries from foreign agents or firms ranked third with these owner–managers. Like their manufacturing counterparts, they too believed that the majority of such inquiries sought entry into EC countries other than Britain.

The saturation of domestic markets ranked fourth (21.74 per cent) among service sector owner–managers. Ranking fifth, with both manufacturing (14.05 per cent) and service (17.39 per cent) owner–managers, was their awareness of the globalization efforts of known competitors. Personal and/or professional contacts abroad only motivated the globalization efforts of a small proportion of these owner–managers (5.79 per cent and 4.35 per cent, respectively). A similar proportion of respondents (4.96 per cent and 4.35 per cent) claimed that competitive pressures from large firms were increasingly driving them to seek marketing opportunities abroad. Just over 13 per cent of respondents provided other reasons for their globalization efforts, such as the opportunity to travel, to learn foreign languages, to meet interesting people or to enrich their personal and professional lives. There are considerable similarities between the globalization reasons given by small business owner–managers operating in the manufacturing and service sectors of the British economy. This cohesion of motives to globalize could reflect similarities in owner–manager perceptions regarding domestic and international markets or be attributable to socioeconomic and cultural factors, which ultimately appear to affect their attitudes towards and perceptions of globalization.

FACTORS AFFECTING THE GLOBALIZATION TENDENCIES OF SMALL BUSINESS OWNER–MANAGERS

When questioned about the main factors that affected their globalization tendencies, the respondent owner–managers in the research sample identified two main types of factors, 'internal' and 'external' to their firms (Table 11.6). There were considerable similarities between the responses given by manufacturing owner–managers and their service sector counterparts.

The main internal factor to affect globalization tendencies in micro- and small businesses involved the knowledge and competencies of owner–managers. About three-quarters of respondents (78.26 per cent in manufacturing and 73.20 per cent in services) admitted that their own knowledge of globalization issues and related competencies influenced their decision-making processes. As owner–managers in micro- and small businesses were the main, and often the only, decision makers in their firms, personal knowledge and competencies were perceived to affect globalization-related outcomes significantly. Lack of relevant knowledge/competencies affected the whole globalization process, beginning with the early stages of initiation, planning and inception, right up to completion. If these owner–managers

Table 11.6   Factors affecting the globalization tendencies of small business owner–managers

Factors affecting the globalization tendencies of small business owner–managers	Respondents operating in manufacturing (%) (N=2157)	Respondents operating in services (%) (N=3683)
Internal factors		
Owner–manager knowledge/competencies	78.26	73.20
Skills and human resources	67.13	66.41
Internal financial resources	53.87	55.99
Other internal factors	11.68	16.43
External factors		
Global networks and contacts	46.27	48.87
Specific global marketing information	44.14	45.72
Global distribution channels	41.49	42.87
Economic conditions	36.72	31.25
Availability of external sources of finance	26.38	22.18
Risks associated with exports	17.48	9.45
Other external factors	7.83	9.86

could not find reliable sources of relevant information or support, perceived knowledge and competence inadequacies would often frustrate or even curtail globalization tendencies at an early stage in the process. Some determined respondents claimed to have approached a variety of private, public and official support agencies, only to fail to satisfy their specific needs. Interestingly initial globalization successes, regardless of their scale, would considerably boost the confidence of an owner–manager and, therefore, encourage him or her to seek further knowledge, competencies and relevant experience in this field. Conversely globalization failures, at interim and, in particular, at the closing stages of the process, proved to have had severe curtailing effects upon the globalization tendencies of these respondents. Owner–managers who exhibited high levels of target market knowledge and understanding also employed innovative and/or high-growth business strategies that ensured the success of their globalization efforts. Positive attitudes towards business success, and the promise of commensurable rewards, appeared to provide not only the springboard for high-growth global strategies, but also the motivation and stamina needed to implement them.

The second most important internal factor, affecting 67.13 per cent of manufacturing and 66.41 per cent of service owner–managers, reflected the existing levels of relevant skills within their firms. Owner–managers typically viewed globalization with apprehension, not only because of their own perceived limitations but also because of the pool of available skills within their workforce. Surprisingly, very few of the respondents considered their workforce sufficiently skilled for the proposed globalization task. Most respondents perceived the level of existing skills in their micro- and small businesses to be barely adequate or, at best, just sufficient to satisfy the demands of the domestic market. The prospect of identifying, evaluating, planning and upgrading training and human resource development (HRD) needs proved too daunting for a large proportion of these owner–managers. Furthermore even those few respondents who overcame initial HRD difficulties claimed to have encountered considerable obstacles in matching their specific needs to the existing supply of relevant training. Customized training, which arguably could have satisfied at least some of their firm-specific needs, proved too costly for most of these owner–managers, when evaluated in relation to the perceived outcomes and benefits attributable to proposed globalization strategies.

The third most important internal factor to affect globalization was the financial resources available within a firm. In the research sample, 53.87 per cent of owner–managers operating in manufacturing and 55.99 per cent in the service sector claimed that the availability of internal financial resources played a substantial role in their globalization efforts. It appears that more than half of the respondents were reluctant to fund their globalization process from external sources of finance. In their view, globalization could be equated with diversification abroad and, as such, posed similar or even greater risks than business expansion within the domestic market. Furthermore they felt that diversification in general, and globalization in particular, carried relatively low rates of returns on investment (ROI), and would only be undertaken when internal financial resources could be made available for that particular purpose. Only about one-quarter of respondents were prepared to fund their globalization efforts from external sources. Even when the funding was available internally, conflicting demands on cash reserves, and the effects of contingency plans, would often result in the postponement of globalization activities and related financial decisions. Interestingly investments in globalization from personal and/or family resources were invariably considered as originating from 'internal' rather than 'external' sources of finance. On the principle of 'nothing ventured, nothing gained', the expected rates of return on personal investments in globalization were either very low or non-existent. Paradoxically, however, investments in globalization were perceived as important strategic decisions that could significantly affect the survival and expansion opportunities of these firms.

A small proportion of respondents (11.68 per cent in manufacturing and 16.43 per cent in services) mentioned other internal factors that affected their globalization tendencies. For example, time constraints and conflicting priorities appear to have forced some of these owner–managers to delegate, against their better judgment, some routine tasks to other employees or to 'shadow managers'. Mostly their trust in these individuals proved disastrous, and it often resulted in an unacceptably high waste of time and resources. Family and social responsibilities also affected some of these owner–managers' commitment to globalization. A minority of owner–managers mentioned xenophobic attitudes, the fear of flying and the dislike of foreign food and drink as factors affecting their globalization tendencies. These factors, however, were of minor importance and only influenced the attitudes of a very small number of respondents.

Active participation in global networks, and business/personal contacts abroad, was acknowledged by respondents (46.27 per cent in manufacturing, and 48.87 per cent in services) as the most important external factor to affect their tendencies to globalize their activities. Business and personal contacts formed an integral part of the managerial style of a large number of owner–managers in the research sample. The importance of international networks, to the globalization of almost half of the respondents, was confirmed both by the owner–managers who managed to complete their globalization efforts successfully and also by those who gave up owing to a lack of relevant contacts abroad. Successful respondents claimed to have made their initial contacts at conventions, conferences and exhibitions both in Britain and abroad. 'Like-minded' entrepreneurs tended to seek international contacts to explore business opportunities, and to exchange 'valuable information'. Science parks and university campuses also proved fertile grounds for international exchanges and collaborations. English language trade and specialist journals carried a wealth of pertinent advertising, as well as information for joint venture projects. Similarly most chambers of commerce in Britain, and their equivalent organizations abroad, facilitated global collaboration through advertising, publicity and social events. Cultivating international contacts occasionally facilitated entry to both domestic and global 'closed' or 'by invitation only' networks, which would offer tremendous business opportunities to 'insiders'. Both types of networks were otherwise very difficult to enter. Conversely a lack of access to global networks and international contacts acted as an effective barrier to entry into foreign markets. Few of the responding owner–managers managed to establish useful contacts abroad by either 'cold calling' or placing 'chance inquiries'. Interestingly, however, 'serendipity' and being 'in the right place, at the right time' would occasionally result in 'fortuitous collaborations' that facilitated the globalization tendencies of some owner–managers.

Specific global marketing information constituted an important external factor in the case of 44.14 per cent of manufacturing owner–managers and 45.72 per cent of their service counterparts. Without a reliable source of up-to-date information on relevant international markets, as well as specific data on niche opportunities, globally-oriented owner–managers would be unable to gauge the effectiveness and the focus of their chosen globalization strategies. Owner–managers attempted to gain access to a wide variety of information sources. Their efforts, however, resulted in varying degrees of success: official data available from domestic sources were reliable, but mostly out of date. Similar sources located abroad were difficult to identify and access, mainly because of language barriers. Private and commercial sources that could provide useful specific information to the owner–managers invariably charged an economic price for their services. Few of the respondents in the sample chose to purchase from such sources, mainly because of a reluctance to pay the price. Unrealistically most owner–managers expected specific marketing information to be easily accessible and freely available in English in official databases or in the public domain.

Both manufacturing (41.49 per cent) and service sector (42.87 per cent) owner–managers appeared to rely upon global distribution channels in their quest for globalization. Typically these global distribution channels varied considerably, both in size and in influence. Access to and detailed knowledge of local, regional and national channels of distribution proved to be of crucial importance to the ambitions of globally oriented owner–managers. Respondents who had successfully developed a global portfolio relied considerably upon detailed knowledge of local channels of distribution. They claimed to have used a variety of formal and informal means of maintaining existing channels of distribution or even initiated and developed new ways of marketing their products and services. Local agents, contacts and distribution managers were employed (on a full- or part-time basis) to ensure the smooth operation of these channels. Naturally distribution channels contributed significantly to other important aspects of the globalization process, including the collection of reliable and up-to-date marketing, economic and sociopolitical information, which often proved indispensable to the success of globalized businesses.

Owner–managers' perceptions of the prevailing economic conditions, in both domestic and international markets, affected 36.72 per cent of the respondents in the manufacturing sector and 31.25 per cent in services. Recessionary conditions negatively affected these owner–managers' tendencies to globalize their products and services. Conversely periods of recovery and growth motivated some of the respondents to invest their time and resources in globalization processes that relied upon a perceived excess demand for the type of products and services they held in their sales portfolios. A combination of recession in the domestic market and growth conditions prevailing abroad constituted an ideal economic situation conducive to overseas expansion, and diversification. The accuracy of these owner–managers' analyses of domestic and overseas economic conditions depended on the quality of information at their disposal. Unfortunately quality information was not always easy to obtain, evaluate or 'double check' for accuracy. For the majority of globally oriented owner–managers, the cost of 'red hot' information most often proved an obstacle difficult to overcome. Nevertheless some of these owner–managers claimed that 'practice makes perfect' and that they could occasionally obtain free or reasonably priced quality and reliable information relevant to their globalization efforts.

In their pursuit of globalization about one-quarter of the respondents in the manufacturing (26.38 per cent) and service (22.18 per cent) sectors relied on external sources of finance. The degree of difficulty involved in locating, analyzing, and actually raising the necessary funds affected the globalization tendencies of these owner–managers. This factor was closely linked to the availability of internal financial resources as it represented an alternative strategy for those reluctant to use external resources for funding their globalization efforts. Most owner–managers in this category complained about the difficulties they had encountered in raising the necessary funds from a variety of sources, including high street and merchant banks, venture capitalists, business angels and credit houses. It appears that, in most cases, they were unable to satisfy the prospective lender's requirements for relevant business plans, cash flow forecasts or disclosure of profit and loss statements. Owing to language, cultural and information barriers, none of the respondents appeared to have considered tapping into financial resources available abroad. Furthermore very few of the respondents managed to obtain loans that would have funded, wholly or in part, their proposed globalization strategies.

The perceived risks associated with the export of products and services affected 17.48 per cent of manufacturing owner–managers and 9.45 per cent of the respondents from the service sector. The risk aversion typically exhibited by micro- and small business owner–managers was also evident in relation to their globalization tendencies. Few of these respondents were willing to allow extended credit for goods and services sold abroad, even when these were customarily available in their proposed target market. Most of them sought credit guarantee agreements or risk-free contracts with third parties already operating in the chosen international niche market. When these agreements proved to be unrealistic options to safeguard their export contracts, a large proportion of respondents preferred to pull out from the chosen target market, rather than risk 'ending up with nothing'. A small proportion of respondents (7.83 per cent in manufacturing and 9.86 per cent in services) claimed to be affected by globalization factors other than those listed above. The factors mentioned in this category mainly reflected their personal preferences, attitudes, beliefs and fears, which were indirectly related to their globalization intentions and tendencies.

CONCLUDING REMARKS

A number of interesting findings have emerged from this research study. As expected, owner–managers make most, if not all, of the decisions in relation to globalization processes in micro- and small firms. The globalization tendencies of small business owner–managers were affected by both internal and external factors. Internal factors were related to an owner–manager's knowledge and competencies, as well as the skills and human resource development needs of their workforce. The availability of internal financial resources affected the globalization tendencies of micro- and small firms at all stages of the process. External factors that affected globalization in these firms related to an owner–manager's ability to participate in global networks, gather specific marketing information and have access to relevant channels of distribution. The economic circumstances prevailing in the domestic and international markets also influenced their decision-making processes and in particular the choice and timing of their globalization efforts. The availability of external sources of finance was only important to those owner–managers who had overcome their fears and developed a preference for using these resources to finance their global strategies.

Those entrepreneurs who exhibited high levels of target market knowledge and understanding also employed innovative and/or high-growth business strategies. More importantly they were able to read and interpret market developments, identify opportunities and reallocate human and financial resources to achieve or surpass their globalization targets. Conversely an entrepreneurial inability to read and react to changes in the global market invariably resulted in organizational stagnation and/or decline. Human resource development strategies and access to financial resources appeared to affect strategic outcomes significantly. Proactive human resource development procedures formed an integral part of the business strategies of high-growth firms. In contrast, reactive strategies were perceived to hinder organizational growth in these firms. An entrepreneurial ability to raise funds from a variety of commercial and personal sources facilitated the achievement of ambitious short-, medium- or long-term growth strategies. Entrepreneurial attitudes towards business success and the promise of commensurate rewards appeared to provide, not only the springboard for high-growth global strategies, but also the motivation and stamina needed to implement them.

REFERENCES

Archibugi, D. and J. Michie (eds) (1997), *Technology, Globalisation and Economic Performance*, Cambridge: Cambridge University Press.

Barney, J. (1991), 'Firm resources and sustained competitive advantage', *Journal of Management*, **17**, 99–120.

Bell, J., D. Crick and S. Young (1998), 'Holistic perspective on small firm internationalisation', *Proceedings of the AIB (UK Chapter) Conference*, April.

Bloodgood, J., H. Sapienza and J. Almeida (1996), 'The internationalisation of new high-potential US ventures: antecedents and outcomes', *Entrepreneurship Theory and Practice*, **20**, 61–76.

Bruland, K. (1989), *British Technology and European Industrialisation*, Cambridge: Cambridge University Press.

Casson, M. (ed.) (1991), *Global Research Strategy and International Competitiveness*, Oxford: Basil Blackwell.

Coviello, N. and H. Munro (1997), 'Network relationships and the internationalisation process of small software firms', *Scandinavian International Business Review*, **6** (4), 361–86.

Cox, K., (ed.) (1997), *Spaces of Globalisation – Reasserting the Power of the Local*, London: The Guilford Press.

Crick, D. and S. Chaudhry (1995), *Some Aspects of the Export Behaviour of SMEs in the UK Clothing Industry*, Leicester: University of Leicester Management Centre.

Cyert, R.M. and I.G. March (1963), *A Behavioral Theory of the Firm*, Englewood Cliffs, NJ: Prentice-Hall.

D'Souza, D. and P. McDougall (1989), 'Third world joint venturing: a strategic option for the smaller firm', *Entrepreneurship Theory and Practice*, **14**, 19–33.

Dunning, J. (1992), *The Globalisation of Business*, London: Routledge.

EC (1996), 'SMEs: recommendation of the Commission', *Official Journal of the European Communities*, **107**(6), 1–2.

Fiegenbaum, A. and A. Karnani (1991), 'Output flexibility – a competitive advantage for small firms', *Strategic Management Journal*, **12**, 101–14.

Fitzgerald, N. (1997), 'Harnessing the potential of globalisation for the consumer and citizen', *International Affairs*, **73** (4), 739–46.

Hamel, G. and C. Prahalad (1990), 'The core competence of the corporation', *Harvard Business Review*, **68** (3), 79–91.

Hamill, J. and K. Gregory (1997), 'Internet marketing and the internationalisation of UK SMEs', *Journal of Marketing Management*, **13** (1), 9–28.

Hitt, M., R. Hoskisson and J. Harrison (1991), 'Strategic competitiveness in the 1990s: challenges and opportunities for US executives', *Academy of Management Executive*, **5** (2), 7–22.

Howells, J. and M. Wood (1993), *The Globalisation of Production and Technology*, London: Belhaven Press.

Johanson, J. and J. Vahlne (1977), 'The internationalisation process of the firm – a model of knowledge development and increasing foreign market commitments', *Journal of International Business Studies*, **8** (1). 23–32.

Johanson, J. and J. Vahlne (1990), 'The mechanism of internationalisation', *International Marketing Review*, **1** (3), 9–27.

Karagozoglu, N. and M. Lindell (1998), 'Internationalisation of small and medium-sized technology-based firms: an exploratory study', *Journal of Small Business Management*, **36** (1), 44–59.

Lindell, M. and N. Karagozoglu (1997), 'Global strategies of US and Scandinavian R&D: intensive small and medium-sized companies', *European Management Journal*, **15** (1), 92–101.

Mahone, C. (1995), 'A comparative analysis of the differences in perceived obstacles to exporting by small and medium-sized manufacturers and traders', *The International Trade Journal*, **9** (3), 315–32.

Marginson, P., P. Armstrong, P. Edwards, J. Purcell and N. Hubbard (1993), 'The control of industrial relations in large organisations: an initial analysis of the second company level industrial relations survey', Warwick Papers in Industrial Relations no.45, Industrial Relations Research Unit, University of Warwick.

Matlay, H. (1997), *The Globalisation Tendencies of Firms Operating in the Small Business Sector of the British Economy: An Overview*, Oxford: Second Foundation.

Matlay, H. (1998), *The Training Needs of Owner/Managers in Globalized Small Businesses: A Critical Overview*, Coventry: Global Independent Research.

Matlay, H. (1999), 'Internationalisation, competitiveness and growth in tourism SMEs: a pan-European comparison', paper presented at the Small Business and Enterprise Development Conference, University of Leeds, 22–3 March.

McDougall, P. and B. Oviatt (1996), 'New venture internationalisation, strategic change and performance: a follow-up study', *Journal of Business Venturing*, **11**, 34–40.

Moini, A. (1992), 'Europe 1992: a challenge to small exporters', *Journal of Small Business Management*, **30** (1), 11–20.

Morgan, R. (1997), 'Export stimuli and export barriers: evidence from empirical research studies', *European Business Review*, **97** (2), 68–79.

Nothdurft, W. (1992), *Going Global: How Europe Helps Small Firms Export*, Washington: Brookings Institution.

Oberhansli, H. (1997), 'A global agreement for private investment and regulatory competition in globalised markets', *Aussenwirtschaft*, **52** (3), 449–71.

OECD (1996), *Globalisation of Industry: Overview and Sector Reports*, Paris: Organization for Economic Co-operation and Development.

OECD (1997), *Globalisation and Small and Medium Enterprises (SMEs), Vol.1: Synthesis Report*, Paris: Organization for Economic Co-operation and Development.

O'Farrell, P., P. Wood and J. Zheng (1996), 'Internationalisation of business services: an interregional analysis', *Regional Studies*, **30**, 101–18.

Oviatt, B. and P. McDougall (1994), 'Toward a theory of international new ventures', *Journal of International Business Studies*, **25**, 45–64.

Preston, C. (1997), *Enlargement and Integration in the European Union*, London: Routledge.

Reid, S.D. (1983), 'Firm internationalisation: transaction cost and strategic choice', *International Marketing Review*, **1** (2), 45–55.

Robertson, R. (1992), *Globalisation, Social Theory and Global Culture*, London: SAGE.

Scase, R. (1996), 'Employment relations in small firms', in P. Edwards (ed.), *Industrial Relations, Theory and Practice in Britain*, Oxford: Blackwell.

Stewart, D. (1997), 'Domestic competitive strategy and export marketing strategy: the impact of fit on the degree of internationalisation of SMEs', *Journal of Marketing Management*, **13** (1), 105–17.

Storper, M. (1997), *The Regional World: Territorial Development in a Global Economy*, New York: The Guilford Press.

Styles, C. and T. Ambler (1994), 'The first step to export success', PAN'AGRA Research Programme, London Business School.

Taylor, P. (1995), *International Organisation in the Modern World: The Regional and the Global Process*, London: Pinter.

Welch, L.S. and R. Luostarinen (1988) 'Internationalisation: evolution of a concept', *Journal of General Management*, **14** (2), 34–55.

Wiedersheim-Paul, F., H.C. Olson and L.S. Welch (1978), 'Pre-export activity: the first in internationalization', *Journal of International Business Studies*, **9** (1), 47–58.

Willis, G.H. (1981), 'SMEs and globalisation', *International Journal of Manufacturing*, **3** (4), 117–39.

12. Conclusion: the evolutionary patterns of change, the emerging trends and implications for internationalizing small firms

Hamid Etemad

INTRODUCTION

Although slow and evolutionary change has been with us for a long time, systematic change in the business environment started some time in the 1950s. International trade introduced comparatively advantageous goods and services, through exports, from one nation to another and inevitably introduced change, but the rate of diffusion of the change due to trade was comparatively low. International investment followed trade and foreign direct investment (FDI) gradually replaced the initial imports of traded goods.[1] International investment introduced a qualitatively different change with a potentially higher diffusion rate than international trade (that is, exports and imports) because of higher involvement of investors than of traders. Inadvertently the subsidiaries of multinational enterprises (MNEs) became the systematic and consistent change agents as they introduced an innovative portfolio not only of goods and services but also of corporate practices and procedures which originated in their parent company environments (or headquarters).

The early parent companies were mainly based in the United States and European countries. Their corporate research and development (R&D) laboratories created a continual stream of new products and services centrally, mainly in response to competition in their own markets in industrialized countries, and their modern marketing departments commercialized them with a vengeance to keep the competition at home at bay. When they expanded beyond their shores, naturally they took their innovations to other countries as well. This in turn enabled them to enlarge their sales and benefit from the associated scale economies worldwide. As a result the health of the local firms was threatened, as they did not have similar access to such large external scale economies. Servan-Schreiber (1968) forewarned local governments with the publication of the *Le Défi Américain* (*The American Challenge*) in 1968. With the arrival of US-based MNEs in Europe, he suggested that the local businesses and their government would soon be at bay. By a logical extension, the local subsidiary would soon be forced to follow the policies set by corporate headquarters, rather than those of the local governments, and thus some policies would be de facto set abroad. In his book *Sovereignty at Bay* (1971) Raymond Vernon focused on these arguments and started a debate on the topic that is still going on. This debate is no longer about whether or not the sovereignty of the nation state, its institutions and its policies is threatened; it is about the nature, extent and rate of change due to internationalization, if not globalization, of trade and investment environments.

One of the manifestations of the early international expansion of MNEs, starting in the 1950s, and more recently of smaller firms, has been the introduction of an incremental, systematic and purposeful portfolio of products and services to other nations. The introduction of such innovative portfolios either changed and challenged or replaced what was there before; alternatively, it created a new industry where the local enterprises did not, or could not, cope fast enough with the change introduced a short while before. With the advent of MNEs and the expansion of their subsidiaries from the 'center' (mainly in industrialized and developed countries) to the 'periphery' (mainly in developing nations), the international version of the Schumpeterian theory of 'creative destruction' (Schumpeter, 1934) began to work more profoundly outside, rather than inside, the market for which the innovation was originally intended. Subsidiaries propagated the parent's innovative portfolios as well as more efficient competencies to the peripheries in host countries. The local SMEs, already disadvantaged by the diseconomies of market size and scale, were severely affected and suffered even more than the others.

Naturally, where unbridled competition was permitted, the local national firms came under tremendous competitive pressure and were forced to change in order to survive, as implied earlier. Most of these firms were micro- and small-sized enterprises as compared to MNEs by today's standards. In response to the local firms' cry for help, national governments had to create entry barriers to protect them as well as national industries, as documented in the history of international trade and investment. However the predecessor of the World Trade Organization (WTO), the General Agreement on Tariffs and Trade (GATT) set out to liberalize trade and investment barriers gradually and to remove them eventually. Some ten rounds of GATT negotiations have dismantled, and the continuing negotiations among the 140 members of WTO are removing, many of the barriers that segregated markets and offered protection to the local enterprise and national industries in those markets. With the prospects of globalization more real than ever before in the history of mankind, the possibility of local or national protection grows ever weaker and with it goes the viability of local enterprise and national industries.

Another end result of the above process was the introduction of innovation from industrialized countries to the rest of the world. As discussed earlier, along with international trade came innovation (and subsequent change), followed by foreign direct investment (FDI) further supporting the initial trade and the intellectual property embedded in the initial innovation. Barnet and Muller (1974) viewed the phenomenon as tantamount to a systematic and unidirectional control, if not effective takeover, of the periphery by the centre, while Vernon (1966) saw it as an evolutionary progression and used it as the basis for articulating his theory of the international product life cycle (IPLC) and Dunning (1980, 1988) and other scholars of FDI (for example, Buckley, 1989; Buckley and Casson, 1976, Caves, 1982) formulated the various versions of the theory of FDI.

In Vernon's IPLC, new innovative products flowed unidirectionally from the center (that is, the USA) to the periphery. Production followed in the same direction: first, in the USA, then in the developed countries, before moving into the developing countries. The noteworthy point is that innovative ideas, products, FDI and production traveled unidirectionally from the center to the periphery, and so did the control, but profits traveled in the reverse direction. Although not an explicit part of the theory, FDI would flow from capital-rich countries to others so they would have similar unidirectional flow structure and consequences. However that was the pattern prior to the broad liberalization of trade and investments and globalization. The world has come a long way and today's reality is much different. Although a cliché now, continual change is the only unchanging constant; the rate and nature of change has evolved dramatically over time, ever since the 1950s. As compared to the early predictable patterns, the prevailing change is verging on chaos in terms of rate, number and size of players and their respective strategies.

The primary objective of this chapter, therefore, is to review some selective aspects of change and their respective evolutionary pattern over time, and examine some of the forces and drivers of change that are affecting the environment of international entrepreneurship with a view to exploring their combined implications for setting an agenda for informed formulation of internationalization strategy, especially for smaller enterprises, as they attempt to embark on their path of international, if not global, expansion. For reasons of clarity, this chapter will study the change in the environment in four layers, from four different perspectives, each building on the previous one. Each layer is presented as a part and decomposes relevant influential concepts, or constructs of that part sequentially, as follows:

- the patterns of change and the emerging trends in the socioeconomic aspects,
- the patterns of change and the emerging trends in the technological aspects,
- the patterns of change and the emerging trends in the organizational aspects, and
- the patterns of change and the emerging trends in converging factors.

Each part builds on the pertinent concepts, including those presented in the previous chapters, extending them to provide potent conceptual tools for analyzing the complex environment facing smaller firms aspiring to internationalize. While global competition is constantly adding to environmental complexity, each part's conceptual tools and grounded discussions will increasingly unbundle the strategic complexity facing internationalizing firms. The lessons and implications associated with the patterns of change and their corresponding trends are presented throughout the chapter.

THE PATTERN OF SOCIOECONOMIC CHANGE AND THE EMERGING TRENDS

The Rapid Globalization of Environment through Free Trade

Although a slower dynamics of change started in the 1950s, the world had never experienced the much more rapid change, with much more profound impact, before the early 1990s, when the repeated and increasing waves of free and freer trade and investments continually dismantled barriers and facilitated the flow of goods, services and knowledge around the globe. These waves of change have transformed the global competitive environment into multipolar centers of specialized competencies and production that create incremental value through collaboration (Kanter, 1984). They include small and large independent companies (Doz, 1996; Forrest and Martin, 1992) and some are already members of networked companies (Gilroy, 1993), such as multinational enterprises (MNEs).

Ohmae (1985) suggested the concept of 'triads' in the 1980s to introduce the emergence of a tripolar competitive world. In addition to the European continent and North America, Ohmae considered Japan as the third pole in the triad concept. In the interim period, however, much qualitative change has occurred:

First, progressive smaller firms, based in the countries of South and East Asia, have become integral parts of the worldwide supply chains of Japan-based MNEs, and other MNEs based elsewhere to a lesser extent. As a direct result, not only have many smaller firms acquired the competencies to satisfy the quality requirements of Japanese MNEs (and others) but also they are selling their original equipment manufacturer (OEM) product globally through these MNEs. This points to a pervasive development: inter- and intrafirm trade with a functionally profound impact matching that of regional free and freer trade agreements.

Second, greater China, including the People's Republic, Hong Kong and Taiwan, has become a global powerhouse in its own right. Additionally the globally-oriented firms in greater China, especially in Hong Kong and Taiwan, have progressed far beyond inter-firm trade and OEM. They have established their brands globally and are competing in the international markets directly. In so doing, they are also updating the basis of competition (Christensen and Bower, 1996) and tightening competition in their wake at home and abroad.

Third, firms in the Indian subcontinent, which used to be relatively lethargic, as they were insulated from global competition through regulatory protection and were not severely challenged, are entering and competing in international markets with their strong resource-based capabilities, including considerable intellectual competencies.

Fourth, firms in South Korea, the Australia–New Zealand Free Trade Area and other developing Asian countries are also joining the internationalization process. Malaysia, Singapore and South Korea have become sectoral power houses in their own right and can easily stand global competition at home and abroad.

Finally, firms in South American countries, especially those in the Southern Cone (Mercesor), are making fast strides in joining global trade and investments. They are becoming progressively more competitive and are participating in globally integrated supply chains of their own, and others.

A consequence of such change is that traditional strategies, explanations and even theories are no longer as applicable, or as potent, as in the past. Consider, for example, Raymond Vernon's (1966) international product life cycle (IPLC). It is incapable of explaining international product life cycles as they are no longer unipolar (or with very few origins in the industrial markets) as proposed by the theory in the 1970s. The theory's proposed flow of new products, initiating at the MNEs' home and radiating to the peripheries, as in a unicentered web, has now become a family of inverted webs of multipolar origins of competencies at the periphery radiating towards their respective centers. Many smaller, internationally oriented and globally competitive firms in the developing world are occupying the periphery. Each of these smaller firms at the periphery is specialized in a part of the total value chain and is fully capable of producing value-loaded products at scale economies for distribution to the rest of the world, not only through the old centers but also directly through their own specialized global networks. Most of these smaller firms are not located in the USA or Europe or dominated by US- or Europe-based MNEs. Instead they are located in developing and industrializing countries. They have given rise to the internationalization of smaller firms on a broad scale (the international entrepreneurship phenomenon), selective aspects of which were examined in the previous chapters of this volume. As a result, both the US- and non-US-based MNEs are forced to change course and serve as the nerve centers of their own inverted webs (Etemad, 2002, 2003c) of international supply chains to control their own interests.[2]

The Emergence of Regional Industrial Clusters

Two aspects of the regional industrial clusters are germane to the transformation of local firms, local environment, industrial organization and competition, with an eventual impact on the region's global competitiveness.

Strategic evolution in the firm

Ample research suggests that the geographical proximity of firms in a regional cluster and the supportive regional environment facilitate cooperation (Saxenian, 1994) and alliances (Gomes-Casseres, 1997; Gulati, 1995a) among local firms. The classic view of the entrepreneur as an independent and self-reliant agent is increasingly challenged and is being gradually transformed to include complementary and collaborative concepts such as interdependence (Etemad *et al.*, 2001), codependence (Acs and Yeung, 1999) and even extreme dependence in terms of symbiotic relations (Etemad, 2003a, 2003b).[3] Increased cooperation, based mainly on proximity,[4] and social embeddedness (Anderson and Johanson, 1996), leading to ease of interactions and trust (Gulati, 1995a, 1995b), have quickened this transition to codependence, which may in turn reinforce further collaboration as the transaction costs (Joshi and Stump, 1999; Williamson, 1979, 1981)[5] of cooperation and collaboration begin to decrease and the prerequisite of increased mutual trust takes further hold (Gulati, 1995a; Barkema *et al.*, 1996; Barkema *et al.*, 1997). Such proximities encourage cooperation, collaboration and joint action, including investment in research and development, which is a requisite of co-learning. Combined, these factors have led to a strategic reorientation in favor of building and optimizing a joint value chain. Joint value chains, based mainly on trust, division of labor and specialization, resulting in improved quality and decreasing costs, are becoming the structural and strategic foundations that give joint action dynamic continuity, especially in the regional clusters.

With the expansion of free and freer trade areas, regional proximity may extend beyond a contiguous geographic region and spread across national boundaries to engulf an industrial sector. What used to be a true regional cluster, in a geographic sense, may now include many multicentered webs of cooperation within a sector around the world[6] (consider electronic parts as an example of such global cooperation and integration among many small, medium and large-sized firms). Such reorientation may further transform the members of the regional (or sectoral) cluster in the direction of increased specialization, which in turn increases their dependence not only on the members of their own supply chain in their regional clusters but also on other clusters (or inverted webs) within their immediate free trade area and possibly beyond.

The above chain of relations provides an explanation for the increased cooperation and competition at the same time (D'Aveni, 1994) among the regional clusters, including those in the Austin-Texas Area, the Ottawa-Carton Area, the North Carolina Area, the San Francisco-Bay Area, Route 128 (Boston Area) and others in the Canada–US Free Trade Area, with the possibility of extending to NAFTA and beyond in the near future.[7] These developments point to the increased involvement of smaller local and regional firms in supply and value chains extending beyond a region, and creating incremental value in international markets. They also point to the increasing dependence of firms, regardless of size, on others. These developments, including regional clusters (see, for example, Chapters 2, 3 and 4 of this volume) provide proven functional models for both higher cooperation and integration across independently owned firms resulting in further internationalization of smaller enterprises around the world.[8]

Transformation of the value chain

The gradual transformation from independent and all-inclusive arrangements to interdependent production through joint value chains in the region has contributed to the increased competitiveness of both the firms and the region as a whole. With the growth of the joint value chains, each firm can further specialize on a particular part of the value chain for maximum scale economies without sacrificing either the product quality or joint scope economies. This will in turn assist all collaborating firms in creating a highly competitive value chain as a basis for increased competitiveness. This increased codependence (Acs and Yeung, 1999) may further stimulate joint actions in order to avoid higher transaction costs (Williamson, 1975, 1979, 1981). The reduced risk resulting from joint action and colearning, supported by the accumulation of trust based on proximity and social embeddedness, gradually transforms firms within the cluster to a coalition resembling, and even acting in a manner very similar to, the constellation of networked firms (Gomes-Casseres, 1996, 1997; Yoshino and Rangan, 1995).

As compared to multinationals, the main difference between regionally networked firms and MNEs is MNEs' unified ownership and governance, which is no longer a compelling basis for increased global competitiveness, as constellations and alliances of many diverse and independently owned firms have achieved higher competitiveness than corresponding MNEs. While the former may be locally bound (for example, based partly on proximity and social embeddedness), MNEs are globally based and locally enhanced (at least in theory). This may result in some competitive edge for the members of the MNE network over the network members of the regional industrial (or sectoral) cluster(s). However the members of the local regional cluster will not be disadvantaged by 'foreignness' (Hymer, 1976), nor are they compelled to compete against one another.

The above discussion suggests that a rich array of competitiveness-enhancing mechanisms that were not feasible a decade ago have become available to smaller local firms. International competitiveness and internationalization do not necessarily depend on physical and geographical expansion to other countries and faraway markets beyond the home markets. Even smaller local firms can take advantage of the enabling change in the environment to pursue novel strategic paths for increasing their respective competitiveness as a basis for internationalization, perhaps no longer having a physical presence in distant geographical locations. These arguments point to an emerging, but inescapable, trend: internationally oriented local firms can globalize at home and enjoy the benefits of internationalization while primarily based in their region. These, and the above, arguments resonate very well with the discussion presented in the previous chapters of this volume.

THE PATTERN OF CHANGES AND THE EMERGING TRENDS IN THE TECHNOLOGICAL ENVIRONMENT

Rapid Technological Developments outside North America (and in the Triad) and Corresponding Migration of Production and Supply Chains

In contrast to the previous technological superiority of the Europe- and US-based firms, the rapid technological developments in Asia generally parallel, if not exceed, those in Europe and the USA. This implies a relative decline in the technological position of the United States, especially in the industries which it previously dominated. In fact many products and technologies created and perfected in the USA have experienced higher growth rates outside the USA (and Europe in some cases) and the US position is no longer dominant, or competitive. Consider, for example, air frames, jet engines, computers, household electronics, kitchen appliances, chemicals and plastics, light and lower technology military industries, to name a few, in which the USA and, in some cases, Europe held worldwide dominance for some time.

The prevailing reality is very different now. Table 12.1 highlights these industries and their respective migration to other locations.

The pattern of the change in dominance, highlighted in Table 12.1, parallels the pattern of competitiveness. Other nations are now either more globally competitive than, or at least as competitive as, the USA and Europe, which dominated industry in the recent past. Producers in each of the industries shown follow their own strategies for increased global competitiveness in order to gain much higher global market shares. As stated earlier the members of their supply and value chains are not all large companies, nor are they joint-venture partners or the license-holders of Europe- and US-based MNEs, as predicted by theories of internationalization (for example, Buckley and Casson, 1976; Cavusgill, 1982; Dunning, 1980, 1988, 1995; Johanson and Vahlne, 1977, 1990, 1992; Johanson and Wiedersheim-Paul, 1975; Rugman, 1982; Vernon, 1966).

Table 12.1   The pattern of change of dominance in selected industries

Industry dominated by USA and/or Europe	Pattern of migration from USA and Europe to designated countries
1. Air frames	From US to Europe (for example, airbus industries) and moving further east and southward to Japan, China and even Brazil
2. Jet engines	From US to UK, France, Italy and to Brazil and beyond
3. Computers	From US to Japan, Korea, Taiwan, PRC and elsewhere
4. Chemicals and plastics	From Europe and US to PRC, oil-producing countries and others
5. Household electronics	From US to Japan, Taiwan, Korea, PRC and their respective supply chains
6. Kitchen appliances	From US to Europe and then to many developing nations
7. Light and lower tech. military industries	From US and Europe to China, Israel, South Africa and other developing nations
8. Steel and ferrous metals	From US to Japan, Korea, PRC, India, other developing nations
9. Shipbuilding	From US and Europe to Japan, Korea, PRC and their supply chain worldwide

In fact, these developments confirm the pattern of change discussed earlier: Such change is, however, transforming the pattern of world production and marketing of the goods and services involved from the unidirectional pattern of the recent past, radiating from the center to the periphery, to their own inverted webs (and networks) of multipolar 'centers of excellence', radiating in the reverse order. As stated earlier, each of the smaller, as opposed to the larger, firms in the network is producing specialized components under special arrangement, including global product mandates (Etemad, 1982; Etemad and Seguin-Dulude, 1986a, 1986b; Rugman and Douglas, 1986). As a result, the members of each of these networks collaborate strongly in order for the network to compete intensively against other similar networks for an ever-larger share of the global markets, rather than competing against each other within such constellations of independent firms (Gomes-Casseres, 1996). The headquarters of US- and Europe-based MNEs no longer dominate the value chain of such constellations. Instead globally-competitive SMEs enable the value chain of their respective flagship enterprises (Rugman and D'Cruz, 2000) to compete globally against similar constellations of firms (Gomes-Casseres, 1996) in inter-constellation, as opposed to inter-firm, competition. The membership of these constellations include innovative and entrepreneurial SMEs scattered throughout the world (Gomes-Casseres, 1997) and offer protection to their members similar to that of the recent past offered by countries, with a fundamental difference: countries offered protection to the weaker firms (relative to global competitors) while the innerdynamics of constellations shield the stronger firms from global competitors, regardless of the firm size.[9]

The Emergence of a Technological Race throughout the World

The flow of information, knowledge and technology, as well as the supporting investments described above, may have in fact triggered a continual quest for technological superiority. However achieving such superiority would require ever-higher R&D expenditures to support further generations of technology to produce ever more advanced products and services. The MNEs' centres of excellence in general, and technologically-oriented SMEs in particular (Etemad, 2003a; Joshi and Stump, 1999; Gupta and Govindarajan, 1994), are deeply involved in such implicit technological races. The economics of 'first mover's advantage' (Lieberman and Montgomery, 1998) motivates competitors to attempt to win the technological race as early and as fast as possible as it confers the 'first mover advantage' on the winner for the early generations. At the same time, others will also be forced to attempt to win the global technological race against the next generation in order to recoup their accumulated large sunk investments, to attain a share of the global markets and to reverse the tide in their own favor as soon as possible. The dynamic of these behaviors will in turn speed up the pace of the global races. The prize for winning such races is not only the acknowledged technological superiority but also competitiveness in international markets.

However these markets are either the home markets of the local firms or the host country markets of MNEs' local subsidiaries. Regardless of the home–host distinction, the firms in these markets will be pressed into competing at the cutting-edge levels of technological products, even if they have refrained from competing in the international markets previously. Consequently these markets are transformed into marketing battlegrounds for market shares that support further R&D expense, which enables the technological race. Ironically the losers are likely to resist pressures from the winners to lock in the prevailing situation and will be more eager to keep the race open in the hope of winning in the next round. While keeping this dynamic open would avoid (or at least postpone) conceding both superiority and market shares to the winners of the previous rounds, it would also force higher R&D expenditures and deeper commitments. Unfortunately, in such high-technology and rapidly changing environments, independent small local firms stand a poor chance of success or even survival. As stated in previous chapters, internationalization has become a forced imperative, regardless of the firm's age, size and location.

The Transformation of the Cost Structure in the Local Markets

Prior to their becoming a part of the global trading system and receiving continuous injections of high-technology flows and ever-increasing pressures for higher R&D expenditure, simple competition dominated in these markets. Firms used simple price mechanisms to compete and to gain market share. The forced deployment of ever-higher technologies to support the family of ever more advanced products (based on and produced by such high technologies) would gradually transform the respective cost structure from a relatively lower fixed and higher variable cost to a much higher fixed cost and relatively lower variable cost regime. The economics of such higher fixed cost regimes requires an increasingly large scale and faster amortization because of the rapid accumulation of high fixed (or sunk) costs of rapidly-obsolescing technologies and the shrinking life cycle of their associated products. This dynamic is one force, among others, that would incite a fresh round in the technological race and increased competition for capturing the necessary incremental market share to support the current operations and, it is hoped, enable the acquisition of a yet higher technological generation and the consequent future expansion(s). As a direct result, the competition in high-technology-intensive products and processes has transformed the rules of production and the basis of competition from simple price and quality relations to competitive battles supported by the technological race and temporal games with only one or two winners (and naturally many losers) in each round of product advancement along their respective IPLC. This dynamics would further urge the losers to try to win in the next generations of products and services in the hope of recouping their previous losses and to survive; the alternative is a slow death under the mounting pressures of ever-higher sunk costs. The extant literature of the 'first mover advantage', as stated earlier, provides ample evidence to suggest that competitors view competition involving the high-technology product market as a multi-period, multi-stage and multi-location competition at the end of which the first movers are not necessarily the ultimate winners. Unless local SMEs understand the nature of such games and the gaming rules governing them, they stand a poorer chance of succeeding in, or even surviving, such competitive dynamics, than otherwise.

ORGANIZATIONAL CHANGES AND THE EMERGING TRENDS

The Emergence of Multipolar IPLCs

Vernon's (1966) theory of the international product life cycle (IPLC) proposed three principal phases in a complete product life cycle.

The first phase
Innovative ideas, originating in US corporate laboratories, would lead to the launch of the new products (or services) on the US markets, in the initial stages of this phase, before being exported to the European markets and then to developing markets after some passage of time. The theory implied that neither the markets in Europe nor those in the rest of the world (ROW), were prepared to purchase the product; nor could they provide the necessary factor inputs (including skilled labor and technology) to manufacture them locally. Therefore the R&D, production and consumption would be concentrated in the USA initially. Demand for the product would emerge later in Europe, followed by the ROW at a later point. All these export markets would be served by US-based production.

The second phase
With the further development of the European environment (mainly on the demand side) and a gradual transformation of production inputs on the supply side in the USA (in favor of less skilled labor and lower technology), a European subsidiary would be set up (with the headquarters' investment and

R&D support) to produce the product locally in Europe for local market consumption and also for exports to developing countries in the second phase of the theory.

The third phase

The next phase comprised a further movement of production to the developing countries as their demand for the product(s) grew sufficiently and further technological transformation allowed for investments in local production facilities, initially to satisfy local consumption, and later on to export to other countries. Considering the higher cost structure in the US and European markets, the product manufactured in developing countries could be imported back to both the US and the European markets in phase three. This phase brought the IPLC to an end as the US-based MNE, which used to export to the ROW in the earlier phases, would now be importing from the rest of the world for US and European consumption. The implicit outcome of the theory was that production would migrate from the US and European markets to developing countries, not necessarily because of improvements in their labor and technological environment, but certainly thanks to a further transformation in the factor input composition due to the R&D efforts in the US laboratories. Thus the US-based R&D was the critical element of the theory as it played a multitude of fundamental roles, such as product and process improvements, which included a transformation in the composition of US production factor inputs to match those readily available in other countries to which production would later migrate.

Stated differently, the US-based R&D played the most critical role in the theory; the power of FDI, which followed in later phases, became equally critical, as it paved the way for migration of production from the USA (with higher costs) to local facilities in Europe and other countries with lower fixed and variable costs. It was this expansion process that enabled the US-based MNEs to lower their variable cost progressively, which allowed them to attain even higher margins and to recover their initial R&D costs (that is, fixed sunk costs). Therefore any dissipation of R&D in any part of such a system would risk compromising the entire system. However progressive firms in the European, Asian and developing countries began to acquire or develop their own R&D capabilities and create their own IPLCs, resulting in the current inverted multi-centered network of organizations governing and regulating supply chain, marketing and sales, and value and wealth creation processes. This emerging decentralized governance and organizational system appears to be more flexible strategically and more powerful competitively than its predecessors. Naturally SMEs aspiring to internationalize and achieve global competitiveness need to understand and take steps to join or to attain such or similar structures in order to benefit from them.

It is instructive to analyze the initial movement of the products, and migration of production along the evolutionary path of IPLC, from the headquarters to other countries, from a different perspective than those of the scholars and students of the theory. The above movements consist of three parallel developments under way at the same time.

The increased production scale   Exports to the ROW contributed to increasing the production scale and reduction of average costs, thereby enabling other lower-income communities to afford the imported product and to join the demand for the product, which in turn contributed to further production and scale economies. We refer to this as the scale economies and market development interaction effect.

As scale economies reduced the costs further, lower-income populations joined the previous market, necessitating further production expansion. The next production facilities could be located elsewhere outside the USA, for example, on a'turnkey' or 'license' basis. The establishment of such facilities did not have to wait for the transformation of factor inputs at home to match the less sophisticated technological environments in a potential host country. Such migrations are readily observable in highly sophisticated products, such as electronic chips, in the South and East Asian countries, where highly sophisticated products are produced in locations at the periphery with lower factor costs rather than sophisticated factor inputs matching those of the center.

The role of factor input composition in the theory   The relative capital and skilled labor intensity of the required input factors initially called for a highly developed location, such as the USA, capable of supplying them. This composition dictated the choice of the initial production site in the theory (in the first phase of the IPLC). The theory implied that the manufacturing processes were simplified with time, the composition of factor inputs began to change in favor of the developed and then developing countries' factor inputs, which motivated production to migrate from the USA to those countries. Vernon's theory assumed that the skill and capability levels outside the USA were not high enough to accommodate production elsewhere in the early phases of IPLC, in spite of their potentially lower costs. However evolutionary changes in production reduced the capital intensity and skill requirements of production and therefore provided for production to migrate to other countries with lower skills, capabilities and costs than the USA. Ironically there was an asymmetry built into the theory: while the theory allowed the US centers to learn how to lower the skill and competence intensity content of the initial factor inputs, other countries could not learn how to improve theirs. We refer to this phenomenon as the asymmetric production requirements and local cap*abilities interaction effect*.

The knowledge and capability transfer The inherent processes in IPLC would result in a flow of knowledge, skills and capabilities from the US-based headquarters to the local subsidiary elsewhere (that is, from the center to the periphery, as articulated in the theory). Although the theory did not discuss competition directly, with the introduction of competitive products by the US-based and other MNEs, the above flow would increase at a much higher rate with time in order to defend the initial investment and market share world-wide. Therefore, beyond the birth stage, progressive phases in Vernon's IPLC would transfer increasingly more knowledge and capabilities to subsidiaries outside the USA. Dunning called such transfer of resources, skills and capabilities the 'ownership-specific advantage or OSA' (Dunning 1980, 1988), which also served as the first pillars of the modern theory of MNEs in Dunning's eclectic theory (Dunning, 1980, 1988, 1995). As a result of such continuous transfers, more skills, expertise, capabilities and knowledge would accumulate at the various subsidiaries at the peripheries of the network of subsidiaries (especially in response to competition, as discussed earlier) and the focal subsidiary would soon be self-sufficient. It is only logical to assume that the content of these transfers would eventually be localized in order to take advantage of local characteristics, including cheaper factor inputs, which could substitute for, or complement, the initial factor inputs transferred from the headquarters to the subsidiary. Dunning (1980, 1988, 1995) referred to this transformation as adding the 'locally-specific advantage' (LSA) to the initial OSA. We refer to the combined process as transfer of ownership-specific advantage (OSA) to a subsidiary and the inevitable localization of such advan-tages (for example, using local resources, skills and capabilities) over time, mainly in response to local conditions, including local competition.

Thanks to the above effects, the subsidiary at the periphery would soon be capable of replicating the US-based advantage (transferred to it initially) with its own resources and producing similar, if not more advanced, versions of goods and services produced originally in the USA for the American markets and the ROW. Not only would this process further contribute to the faster diffusion of knowledge, technology and other capabilities to other locations outside the USA than otherwise, it would also allow the recipients to improve upon the original portfolio of products with time and to introduce more advanced versions on their own, enabling them to meet the local competition and behave as a center for producing their own incrementally improved inno-vative product(s), which would more likely be a product line as opposed to only one isolated product. Although given different names by different authors (for example, centers of excellence, by Rugman and D'Cruz, 2000;[10] world product mandate holders, by Etemad, 1982;[11] global product mandate holders, by Rutenberg, 1981; or subsidiary mandates, by Roth and Morrison, 1992,[12] and others), each of these subsidiaries could become a center capable

of establishing its own network of buyers and suppliers at its own periphery in
its own right. Soon, there will be many such centers, at locations that used to
be peripheries for the headquarters at the beginning of the IPLC, radiating
flows of products, knowledge and possibly investments inwards, as well as
outwards (as opposed to receiving them), and thereby forming an inverted web
of innovation, new products, knowledge and possibly investments, as
discussed earlier.

The Inevitable Transformation of the Local Subsidiary and its Impact on its Competitive and Organization Environment

Naturally such temporal evolution would change a local subsidiary gradually
into an organization resembling its parent headquarters and capable of functioning in that capacity (at least in a limited capacity, based on the initial transfer of products and capabilities). Once a subsidiary becomes capable of
enhancing its initial ownership-based advantages with the locally based (or
acquired) capabilities in order to produce for the local market, and then to
export to its periphery in the rest of the world, it could act as the headquarters
for its specific product mandate (Etemad, 1982). In comparative terms, it
would be resembling its corporate headquarters in the early phases of the
IPLC; and, if desired, it could initiate an IPLC of its own, following in the
footsteps of its own headquarters (Etemad, 1982; Etemad and Seguin Dulude,
1986a, 1986b; Rutenberg, 1981). Following a natural IPLC path, the
subsidiary would be exporting to the rest of the world in the early stages of its
own IPLC, including exporting to the more advanced countries (or richer
markets elsewhere). It could also outsource the necessary supplies from other,
less advanced, countries, thereby reinforcing, if not propagating, its own product mandate (Etemad, 2003b) and establishing its own corresponding supply
chain network as well as a marketing and distribution network within and
outside the sister-subsidiary system. In other words, it could become and act
as a headquarters in its own right and expand its sphere of influence.

Therefore the initial IPLC supply chain that resembled a spider's web with
one central node in a hub-and-spoke structure, with the spokes radiating
outward, would soon be transformed into an inverted web with many nodes at
the periphery radiating inward and outward. Each of these would have its own
capabilities and expertise, acting as a center of excellence with respect to its
specialization (or mandate) in the connected web of sister-subsidiaries (and
possibly others constituting its own respective supply chain networks). This
would in fact truly globalize the original IPLC and transform the MNE into a
constellation-like structure with one fundamental difference: unified ownership.

This extension of Vernon's IPLC appears to be more reflective of the
prevailing reality and will force others within and outside the MNE to at least

emulate it in order to avoid falling behind (Knickerbocker, 1973). Such emulation would change a simple competition into a more sophisticated and strategic one that would include technological and temporal competition. Furthermore competing constellations of firms (Gomes-Casseres, 1996), including MNEs and alliances of independent firms, may attempt to win both competitions by a twin strategy: speeding up the rate of technological change and shortening the life cycle of their products much beyond what was originally implied by either the theory of IPLC (Vernon, 1966) or the eclectic theory of MNEs (Dunning 1980, 1988). Both of these theories attempted to explain internationalization without addressing global competition; but global expansion and its twin concept, global competition, were inadvertently defined at the same time.

One noteworthy implication of the above process is that the initial transfer of the capabilities, knowledge and expertise from the center to the periphery in a globalized environment would inevitably initiate the creation of multi-polar structures, with each center seeking more bargaining power and exerting higher competitive pressures within the shared competitive space, if not beyond, with the passage of time. The ultimate reversed flow of the enriched and enhanced capabilities from the local subsidiary to other locations would potentially begin a new round of IPLC spiralling upward over time. Such developments point clearly to the intensification of competition worldwide and especially in the host country markets within which these subsidiaries are located and the local SMEs must compete to survive. With the presence of MNEs' subsidiaries in their home markets, smaller local firms would soon have no choice but to change their competitive structures: either to join MNE-like institutions and internationalize (for example, become a member of an MNE's local subsidiary's supply chain) or to create a multi-centered institution of their own (for example, join the constellation of interdependent firms) in order to avoid losing further ground, if not suffering wipeout.

The Spread of MNE-like Institutions

The logical extension of the above argument suggests the rise of MNE-like institutions even within MNE structures, as simple subsidiaries can evolve to act as their own headquarters in order to deflect the mounting competitive pressures exerted by other subsidiaries and the local firms competing for ever-higher market shares in the same competitive space. In the process of evolving to meet the local competition (from other constellations and local firms), such subsidiaries may embark on a strategic game that could resemble multi-location and multi-period gaming, as compared to a simple competitive game, in order to exert far higher pressure on all competitors in their shared competitive space, including local SMEs. This will inevitability heighten local

competition and force local SMEs either to compete at the prevailing levels or
to face the eventual risk of elimination from such competitive markets. The
inescapable implication of this fundamental evolutionary pattern is an equal
increase in competitive intensity in both the local and the international
markets. Stated differently, the lowest common denominator of local competition would be the lowest level of competition at which a subsidiary, representing a networked entity, would be willing to compete. This level could still
be highly competitive for an independent, small, local firm. Obviously those
firms which could not meet the challenges associated with these competitive
levels could not expect to survive. Naturally, once a networked enterprise
capable of competing at a higher competitive level appeared on the scene, the
overall competitive intensity would rise again to at least that level to avoid
losses. However this higher competitive level may bring massive attrition in
its wake, especially for those who cannot meet the challenge.

The emerging trend evident from the above discussion is that the international network of firms would possess a higher capability to grow faster and
raise competitive levels to higher levels than others. The clear implication for
the local SMEs is that the members of networked firms would be in a much
better position to set the competitive levels high enough to outcompete the
local SMEs in their own home market. Local SMEs will face a bleak reality
unless they enter into network-type arrangements and internationalize in order
to grow and join the ranks of global players. Other options appear as non-
viable in the long run.

THE CONVERGING PATTERNS AND TRENDS

Convergence of IPLC and the Modern Theory of MNEs

The eclectic, or the OLI, theory of MNEs (Dunning, 1980, 1988, 1995)
suggested that the ownership advantage (that is, the 'O' component of the
theory, for example the IPLC's initial flows of knowledge, expertise and capabilities to the subsidiary) would be transferred to a local subsidiary and integrated with the locally based advantages (the 'L' component of the theory, for
example cheaper local input factors) in the local subsidiary. This combination
would naturally evolve with time into a more enriched advantage than the
ownership advantage transferred initially to the local subsidiary in the early
stages of the subsidiary's life cycle (which coincide with the second stage of
Vernon's IPLC). Furthermore Dunning (1980, 1988) proposed that the
combined (or enriched) advantages would then be internalized (the 'I' component of the theory), that is, reincorporated into the corporate advantage and
made available for trade in the MNE's internal markets, populated by the

MNE's sister-subsidiaries and the headquarters. The concept of an internal market was proposed in the theory to serve the respective needs of the sister-subsidiary system at privileged prices with the headquarters' blessing. Operationally this would imply that the headquarters would be importing at a later time (this is identical to the third stage of Vernon's IPLC) from the local subsidiary to the internal market the enhanced version of capabilities and resources that they had initially transferred to the subsidiary (that is, in the second and third stages, to the developed and then to the developing countries, respectively, in Vernon's IPLC).

The above brief description shows that Dunning's OLI and Vernon's IPLC converge on many aspects, including the initial transfer of capabilities, expertise and knowledge to the subsidiary and later transfer of certain results back to the MNE and other sister subsidiaries. In the OLI theory, the new subsidiary would be given the necessary assets, capabilities and competencies, constituting the initial ownership advantage in OLI, to enable it to establish a local presence and survive. For initiating an international life cycle in Vernon's IPLC, sufficient assets (including technology) would be invested in a developed country (in the second stage) or a developing country (in the third stage) to set up a subsidiary. In other words, the newly established subsidiary would be given all the necessary factor inputs, including technology, to produce the product locally for both local and export markets. Although Dunning's and Vernon's respective motivations may have differed at the outset, the end results would be almost identical: the establishment of a subsidiary for capitalizing on the corporate assets and transforming them with the use of local resources to produce the product for the local market. However, once the subsidiary was set up and functioning, IPLC would require the subsidiary to utilize the transformed factor inputs to produce products for exporting to other markets as well as for local market consumption, that is, produce factor outputs for the local and other export markets, while the OLI would require the subsidiary to produce for the local market and 'internalize', that is, to transfer only the enriched factor inputs to the internal markets for further use by the headquarters and in a multitude of sister-subsidiaries. In both of these theories, even for the US-initiated products, US headquarters would be the recipient of certain transformed factors (a reverse flow of the end-product, or the enhanced and enriched flow of the initial ownership advantage, respectively) at the later stages of the OLI and IPLC. Both theories allow for multiple subsidiaries to possess the initial ownership advantage as well as receiving the enhanced capabilities. Both would even deploy them to produce related products and product lines in other country sites for use in their own and other markets.

Six implications of these two converging theories are of importance to internationalizing SMEs and deserve highlighting.

Exports and internationalization

Preparations for export followed by actual exports can initiate the process of internationalization, even for larger firms. The Scandinavian school of internationalization (Cavusgil, 1982; Johanson and Vahlne, 1977, 1990, 1992; Johanson and Wiedersheim-Paul, 1975), would also start the process of internationalization with simple exporting to psychologically close markets (Stöttinger and Schlegelmilch, 1998) before proceeding to export to other markets or attempt more complex operations in later stages in the process. The primary benefit of exporting according to this school is to collect information and accumulate experience about foreign markets in order to increase responsiveness to the local market needs and mitigate the risk of foreignness at the same time, which are essential to the health of the subsequent expansions (which are the actual domains covered by both Dunning's eclectic and Vernon's IPLC theories). In fact, exporting is an integral part of the first stage of Vernon's IPLC, where the US-based firm begins its IPLC by exporting abroad. Although the process of exporting is not explicitly defined in the theory, the results of such exports and the lessons learned through them are necessary when deciding the location of the first subsidiary in IPLC (that is, the beginning of stage two). It is, therefore, incumbent upon the internationalizing SMEs to explore the benefits, and potential hazards, of exporting before attempting full-fledged internationalization.

Scale and scope economies

Simple exporting remains a low-risk strategy with low resource requirements. As stated earlier, even early exports can help to increase the scale of production and its associated economies to reduce average costs for both domestic and export markets. This can facilitate limited experimentation in international markets to expand target segments and markets beyond the domestic market. It can also supply the necessary information for expanding the portfolio of products in response to demand variations in those export markets, which may in turn lead to further scope economies. These economies can therefore be viewed as valuable savings, upon which smaller firms can easily capitalize, even when they are not prepared to internationalize fully.

Reduced risk and vulnerabilities

The increased scale and scope economies resulting from expanded export markets and responsiveness to those markets' demands, even in the absence of further internationalization, provide for lower risks and vulnerabilities due to the gradually expanded and larger product market portfolio. A methodical export program can therefore easily pave the way for internationalizing a small firm without undue exposure to risk.

Further internationalization
Exports can also provide for systematic experimentation in international markets without undue exposure to risks and therefore facilitate assessing the potential for local production and FDI at later stages. Both the eclectic and IPLC theories transfer ownership advantage in stages along with the economies associated with both increased scale and scope. Once the optimum production capacity at the current site is reached, the acquired economies can serve as the basis for attaining even higher savings at future sites when further products are transferred.

Local competition
Both the eclectic and IPLC theories imply higher local competition due to the introduction of a product, or family of internationally oriented products, to the local market even if global rivals do not participate in the local market. When global rivals participate, they further heighten local competition. The local market would eventually be transformed into a microcosm of the international market with similar competitive intensity. In the absence of exporting, followed by further internationalization, international competitors would have access to the full range of benefits described above, while the local SME would be limited to its own local market on a rapidly shrinking scale. Again local SMEs should read the competitive trends before they become suffocating and start the process of internationalization as a defensive strategy for protecting their own home markets against the marching armies of international competitors.

The network aspects
The appearance of products of IPLC or the subsidiaries of MNEs (the beginning of the first stage in both theories) must be taken as a signal for gradual transformation of competition in the local market. In fact, their presence must be interpreted as an inevitable rise in expectations and heightening of competition in the local market as they represent globally networked firms in the local market. As discussed earlier, members of networked firms can draw upon their access to numerous advantages that are specific to network firms enabling them to compete more rigorously and offer higher value in the local market than the local independent firms, to which these advantages are not available, regardless of their size and scope of activity. It is incumbent upon the local firms to detect the signals early enough, understand their implications in terms of potential impact and prepare proactively for the expected transformation of the market and the heightening of competition.[13]

MNEs Becoming Learning Organizations

Although Vernon, Dunning and other scholars concerned with the growth of MNEs did not explicitly incorporate learning in their conceptualization, a learning capability is inherent in the headquarters–subsidiary structures. It is not difficult to point to the obvious incidents of learning in typical MNE–subsidiary relations and indicate the combined impact of learning in the market place (Nonaka, 1995; Nonaka and Takeuchi, 1996; Gupta and Govindarajan, 1991). For clarity of exposition and for distinction of their impact on the local SMEs, they are examined in three parts, each representing a different process with different implications.

Contextualization of production

For a subsidiary to set roots in the local environment of the host country and compete with the local firms, it is necessary to develop fully a mastery of the ownership-specific advantage (OSA). It is this OSA (in Dunning's terminology, or the initial transfer of technology and other necessary factors in Vernon's terminology) that empowers the young subsidiary to establish a competitive presence against the local and entrenched firms. In order to use the OSA efficiently, the young subsidiary must adapt it to the local context in the early stages of its life (which would be at the beginning of Dunning's eclectic theory and could be in either stages 2 or 3 in Vernon's IPLC conceptualization, depending on the host country's level of development). Such local adaptation would involve at least three sets of qualitatively different learning processes:

1. the learning process involved in characterizing OSA, transferring the inherent tacit knowledge in it from the headquarters to the subsidiary, and deploying it explicitly locally (Eriksson *et al.*, 1997);
2. the learning process involved in identifying the locally specific advantage (LSA, which can complement OSA), which is locally tacit, and also transferring it from the local environment to the subsidiary (Kogut and Zander, 1992);
3. the process of learning inherent in combining and exploiting both advantages to give the young local subsidiary a competitive edge over the other local subsidiaries.

Although all the above processes may be going on at the same time and quite distinguishable at the subsidiary, these are the specific processes involved in learning how to contextualize the ownership advantage to the local environment in creating incremental value above that of the local firms and that obtainable through exports. Naturally the substance of these processes would differ according to the local market environment. We refer to this process as context-seeking learning for incremental local value creation.

Such learning is implicit in and equally essential to both Dunning's and

Vernon's conceptualizations of the way young subsidiaries learn from the corporate parents and others in the early stages of their life in the host country in order to offer the products and services locally for either less than imported prices or with higher value than the local competition, which makes it possible to compete successfully in the local market. In both conceptualizations, the subsidiary must learn how to create value by adapting the OSA (which is defined as a composition of foreign-oriented factor inputs originating from foreign sources rather than a locally oriented composition) to complement the local conditions (for example, using local factor inputs, facing local operating conditions and market characteristics) in order to create higher value than the locally entrenched firm and also the local subsidiaries of other MNEs present in the local markets.

The cross-transfer and exportation

Dunning's theory implies that the MNE's internal market is populated by only the sister-subsidiaries and the headquarters and is regulated by the corporate parent company. Goods and services exchanged, or traded, in such an internal market are demanded, supplied and supported by both the parent company and the sister-subsidiaries. In order for the internalization concept in Dunning's theory to function consistently over time, a combination of the parent company and subsidiaries must actually learn, or acquire the capability of learning, how to deliver incrementally higher value to the internal market (in the case of subsidiaries supplying/selling) or extract it from the internal market (in the case of subsidiaries demanding/buying) at advantageous prices as compared to similar transactions with other markets at arm's length. This in turn entails, first, creating incremental value through exchange in the internal market as compared to general markets and, second, supporting their transactions within the internal market (transfers both to and from the internal markets) by controlling their transaction costs especially in the case of services.

At the subsidiary level, this support implies that at least some of the particular capabilities learned and competencies gained locally (for example, those capabilities and competencies learned or gained in the contextualization process, as discussed above) would be supplied to the internal markets to meet the potential demands of other subsidiaries in need of those competencies. As a result, the internal market can be viewed as a market place for selling and acquiring new or enhanced capabilities and competencies that are capable of (a) providing for the competitive needs of a typical sister-subsidiary to stimulate its competitiveness; and conversely (b) supplying locally developed (or acquired) potent competencies to the internal market for distribution to other sister-subsidiaries that can utilize them.

Recontextualization

The above characterization is implied in Dunning's eclectic theory and resonates well with Vernon's IPLC. For example, in the second (or the third) phase of Vernon's IPLC theory, the production capability is transferred from the parent (or a subsidiary in a developed country) to a new site in a developing country to produce for the local market consumption and exports to other countries. This transfer is similar to a transfer of OSA in the eclectic theory, not from the corporate parents, but from a subsidiary instead. The supplying subsidiary in the developed country must have either already acquired, or acquire during the transfer process, all the necessary expertise to support the transaction (similarly to the parent company transferring original OSA to a young subsidiary in Dunning's theory) in order to enable local production in the developing country and the subsequent exporting of the product(s) to all the other markets. We refer to these capabilities as *recontextualization* as they entail learning how to transfer certain locally enriched and enhanced competencies (with locally specific resources or capabilities) to other locations and markets which do not have the same or similar characteristics. Recontextualization entails a few learning processes, including (a) learning how to *identify the local components* (that is, knowledge, capabilities and/or competencies) that have enhanced and enriched the original OSA and have become integral parts of the local capabilities and competencies (that is, gained during the local adaptation of the original OSA in the *contextualization process)*; and (b) learning how to *decontextualize* for redeployment by other subsidiaries and even how to *recontextualize* for the local factor inputs. The form and composition of these local components are mostly implicit, tacit and embedded in the local environment or entwined with the competencies that a subsidiary wishes to supply to another. Therefore such capabilities and competences will have to be prepared before a successful transfer from an older subsidiary to a younger one (in Vernon's conceptualization) or reverse-transfer to the internal market (in Dunning's conceptualization) can be accomplished.

Therefore contextualization and decontextualization may be viewed as strategic learning processes for incremental value creation in international markets and throughout the internal markets. In contrast to the passive learning mode (by one subsidiary from the others) in IPLC theory, the learning must be active in the OLI theory in order for the internal markets to function effectively. The previous discussion points to the institution wishing to gain or possess incremental capability (for example, a progressive subsidiary or a subsidiary under competitive pressures) above and beyond what the corporate headquarters would be able to offer it at the time. Conversely, the internal markets must be able to offer an increasingly more advanced set of expertise, capabilities and competencies than the headquarters' classic ownership advantage to stay relevant to the sister-subsidiary network as time and technology march on. The OLI theory is not clear whether the internal markets are time-sensitive and evolve with time or not. However, without a reverse-transfer of enriched and enhanced initial competencies, there will soon be no demand for the headquarters' initial OSA; and headquarters will eventually be out of the business of supplying OSAs. In other words, if the enhancements, due to contextualization of OSA, combined with enrichments, due to integration of the subsidiary's local advantage with OSA, are not decontextualized to be reutilized elsewhere, not only will the network advantages of MNEs (conceptualized and captured by the concept of internal markets) gradually vanish but also the headquarters will no longer be the supplier of OSA if and when technological obsolescence prevails. Should headquarters fail to supply updated and cutting-edge OSA, the eclectic theory would have very little to offer and the ownership advantage of the corporate parent would be reduced to unified ownership: the MNE would be transformed into a holding company.

The local enhancements and enrichments, along with the transfer and reverse-transfer of capabilities, are therefore the necessary and integral parts of the concept of internal markets as they provide for the OSA's renewal with time and corporate expansion, which can in turn be made available to the internal markets again in order to initiate the birth of a new subsidiary and a potential cycle of renewal along with it. Without such renewal cycles, the OSA will experience obsolescence, similar to other assets, and cannot be reutilized, for example, for establishing new subsidiaries, for upgrading the sister-subsidiary's current capabilities, or even for building new capabilities as a basis for introducing a new or more advanced generation of goods and services, which are all the necessary currencies of the global markets, as discussed in the earlier parts of this chapter. The noteworthy point is that various forms of learning underlie the above process and enable the MNEs as networked firms to advance and expand successfully with the march of time and technology. Alternatively, effective inter- and intra-firm learning in multi-point, multi-product and multi-objective operations in networked constellations and alliances can enable their sustained competitiveness over time. This conceptualization characterizes dynamic capabilities (Teece *et al.*, 1997) and resonates very well with that tradition. The inevitable implications of the above arguments for smaller firms are crystal-clear:

1. internationalizing SMEs must create the requisite conditions for both the intra-firm and inter-firm learning capabilities; and
2. internationalizing firms can learn from members of multi-point, multi-product, multi-technology and multi-mandated constellations of interdependent firms and leverage them for still higher capabilities in response to sustained competition.

The conclusion to this closing chapter is necessarily short. This chapter was designed to build on and extend the rich family of concepts in the previous 11 chapters, organized in four different categories of change and emerging trends, to examine them from the various perspectives discussed in the book in order to extract the logical lesson, compelling implications or long-lasting conclusion from them. The essence of these extractions was made clear at the end of each section for immediate effect as the chapter unfolded.

In the final analysis, learning appears to be the unavoidable key to preserving SMEs' survival in the face of intensifying competition and globalization. While learning within constellations offers higher chances of success within the group's common security, managing relations with others will remain the most valuable currency within such constellations.

NOTES

1. 'Goods' and 'goods and services' are used interchangeably in this chapter. For reasons of simplicity, we use goods to signify both goods and services.
2. This control is accomplished in part by directing investment and knowledge to the centers at their own peripheries within their supply networks. This may further enhance their intrafirm trade, developments and competitiveness worldwide.
3. Symbiosis is defined as the living together in intimate association, or even close union, of two dissimilar organisms. Ordinarily it is used for cases where the association of at least two entities is advantageous, or often necessary, to one or both, and not harmful to either.
4. The concept of proximity appears to be multidimensional: participating in the same regional industry and social associations, sharing the same cultural events, dealing with the same buyers and suppliers in the region, and being embedded in the same sociocultural and economic environment.
5. For full treatment of the subject of Transaction Cost Theory see Williamson (1975).
6. Computer electronics is concentrated in a few regions but traded globally almost free of tariff and non-tariff barriers.
7. In some cases, suppliers of certain electronic parts in the Orient are integral parts of regional clusters in North America.
8. Ironically, Ford Motor Company tried, and achieved, close to full integration in production and marketing in the late 1920s, before they recognized the strategic inflexibility of such arrangements.
9. The history of alliances is replete with examples of alliances protecting smaller innovative firms, for their potential contributions to the constellation, from other alliances and constellations (see, for example, the case of Tiny Mips in Gomes-Casseres, 1996).
10. See Alan Rugman and Joseph D'Cruz (2000).
11. See Hamid Etemad (1982) for further details of world product mandates.
12. See Roth and Morrison (1992) for full discussion of subsidiary mandates.
13. The migration of production to local markets portrays the evolutionary path of competition towards simple price competition globally (that is, in the Fordist view as advocated). The IPLC should be viewed as a reflection of MNEs' striving for efficiency, cost reduction and increased competitiveness globally, owing to lower costs and prices due to learning, scale and scope economies in a contemporary view of strategy.

REFERENCES

Acs, Zoltan and Bernard Yeung (1999), 'Entrepreneurial discovery and the global economy', *Global Focus*, **11** (3), 63–72.

Anderson, U. and J. Johanson (1996), 'Subsidiary embeddedness and its implications for integration in the MNC', *Proceedings of the European International Business Association*, 235–56.

Barkema, H.G., J.H.J. Bell and J.M. Pennings (1996), 'Foreign entry, cultural barriers and learning', *Strategic Management Journal*, **17**, 151–66.

Barkema, H.G., O. Shenkar, F. Vermeulen and J.H.J. Bell (1997), 'Working abroad with others: how firms learn to operate international joint ventures', *Academy of Management Journal*, **40** (2), 426–42.

Barnet, Richard J. and Ronald E. Muller (1974), *Global Reach: The Power of the Multinational Corporations*, New York: Simon and Schuster.

Buckley, Peter J. (1989), 'Foreign direct investment by small and medium-sized enterprises', *Small Business Economics*, **1**, 89–100.

Buckley, Peter J. and Mark Casson (1976), *The Future of the Multinational Enterprise*, London: Macmillan.

Caves, Richard E. (1982), *Multinational Enterprise and Economic Analysis*, Cambridge: Cambridge University Press.

Cavusgil, S.T. (1982), 'Some observations on the relevance of critical variables for internationalization stages', in M. Czinkota and G. Tesar (eds), *Export Management: An International Context*, New York: Praeger, pp. 276–85.

Christensen, C.M. and J.L. Bower (1996), 'Customer power, strategic investment and the failure of the leading firms', *Strategic Management Journal*, **17** (3), 197–218.

D'Aveni, Richard (1994), *Hypercompetition: Managing the Dynamics of Strategic Maneuvering*, New York: The Free Press.

Doz, Y.L. (1996), 'The evolution of cooperation in strategic alliances: initial conditions or learning processes?', *Strategic Management Journal*, **17**, 55–83.

Dunning, John H. (1980), 'Toward an eclectic theory of international production: empirical tests', *Journal of International Business Studies*, **11** (1), 9–31.

Dunning, John H. (1988), 'The eclectic paradigm of international production: a restatement and some possible extensions', *Journal of International Business Studies*, **19** (1), 1–31.

Dunning, John H. (1995), 'Reappraising the eclectic paradigm in the age of alliance capitalism', *Journal of International Business Studies*, **26** (3), 461–91.

Eriksson, K., J. Johanson, A. Majkgard and D. Sharma (1997), 'Experiential knowledge and cost in the internationalisation process', *Journal of International Business Studies*, **28** (2), 337–60.

Etemad, H. (1982), 'World product mandates in perspective', in A. Rugman (ed.), *Multinational and Technology Transfer: The Canadian Experience*, New York: Praeger, pp. 108–25.

Etemad, Hamid (2002), 'Strategies for internationalization of entrepreneurial firms facing different competitive environments', in Hamid Etemad (ed.), *The Proceedings of the Third Biennial McGill Conference on International Entrepreneurship: Researching New Frontiers*, vol. 1, McGill University, Montreal.

Etemad, Hamid (2003a), 'Managing relations: the essence of international entrepreneurship', in Hamid Etemad and Richard Wright (eds), *Globalization and Entrepreneurship: Policy and Strategy Perspectives*, Cheltenham, UK, and Northampton, MA, USA: Edward Elgar Publishing.

Etemad, Hamid (2003b), 'Marshalling relations: the enduring essence of international entrepreneurship', in L.P. Dana (ed.), *Handbook of International Entrepreneurship*, Cheltenham, UK, and Northampton, MA, USA: Edward Elgar.

Etemad, H. (2003c), 'The typology of competitive intensity, evolutionary path of the local subsidiary and the local SME's internationalization strategies', *2003 Proceedings of the Administrative Association of Canada, International Business Division*, 12–14 June.

Etemad, H. and L. Seguin–Dulude (1986a), 'The development of technology in MNEs: a cross-country and industry study', in A.E. Safarian and G.Y. Bertin (eds), *Multinationals, Governments and Technology Transfer*, London: Croom Helm Publishers.

Etemad, H. and L. Seguin-Dulude (1986b), 'Inventive activity in MNEs and their world product mandated subsidiaries', in H. Etemad and L. Seguin-Dulude (eds), *Managing the Multinational Subsidiary: Response to Environmental Change and Host Nation R&D Policies*, London: Croom Helm, pp. 117–206.

Etemad, Hamid, Richard Wright and L.P. Dana (2001), 'Symbiotic international business networks: collaboration between small and large firms', *Thunderbird International Business Review*, **43** (4), August, 481–500.

Forrest, Janet E. and M.J.C. Martin (1992), 'Strategic alliances between large and small research intensive organizations: experience in biotechnology industry', *R & D Management*, **22**, 41–53.

Gilroy, Bernard M. (1993), *Networking in multinational enterprises: the importance of strategic alliances*, Columbia: University of South Carolina.

Gomes-Casseres, Benjamin (1996), *The Alliance Revolution: The New Shape of Business Rivalry*, Cambridge, MA: Harvard University Press.

Gomes-Casseres, Benjamin (1997), 'Alliance strategies of small firms', *Small Business Economics*, **9** (1), 33–44.

Gulati, R. (1995a), 'Does familiarity breed trust? The implications of repeated ties for contractual choice in alliances', *Academy of Management Review*, **38** (1), 85–112.

Gulati, R. (1995b). 'Social structure and alliance formation patterns: a longitudinal analysis', *Administrative Science Quarterly*, **40**, 619–52.

Gupta, A.K. and V. Govindarajan (1991), 'Knowledge flows and the structure of control within multinational corporations', *Academy of Management Review*, **16**, 768–92.

Gupta, A.K. and V. Govindarajan (1994), 'Organizing for knowledge within MNCs', *International Business Review*, **3** (4), 443–57.

Hymer, Stephan (1976), *International Operations of National Firms: A Study of Direct Foreign Investment*, Cambridge, MA: MIT Press.

Johanson, J. and J.E. Vahlne (1977), 'The internationalization process of the firm: a model of knowledge development and increasing commitments', *Journal of International Business Studies*, **8** (1), 23–32.

Johanson, Jan and Jan-Erik Vahlne (1990), 'The mechanism of internationalization', *International Marketing Review*, **7** (4), 11–24.

Johanson, Jan and Jan-Erik Vahlne (1992), 'Management of foreign market entry', *Scandinavian International Business Review*, **1** (3) 9–27.

Johanson, Jan and Finn Wiedersheim-Paul (1975), 'The internationalization of the firm: four Swedish cases', *Journal of International Management Studies*, **12** (3), October, 36–64.

Joshi, Ashwin W. and Rodney L. Stump (1999), 'Determinants of commitments and opportunism: integrating and extending insights from transaction cost analysis and relational exchange theory', *Canadian Journal of Administrative Sciences*, **16**, December, 334–52.

Kanter, E.M. (1984), 'Collaborative advantage: the art of alliances', *Harvard Business Review*, July–August, 96–108.

Knickerbocker, F.T. (1973), '*Oligopolistic Reaction and Multinational Enterprise*, Boston, MA: Harvard University Press.

Kogut, B. and U. Zander (1992), 'Knowledge of the firm, combinative capabilities and the replication of technology', *Organization Science*, **3**, 383–97.

Lieberman, M. and D.B. Montgomery (1998), 'First-mover (dis)advantages: retrospective and link with the resource-based view', *Strategic Management Journal*, **19**, 1111–25.

Nonaka, I. (1995), 'A theory of organizational knowledge creation', *International Journal of Technology Management*, **11** (7/8), 833–45.

Nonaka, I. and H. Takeuchi (1996), *The Knowledge Creating Company: How Japanese Companies Create the Dynamics of Innovation*, New York: Oxford University Press.

Ohmae, Kenichi (1985), *Triad Power: The Coming Shape of Global Competition*, New York: The Free Press, pp. 8–20.

Roth, K. and A. Morrison (1992), 'Implementing global strategy: characteristics of global subsidiary mandates', *Journal of International Business Studies*, **23**, 715–36.

Rugman, A. M. (1982), *New Theories of Multinationals*, London: Croom Helm.

Rugman, A. and J. D'Cruz (2000), *Multinationals as Flagship Firms: A New Theory of Regional Business Networks*, Oxford: Oxford University Press.

Rugman, A.M. and S. Douglas (1986), 'The strategic management of multinational and world product mandating', in H. Etemad and L. Seguin-Dulude (eds), *Managing the Multinational Subsidiary*, London: Croom Helm, pp. 99–101.

Rutenberg, David (1981), 'Global product mandating' in K.C. Dahwan, H. Etemad and R.W. Wright (eds), *International Business: A Canadian Perspective*, Don Mills, Ontario: Addison-Wesley, pp. 853–60.

Saxenian, Annalee (1994), *Regional Advantage. Culture and Competition in Silicon Valley and Route 128*, Cambridge and London: Harvard University Press.

Schumpeter, Joseph Allois (1911), *Theorie der wirtschaftlichen Entwicklung*, Munich and Leipzig: Dunker und Humblot; translated (1934) by R. Opie, *The Theory of Economic Development*, Cambridge, MA: Harvard University Press.

Servan-Schreiber, J.J. (1968), *The American Challenge (Le Défi Americain)*, New York: Atheneum.

Stöttinger, B. and B. Schlegelmilch (1998), 'Explaining export development through psychic distance: enlightening or elusive?', *International Marketing Review*, **15** (5), 357–72.

Teece, D.J., G. Pisano and A. Shuen (1997), 'Dynamic capabilities and strategic management', *Strategic Management Journal*, **18** (7), 509–33.

Vernon, R. (1966), 'International investments and international trade in the product cycle', *Quarterly Journal of Economics*, **80**, (2), 190–207.

Vernon, R. (1971), *Sovereignty at Bay: The Multinational Spread of US Enterprises*, New York: Basic Books.

Williamson, O.E. (1975), *Markets and Hierarchies: Analysis and Anti-Trust Implications*, New York: Free Press.

Williamson, O.E. (1979), 'Transaction cost economics: the governance of contractual relations', *Journal of Law and Economics*, **22**, 3–61.

Williamson, O.E. (1981), 'The economics of organization: the transaction cost approach', *American Journal of Sociology*, **87**, 548–77.
Yoshino, M. and U.S. Rangan (1995), *Strategic Alliances: An Entrepreneurial Approach to Globalization*, Boston, MA: Harvard Business School Press.

Index